SO-BEA-820

FRONTIER PROFIT
AND LOSS

Recent Titles in
Contributions in American History

FRONTIER PROFIT AND LOSS

The British Army and the Fur Traders, 1760–1764

WALTER S. DUNN, JR.

Contributions in American History, Number 180

Greenwood Press
Westport, Connecticut • London

Library of Congress Cataloging-in-Publication Data

Dunn, Walter S. (Walter Scott), 1928–
   Frontier profit and loss : the British army and the fur traders,
1760–1764 / Walter S. Dunn, Jr.
     p. cm.—(Contributions in American history ; ISSN 0084–9219 ; no. 180)
   Includes bibliographical references (p.) and index.
   ISBN 0–313–30605–2 (alk. paper)
   1. Northwest, Old—History—To 1775. 2. Northwest, Old—Economic
conditions. 3. Fur trade—Northwest, Old—History—18th century.
4. Great Britain—Colonies—America—Commerce—History—18th
century. 5. Great Britain—Armed forces—Northwest, Old—
History—18th century. 6. Great Britain—Commercial policy—
History—18th century. I. Title. II. Series.
F482.D86   1998
977'.01—DC21   97–48580

British Library Cataloguing in Publication Data is available.

Library of Congress Catalog Card Number: 97–48580
ISBN: 0–313–30605–2
ISSN: 0084–9219

First published in 1998

Greenwood Press, 88 Post Road West, Westport, CT 06881
An imprint of Greenwood Publishing Group, Inc.

Printed in the United States of America

The paper used in this book complies with the
Permanent Paper Standard issued by the National
Information Standards Organization (Z39.48–1984).

10 9 8 7 6 5 4 3 2 1

To Henry D. Brown, Director, Detroit Historical Museum

Contents

Preface

This is not another book trying to establish the cause of the American Revolution. Instead it is an attempt to describe and interpret one narrow facet of activity—experience on the frontier from 1760 to 1764—that contributed to the change in attitude of some of the colonists toward England. The change had antecedents dating back to the seventeenth century and there is no intent to prove that the change in attitude was confined to these five years, only that much that contributed to the change occurred in this brief period. The clash of four cultures (Indian, Colonial, French Canadian, and British) on the frontier after 1760 was not unique in world history, but the multifarious character of the clash was not common. The geographical scope of the action (about the size of Europe minus Russia) and complex mixture of economic, ethnic, social, and economic groups make it difficult to comprehend. The secondary economic impact of the events that opened and closed significant markets reached from the new factory towns throughout England to the cotton producers of India and the slave coast of Africa. The results of the decisions made as a result of these events would impact world history for two centuries.

Little attempt was made to achieve a "balanced" presentation of all that occurred in America during those five years. Much has been published presenting overall interpretations and descriptions of specific pieces of the puzzle. To summarize all here at the sacrifice of presenting data pertinent to the thesis would seem unprofitable.

The thesis presented is that the shift of the British Army's role from protecting the colonists to an alliance with the French and Indians to drive the colonists out of frontier commerce changed the attitude of the colonists. The frontier experience had an impact on the colonial economy equal to 10% to 25% of colonial trade with Britain. An analysis of the social and economic conflicts that created the changes has been lacking.

A major source of information was the financial records of the period. Reading financial records is not normally considered an exciting pastime, nor are the records usually equated with adventure or pathos, yet the search for clues in the records of a company on the path to bankruptcy has all the elements of a detective story. The promise of unfulfilled dreams found in the records of an expanding company has elements of an adventure novel, and the human misery depicted in the letters of unfortunate traders has some elements of a Dickens novel. Deciphering the tales told by the current balance sheets is not an easy task for the researcher, and the problem is compounded by eighteenth century financial records using methods long abandoned and filled with abbreviated references to services, products, and techniques that everyone understood in 1760, but that must be painfully unraveled in 1998.

Many historians ignore the value of business records; one author dismissed a manuscript collection of an important merchant as "mostly financial records" with the clear implication that little if any useful information would be found in that collection. Financial records are often ignored because the individual has not taken the time to learn how to use them. Imagine writing the history of the twentieth century giving more emphasis to a local hardware store than U.S. Steel because the store owner left descriptive letters about his affairs.

The sheer volume of eighteenth century financial records is daunting. However, the basic framework of a daily journal, accounts, and fund balances are there to be explored. Business correspondence was filled with references, often in abbreviated terminology, that provide the reader with a detailed description of how business was conducted.

Further compounding the interpretive task was the use of multiple currencies in financial records concerning frontier commerce. Although English sterling was commonly used in conjunction with the local colonial or provincial currency in most American cities, on the frontier, agents from three or more colonies or provinces would be conducting business in the same area. Quebec, New York, Pennsylvania, and French paper money circulated and was used along with English sterling in the accounts. In addition, Spanish, English, and Portuguese metallic currency was commonly used in cash transactions. The rates of exchange between the various currencies fluctuated but within a limited range during the brief period covered by this study.

For the convenience of the reader, some amounts have been converted to the approximate value in 1998 dollars at the rate of one pound sterling to $200. The equivalents are presented in parenthesis following the sum in the currency used in the source. A pound sterling consisted of twenty shillings each worth twelve pence. The penny was also divided into half pennies (½p) and farthings (¼p). Colonial currencies were divided in the same manner.

My sincere thanks to the personnel of more than twenty historical societies who were unstinting in their help locating relevant collections. Of particular help were the State Historical Society of Wisconsin, the Pennsylvania Historical Society, and the Burton Historical Collection of the Detroit Public Library.

William Robins read the manuscript and offered valuable suggestions. My wife Jean has tirelessly edited draft after draft, pointing out lapses that occur when one is close to a subject and assumes too much of the reader.

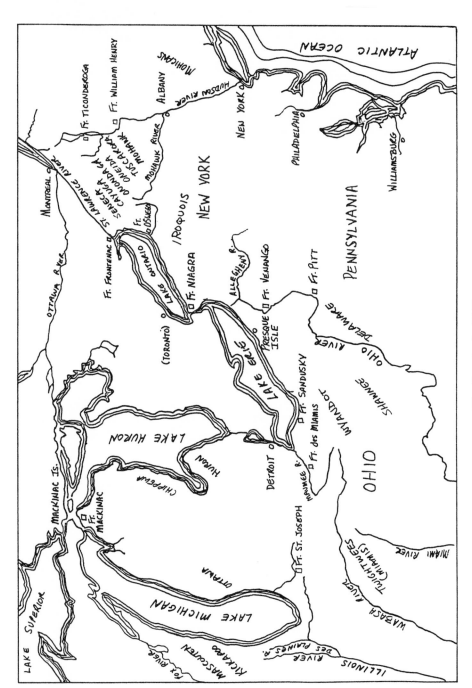

The frontier in 1760.

Introduction

Before 1763, many colonists supported British policies that opened the frontier to exploitation, but the disaster of Pontiac's Rebellion and British imperial reaction after 1763 changed their positive attitudes toward the British government. Many merchants became opponents after the new policies in 1763 and 1764 restricted colonial activities on the frontier, and later were leaders in the resistance to British policy.

Many historians believe that the change in attitude resulted from colonial reliance on Britain for protection against an eminent French threat before the Seven Years' War, and that after 1763 when the threat was removed, British protection became unnecessary and objectionable. The thesis presented here is that the French never threatened seriously the existence of the thirteen colonies. Prior to 1760, the inhabitants of French Canada (which stretched along the St. Lawrence and also included the area between the Allegheny Mountains and the Mississippi River) and the Indians had been supported by the military and financial resources of the French government and physically blocked colonial westward expansion. The Capitulation of Montreal in 1760 removed two of the obstacles to colonial expansion, the French financial support and the French army, but not the French Canadians and the Indians, both of whom continued to impede the colonists.

The conflict in the New World between the French and Indians, on the one hand and the colonists on the other, had been growing in intensity for many years. During the 1740s, the French and the colonists were competing in the Ohio Valley, and Indian traders from the colonies of Virginia, Pennsylvania, and Maryland threatened the French fur trade and their communication lines between Louisiana and Canada. In 1754, a French expedition established Fort Duquesne at the site of the future Fort Pitt, and captured the Virginians under George

Washington, leading to the Seven Years' War between the two major powers, France and Britain.

Although in 1754 the colonists wanted British protection from this French incursion on the frontier at Fort Pitt, General Edward Braddock's expedition received very little support from Virginia or Pennsylvania and ended in disaster. During the Seven Years' War, the colonists were unwilling to provide for their defense and did so only after the promise that the individual colonies would be reimbursed for any expense.

When hostilities between France and England in Canada ended in 1760, trade on the frontier was opened to all with minimum regulation. Before the war, each colony was free to enact its own rules, but in August 1754 the British Board of Trade outlined the need for an imperial policy for the West to prevent French encroachment. The suggested policy included defense of the colonies, management of Indian affairs with imperial officials, and construction of frontier forts with garrisons provided by the colonies. The presents for the Indians and salaries for commissaries, the commander-in-chief, and the commissary general of the Indian Department were to be financed with colonial taxes based on the wealth and population of each colony as set by a board of commissioners.

Although the Plan of 1754 was not implemented, in 1756 Sir William Johnson was made superintendent of Indian Affairs for the northern department, and in 1762 John Stuart replaced the first southern superintendent, Edmund Atkin. Several colonies attempted to place the fur trade under public control, but none was successful because each colony passed different laws. A trader was responsible only to his own colony and might trade in other areas with impunity.

Centralized control was needed, but the issue was whether the colonists would provide joint financial support for trade regulation and for the military presence on the frontier. In Pennsylvania, the frontier farmers wanted protection from the Indians who were supplied by the French, while the peaceful Quakers opposed any military measures.[1] Some colonists did not believe that the French posed any threat to the colonies, that the conflict was between the two imperial powers and was not a colonial concern. In their view, the Seven Years' War with France was fought for British imperial interests. According to Benjamin Franklin in 1766, the fighting in Canada was an attempt to defend the imperial fur trade, not to protect the colonists who were at peace with the French and Indians. The Ohio Valley, according to this interpretation, was imperial property (not belonging to any colony) and its retention was not an essential interest of any colony.[2] This argument denied the intense interest of many colonists in westward expansion and illustrated the conflict among them.

The events and financial transactions that shaped some colonial attitudes occurred on the open and unrestricted frontier in the area bounded roughly by the Allegheny Mountains, the Ohio River, the Mississippi River, the Great Lakes, and the St. Lawrence River. The territory in question was large and sparsely populated, making its control difficult for either the French or the British.

The surrender of the French at Montreal in 1760 presented colonial merchants with the possibility of obtaining a vast quantity of fur that had been accumulated while Canada was cut off from France. In Detroit alone, the accumulated furs were worth £100 thousand sterling compared to only £761 thousand sterling for all goods from all thirteen colonies exported to England in 1760. Leading merchants from Philadelphia and New York City sent agents to Canada in 1761 and 1762 to buy the furs, but the French refused to sell, and under the terms of the Capitulation of Montreal, furs belonging to the South Sea Company were sent to France after the peace treaty was signed.

However, each year the Indians brought in a new harvest of fur that was available to the colonial traders from Pennsylvania and New York who flocked to the former French trading posts to buy both from the French and directly from the Indians in exchange for dry goods and rum. The colonial traders, although rebuffed by the French at the posts, were able to obtain large quantities of furs directly from the Indians through liberal use of rum, in contrast to the French traders who limited the amount of brandy given to the Indians.

Life in the forest was extremely dangerous, subject to Indian attack at any time. Europeans could survive in the wilderness only with the consent of the tribes. If the Indians chose to resist, a few thousand soldiers and a few hundred traders could not control the vast expanse of Canada. The traders were allowed because the Indians desired the European goods. Their desire for rum in 1760 was related to the epidemics that struck terror as entire native villages were destroyed by smallpox introduced by the Europeans. The fear of the unknown created stress that broke down Indian culture, and rum provided a palliative, a means to escape from fear. On the other hand, the rum made the Indians even less able to cope with their problems, but the French and colonials, with a vested interest, also provided clothing and blankets to keep them warm and guns to simplify the task of hunting for food. With comparative ease, an Indian hunter could kill enough beaver and other fur-bearing animals to purchase whatever was needed for the year from the traders. The guns also were useful in warfare with neighboring tribes. Therefore, in 1760 the Indians were eager to deal with any trader.

However, the French were unwilling to share the fur trade with the New York and Pennsylvania traders. The abuse of the Indians by the colonial merchants simplified the French task of inciting Pontiac's Rebellion in 1763. To drive out the colonial traders, beginning in 1762, the French conspired with the Indian leaders, who recognized, themselves, the destructive impact of rum on their tribes and resented their ill treatment. In 1763, after nearly four years of unbridled colonial exploitation, Pontiac's Rebellion was a great victory for the French and Indians. The British army was driven into three forts—Niagara, Detroit, and Fort Pitt—and the colonial traders were robbed and murdered in the smaller posts and forests. The French collaborators were unharmed, often sharing in the loot taken from the plundered colonists.

The cost to Britain of the punitive expeditions against the Indians was high, and the colonists were reluctant to provide more than token assistance. Therefore, the British government, in an austerity mood, changed its policy from supporting the colonists, to working with the Canadians and Indians to block colonial advances. The Proclamation of 1763 prohibited settlement west of the mountains, and the Plan of 1764 that restricted the colonial traders, although never officially adopted, was in fact implemented using military funds. In addition, the cost of the Indian bribes and the cost of maintaining an army on the frontier to maintain peace were also factors causing the British government to reverse the open door policy to traders granted in 1760 and to place heavy restrictions on colonial trade in the West. The restrictions (prohibition of the sale of rum to the Indians and no trading beyond the garrisoned posts) were insurmountable and drove the colonists from the fur trade, which then passed to the Canadians and the Scottish merchants, discharged officers in Montreal and Quebec who cooperated with the French, providing a source of goods and a market for the fur. In the eyes of the colonial merchants who suffered heavy losses in Pontiac's Rebellion, the British government had allied itself with the enemy: the Canadians and the Indians. The British government had actually replaced the French in supporting the Canadians and Indians to block the colonists. This alliance of the British government, the Canadians, the Scottish merchants, and the Indians lasted well into the nineteenth century. In defense of the British policy, the government was concerned about the abuse of the Indians by the colonials, and could see no alternative to maintaining peace with the Indians and control over the French, other than to ally the army with the French inhabitants and Indians against the colonials.

The colonial merchants were outraged by the unpunished deaths of their countrymen and their enormous financial losses, including £80 thousand sterling by a group of Pennsylvania merchants. Some sought compensation in land grants. The frontier business activity from 1760 to 1763 made the New York, Pennsylvania, and Virginia merchants aware of possible land speculation, despite the fact that they had lost money in the fur business. Even before 1760 the colonists, especially from Virginia and Pennsylvania, saw the value in land. In Virginia, George Washington was staking claims and buying up soldiers' grants awarded for service in the Seven Years' War. The Proclamation of 1763 was intended to stop the land speculators from encroaching on the Indian land and interfering with the fur trade.

A major item of contention in the early 1760s was what constituted the status quo, the position before the British government began to change the relationship between the colonies and the mother country. Prior to the events on the Ohio River in 1754, the British government had made little contribution to frontier defense because the claims of the French and the colonists were seldom physically contested. The incursions of the French in the Ohio Valley altered the situation when the Virginia governor failed to drive out the French, and the support of the British government was required to remove the French threat to the colonial frontier. However, when the Treaty of Paris officially removed the French presence in Canada, the colonists expected that all restraints on western commercial and territorial expansion would be removed also and that there would be little need for a British military presence other than the Royal Navy to prevent the French government from returning. The status quo of 1760, an open frontier without restrictions, was the situation the expansionists wished to restore in the following years.[3] After Pontiac's Rebellion in 1763, the British regular army troops, with very little assistance from the colonies, restored the conditions that existed in 1754, with the French in control of the fur trade and the frontier closed to settlement. The situation of 1754 was the status quo sought by the British government with a continued British military presence on the frontier to protect the Indians from the colonists.[4]

The British policy after 1763 reflected the fear of a repetition of Pontiac's Rebellion and the desire to reduce expenses. To encourage peace with the Indians, the British government regulated the fur trade to remove some of the abuses and restricted western settlement. However, this new British policy permitted the French Canadians to maintain their close ties with the Indians and to exclude the colonials from the fur trade. This policy also conciliated the French Canadians to British rule and reduced the possibility that the Paris government would try to maintain the loyalty of the French Canadians and make life difficult for the British officials by encouraging Indian resistance. Although the French Canadians and the Indians were not a major threat to British control of Canada, measures to pacify the Indians militarily were extremely expensive, and the colonists were reluctant to finance military action against the Indians. Given the choice, the British government opted to conciliate the French Canadians and the Indians with fur trade regulations unfavorable to the colonists and issued the Proclamation of 1763 that limited westward expansion. The shift of the alliance of the British army from the colonial merchants to the French Canadians and the Indians forebode the division of the American colonies from England and the formation of a strong tie between Canada and London.

The most unfortunate victims of these political, military, and economic policies were the Indians who were deprived of their culture and land, and were destroyed by smallpox, typhus, and other diseases from the time the Europeans arrived in America. In the face of epidemics that killed ninety percent of a tribe, the Indians lost faith in the ability of their medicine men to restore health, and their ancient traditions, including their self-imposed limitation on hunting, began to crumble. Native American culture was sacrificed as their desire for European weapons, clothing, household goods, tobacco, and particularly alcohol drove them to hunt far more aggressively. Many animal species east of the Mississippi River were near extinction. Previously, the French Canadians' policy of restricting the amount of alcohol had reduced Indian incentive and spared the extinction of the animals. Under the British, on the other hand, the unlimited supply of alcohol encouraged unrestrained hunting.

This study begins with a description of the mechanics of the British occupation of the Great Lakes area. The new, more sensitive relationships formed with the Indians previously under French rule provides a background, followed by an analysis of the merchants, traders, and Indians that made up the cast of characters on the frontier in 1760. How commerce was conducted, beginning with the European suppliers and ending with the varied consumers on the frontier, will reveal the intricate commercial relationship between the colonies and England.

The frontier was divided by geography into four distinct areas: the northwest linked by the Ottawa River with Montreal on the St. Lawrence River; the upper lakes reached by way of the Mohawk River and Lake Erie, as well as the Ottawa River; the Ohio River valley; and Illinois connected by the Mississippi River to New Orleans and by the Ohio River to Fort Pitt. The Hudson Bay Company was already in competition with the Montreal traders in 1760 in the far north, but had little impact on the colonial economy. The Great Lakes area was a common destination for traders using all of the routes. Goods could enter the Indian country through one route and be exchanged for furs that would then return to the sea by one of the other routes.

The events that transpired on the frontier from 1760 to 1764 were disastrous to the colonial merchants and costly to the British government. The need became obvious for centralized control of settlement and regulation of commerce west of the Allegheny Mountains. However, the limits and rules imposed to re-establish sanity on the frontier deprived the colonists of the forbidden fruit of unlimited economic exploitation and the promise of enormous gains with minimum investment but maximum risk. Despite the huge investment of time and money, and the loss of lives, few fortunes were made on the frontier in the 1760s, but the techniques had been mastered. When the British government interposed rules and regulations to stop the unruly process, some, if not most of the colonial merchants, must have considered removing that strict barrier to their exploitation of a seemingly limitless opportunity. Although the colonial merchants' advance was halted east of the Allegheny Mountains, they would resume a developing scenario that would not stop until the frontier vanished.

NOTES

1. Merrill Jensen, *The Founding of a Nation* (New York: Oxford University Press, 1968), 26–28.

2. Robert W. Tucker and David C. Hendrickson, *The Fall of the First British Empire, Origins of the War of Independence* (Baltimore, MD: The John Hopkins University Press, 1982), 58.

3. Ibid. 59–65.

4. Ibid. 72–75.

1

The Financial Framework

The British conquest of Canada in 1760 ended the Seven Years' War in North America and opened the frontier to American and British merchants. The fur trade was only one part of a complex economic structure that brought manufactured goods from Europe, food from the colonial farms, and molasses from the West Indies to be distilled into rum to supply the army, the Indians, and the French inhabitants. Furs were carried to the seacoast and were either shipped to Britain or used in the expanding domestic market for fur and leather accessories.

Thousands of men were employed in moving the merchandise to the interior and returning the peltry. More than ten thousand individuals have been identified as participants: manufacturers and agents in England, wholesale merchants on the seacoast, traders in the Indian country, boatmen, and *voyageurs*. The impact of the beginning of a transportation and financial system that was to span a continent spurred the growth of the colonial economy. Wagons, packhorses, boats, canoes, and sailing ships carried the goods, and the lengthy transactions were financed on credit. In the early years, the frontier was transformed from a wilderness closed to colonial merchants to an area ripe for their exploitation.

Considerable economic change occurred in North America in 1760. As long as active hostilities had continued, direct trade with the Indians was legally closed for fear that the military supplies would reach Indians allied to the French. However, the demands of the army for supplies for the troops and gifts for the Indians kept the merchants interested in western trade with a good market. With the tapering off of the war at the end of the year, the shift from war to peace began in the colonial economy.

Every economy needs some form of cash crop to pay for the items that it must import because of climate or lack of ability to manufacture. The Seven

Table 1.1

British Expenditures in North America and Trade Balance

(All amounts in thousands of £ sterling)

	1759	1760	1761	1762	1763	1764	1765
Total Imperial Military Expense	£10,271	£12,759	£14,665	£15,252	£6,849	£5,264	£5,992
Regiments in N. America	26	28	24	10	17	20	20
Military Expense in N. America	£1,118	£1,182	£1,044	£525	£753	£376	£430
Indian Dept.	£11.7	£5.4	£6.6	£8.7	£7.3	£26.9	£15.0
Exports to Br.	£640	£761	£848	£743	£1,106	£1,111	£1,151
Military plus Exports	£1,758	£1,943	£1,892	£1,268	£1,859	£1,487	£1,587
Imports from Br.	£2,345	£2,612	£1,652	£1,377	£1,632	£2,250	£1,944
Surplus (Deficit)	(£587)	(£669)	£240	(£109)	£227	(£763)	(£357)

Sources: George L. Beer, *British Colonial Policy, 1754–1765* (New York: Peter Smith, 1933), 214; Public Record Office, Group 348, T64, Bundle 276A and 691, II, 20; Murray G. Lawson, *Fur, A Study in English Mercantilism, 1700–1775* (Toronto: University of Toronto Press, 1943), 87–88, 108–109, 134–35; Indian Trade, *Canadian Archives*, Colonial Office 323, XV, 182–84; Note C, *Canadian Archives Report*, 1882, 60–61; Colonial Office 378, II (extract); Exports, North America, Great Britain, 1768–1772, Public Record Office, Customs 16, I; Merrill Jensen, ed., *English Historical Documents, American Colonial Documents to 1776*, vol. IX (New York: Oxford University Press, 1955), 392–93.

Years' War had introduced a large cash crop in the form of British army bills of exchange used to purchase goods and services in the colonies. With the ready availability of these bills of exchange to pay debts in England, the colonial economy rapidly expanded its import of luxury merchandise from England. When the supply of army bills of exchange was reduced with the slackening of military operations in North America, the colonial merchants were less able to balance their accounts in England.

The general tapering off in the economy was reflected in the decrease in exports from America to Britain that totaled only about £760,000 in 1760. The war boom was coming to a close, although goods ordered in 1759 flowed into the colonies in tremendous quantities, and exports from Britain to America during 1760 were more than £2,611,000 (See Table 1.1 on p. 8).

The state of the economy placed the merchants of New York and Philadelphia in a mixed mood. One could sell the imports for colonial currency, but there was a shortage of sterling bills of exchange to pay the suppliers in England. In October 1760, Daniel Clarke, a Philadelphia merchant, wrote William Neate, his London correspondent, that the demand for goods was so great that he could sell up to £10,000 sterling worth. However, Clarke complained of the high cost of goods sent to him, and of the high cost of sterling bills. He wished there were some other way to remit payment for goods.[1]

The competition between the merchants in Albany was reflected in the correspondence of John Sanders of Schenectady who with his suppliers, Champion & Hayley, handled a little more than £140 New York; and James Bonbonous, who handled less than £300 New York. Throughout the rest of the 1760s, Sanders seldom dealt in orders more than £200 New York in the single year, but he did pay promptly, unlike many of the others.[2] Sanders was able to make his remittances equal to £275 New York in bills of exchange to England, but for the next ten years, the greatest sum in bills that he was able to remit was equal to £165 New York; for the rest he had to resort to produce or cash. Sales were good, but the era of a plentiful supply of sterling bills, usually drawn to meet the expenses of the army, was ending.

The radical change in the frontier experience was the aftermath of the French army defeat in 1759 that created a political and military vacuum west of the Allegheny Mountains. Colonial merchants, entrepreneurs from England, and discharged soldiers were free to compete with the French Canadians in trading with the Indians. The British army played a vital role in establishing military posts at strategic points, providing safe havens for the British and protecting the colonial traders.

In 1760, the thirteen continental colonies were in the midst of a commercial boom created, in part, by the lavish expenditures for provisions and other supplies for the army during the Seven Years' War. The iron industry, shipbuilding, fishing on the banks of Newfoundland, the carrying trade, distilling, meat packing (beef and pork), and lumbering flourished. Although there was some English regulation of economic life, the merchants were prospering under the protection of the Empire.[3]

Much of the economic growth was concentrated in New York and Pennsylvania where the greatest share of the seaboard development was garnered and formed an essential link to the frontier. New York and Philadelphia merchants broadened their business to include supplying the army, settlers on the frontier, the Indians, and the French Canadians. The result was an increasing tempo of business with the west beginning in 1760, despite an initial decrease in the number of furs exported to England. In 1760, western trade moved from the hands of a few adventurers to become the province of the major entrepreneurs.

The trade with the Indians was seen by most of the new participants primarily as a high-risk opportunity to make a great deal of money with a limited investment of capital. There was no redeeming social objective; the end product was a stylish hat of no practical use or intrinsic value, which served as a status symbol for a few thousand wealthy Europeans. Very few of those hats, which cost the lives of thousands of native Americans, colonists, and Europeans, have survived after 200 years.

The major economic value of the fur trade was that it provided a commodity, along with tobacco, rice, and lumber, that could be sold in England to balance the colonists' purchases of British manufactured goods. The American colonies, with a rapidly increasing population, nearly doubling every twenty years, were the major export market for British products, In 1760, in the thirteen colonies, there were about 1.5 million people including four hundred thousand slaves, compared to eleven million in the British Isles, a number that was growing rapidly as well.[4]

Although western New York was sparsely settled with military garrisons at Niagara, Oswego, and other points, the Mohawk Valley had a considerable agricultural settlement, and towns were developing at Schenectady and Albany. The population of the Province of New York, according to the census of 1756, was 96,765 with 17,424 in Albany County; the other eighty thousand lived within eighty miles of New York City. According to the census of 1771, the population of the province had grown to 182,247 of which 47,375 lived in frontier counties. These statistics indicated a rapid growth in the comparatively undeveloped areas of New York within a period of only fifteen years. Expansion at this rate created a busy market for the merchants of Albany and Schenectady.

The population of Pennsylvania, according to estimates, grew from 217,000 in 1760 to 276,000 in 1770. Although most lived in the immediate area of Philadelphia and along the Delaware River, up to 40,000 settlers lived in the west in 1760. The Province of Quebec, according to one estimate, had a population of 65,000 in 1762, concentrated in the St. Lawrence valley. Using an estimate for New York of 117,000 in 1760, the combined population for the three provinces was about 397,000 in 1760 with fewer than 70,000 beyond the coastal area. Even though only a small percentage of Americans lived on the frontier, they would form a growing threat both to the Indian population and the fur trade in the near future.[5]

Britain needed the colonial market to absorb the ever growing output of her industries. The industrial revolution was transforming the British economy and providing an enormous surplus of manufactured goods. By 1750, large-scale production, the mark of the industrial revolution in Britain, was common in the textile and metals trade, made possible by the mechanical loom, the process of printing cotton, the hot metal press, the coke smelter, the paper mill, the rolling mill, and improved coal mining techniques.[6]

The industrial revolution prospered in England in the eighteenth century because all of the components needed were available: a ready supply of capital, raw materials, labor, and markets, both at home and overseas. Some of the necessary raw materials (iron ore, wool, and leather) were available in England, whereas steel came from Sweden and other products from the American colonies. The rapidly growing English population provided ample quantities of labor and a huge expanding market for many types of consumer goods. The capital came from the huge profits made by the upper classes in overseas trade and in rents in the London area. The capital was available thanks to the Bank of England and the financial structure in England that facilitated loans. The Bank of England extended commercial credit and made trading based on credit rather than cash the customary way of doing business.[7]

Colonial and foreign commerce was the basis of British prosperity. Supplying Spanish colonies in America provided Spanish specie (silver and gold) that was used to buy cotton and calico in India. The cloth from India along with rum from the West Indies and Spanish gold was used in turn to buy slaves in Africa. Because of the poor conditions, the average slave lived only seven years after reaching the New World and very few Black children were born. As a result, there was a steady demand not only to replace slaves who had died from overwork, but to open new plantations to satisfy the growing demand for sugar in Britain and America. The British supplied an average of twelve thousand slaves per year from their slave stations in Africa, and the French sent about seven thousand each year to the West Indies.[8] The trade in cotton, slaves, and sugar created the fortunes that financed the industrial expansion in England.

British merchant shipping was the means to reach the overseas markets, with more than three thousand British ships carrying goods to the British colonies. By 1774, one-third of all British trade, based in London, Bristol, Liverpool, and Glasgow, was with its colonies. Exports from England to the colonies were primarily cloth and wearing apparel, worth £2,355,000 sterling of the total exports of £5,155,000 (over $1 billion) in 1772. Of the rest, ironware was £500,000; foreign goods re-exported to colonies was £770,000; and miscellaneous other products were £1.5 million. British exports to the thirteen colonies in the mid-eighteenth century were three-fourths British manufactures and one-fourth re-export of goods from other countries, including cloth from several European countries.[9]

The 1.5 million Americans formed a mass market, free and clear of any foreign competition, but how the Americans would pay for the British goods was a concern. In the thirteen colonies, ninety percent of the people were farmers, and the main business was the export of farm produce including wheat, corn, rice, indigo, tobacco, bread and flour, packed beef and pork, rum, lumber, and fish.[10] Only indigo, tobacco, lumber, and rice found significant markets in Great Britain. Most of the other products went to Mediterranean countries and the West Indies. Even though exports of fur from north of the Ohio River averaged only about £109,000 sterling annually and ranked third behind tobacco and rice in exports to England, fur had a considerable political and economic impact because of its value in England.

Rum was a crucial component of colonial commerce. The British West Indies used their molasses, a byproduct of the manufacture of sugar, to make rum that was exported to England. To protect their rum market in England, the British West Indies' sugar producers pressured Parliament in 1733 to pass the Molasses Act that placed a prohibitive duty of 6p per gallon on foreign molasses imported by the English colonies. A duty was prohibitive if placed so high that it made import of the taxed product uneconomical and resulted in no legal imports. In contrast, a duty designed to raise money was placed at a low level to ensure the greatest monetary return through volume. A tax of 6p ($5) per gallon significantly increased the cost of a gallon of rum (about $30 on the seacoast), encouraging extensive smuggling from the French West Indies. Export of rum from the French West Indies to France was prohibited to protect the French wine makers, and there was no legal market for the French molasses. Therefore, the large quantities of molasses available at a low price could be exchanged for lumber and food products, making smuggling molasses into the mainland colonies very profitable. Colonial produce was carried by ships with forged papers to Monte Christi in Spanish Santo Domingo and then sent to the French islands. The French molasses returned by the same route. In 1763, an attempt to enforce the Molasses Act failed, and in 1764, although the duty was reduced to 3p per gallon, the tax was still prohibitive and smuggling continued. In 1766, a duty reduced to 1p per gallon of molasses made paying the duty cheaper than smuggling. The magnitude of the previous smuggling was clearly revealed in 1772 when 4.8 million gallons of molasses were imported by the mainland colonies from the French West Indies, whereas only one hundred thousand gallons, slightly more than two percent, came from British islands.[11]

Molasses reaching the American colonies was distilled into rum for the colonists and the British army. However, by 1760, the Indians offered a new market for rum. The colonial traders quickly discovered that rum was a powerful inducement in trade with the Indians and could divert the fur trade into colonial hands. The French Canadians, on the other hand, had operated an extensive trade with the Indians for more than 150 years, and French methods had provided a steady flow of fur with a minimal use of brandy. With the copious supplies of rum, the traders from New York and Pennsylvania broke the

French monopoly. The profits derived from distilling molasses into rum and selling it to the Indians were enormous.

Rum and other Indian goods had another market that was far less risky than direct sale to the Indians. In response to French activity on the frontier in 1754, the British government created the Indian Department and committed the British army to the defense of the frontier. In an attempt to keep the Indians quiet and amenable to trade, the Indian Department supplied the Indians with weapons, clothing, blankets, and a limited amount of rum, usually two gallons for each warrior each time they came into contact with the Indian Department agents. In addition, the army greatly stimulated the American economy with their large purchases of provisions and other supplies. The military and the Indian Department purchased as much as £300,000 sterling ($20 million) a year, mostly from colonial merchants in the years before 1768. From 1754 to 1769, these expenditures played a favorable role in balancing the trade between England and the colonies.

Only a few British regiments were sent to America prior to 1754, and they were withdrawn after each war, because each colony had been responsible for policing its own frontier. After the cessation of hostilities in 1760, a sizable force of British regular troops remained to occupy frontier forts. The colonists believed that they had no need for this protection before the war and even less after the war. The only need for garrisons was in Canada and Florida. The army found itself with the impossible task of trying to protect the colonial traders—impossible because most of the transactions were outside of the forts where the soldiers did well to survive themselves. During a period of increasing British government expenditures in America, sterling bills of exchange became more plentiful. With sterling balances in England, annual imports increased as well from 1759 to 1761. A great demand for European goods developed in the colonies, and imports from England rose sharply from £1.7 million sterling in 1758 to £2.3 million in 1759 and £2.6 million in 1760.[12]

Although cash was plentiful in 1761, and remittances to England were made easily, reduced military spending in 1762 was accompanied by an overall economic slowdown in the colonies.[13]   Exports to England rose slightly, to £847,000 sterling, whereas imports from England dropped sharply to £1.65 million. A sharp increase in the rate of exchange between colonial currency and sterling may have resulted from the need to purchase sterling bills to pay for the large amount of goods received in 1760 from England, while few commodities were being sent to England to balance accounts. Balancing of accounts often took many months in the eighteenth century (see Table 1.1, p. 8).

The sharp reduction in imports from England fell heavily on the merchants of New York and Pennsylvania. Of the slightly more than £1 million sterling of imports listed in 1761 compared to the 1760 total, nearly £600,000 sterling of this loss occurred in New York and Pennsylvania. However, in the following years, most of the silver and gold in the colonies was sent to England to pay off debts. New loans were difficult to obtain because in 1762 many regiments went to fight in Cuba taking with them the market for food and other supplies that had previously provided bills of exchange on London. The immediate result was a severe shortage of cash in Philadelphia and New York, and many merchants were forced into bankruptcy. Six Quaker merchants in Philadelphia declared bankruptcy in 1763, including Scott & McMichael with debts of £30,000 sterling.[14]

Cash again became plentiful in 1763 when the troops returned from Cuba after the capture of Havana with £3 million prize money that was distributed among the troops. Military expenditures in America dropped from £1 million in 1761 to half a million pounds sterling when most of the army went to Cuba in 1762. The economy recovered the following year when the army returned, and exports to England totaled £1.45 million sterling, the best of the seven years from 1760–1766.

At the end of 1763, the cost of the army to Britain was about £231,000 per year for the infantry regiments and garrisons and £23,000 for the artillery companies and other charges. Additional expenses for the newly acquired colonies of Florida, Canada, and others, would have to be paid by Britain. The imperial expense in North America was estimated at £350,000 sterling. Existing colonial revenue would produce only £40,000 to £50,000, so the colonial taxes proposed in 1763 were intended to raise £400,000 annually ($80 million) to maintain ten thousand troops.[15]

Britain's financial problem multiplied during an economic slump in England in the early 1760s. In order to sell goods, credit had been given to Americans by British merchants with the time of payment extended from the previous standard of six months to one year. Production was increasing sharply in Britain as a result of labor-saving machines, creating a need for markets for the flood of manufactured goods. Therefore, the English were willing to trust American merchants with doubtful means to repay loans or to pay for goods purchased on credit. The Americans in turn responded with a buying spree that improved the standard of living in the thirteen colonies.[16]

By 1760, the American colonies owed an enormous debt to England. In 1766, the British merchants who traded with North America, estimated £4,450,000 sterling ($890 million) owed to merchants in London, Bristol, Glasgow, Liverpool, and Manchester. These totals excluded ports such as Plymouth that also traded extensively with North America.[17]

The English financial crisis after 1760 was caused by the slowing of the economy as a direct result of the reduction in the needs for the British army. Suppliers to the army reduced the number of employees and the ripple effect slowed the entire economy. As a result, refinancing (obtaining a new loan to pay off a loan that was due) was difficult to obtain. Demands were made for repayment of old debts, and payment for new purchases was required in a shorter time.[18]

The cost of defending the Empire was reflected in the sharp rise in Britain's military expenditures. Charges on the British government increased from an average of £6.5 million sterling annually from 1750 to 1755, to an annual average of £14.5 million sterling from 1756 to 1766. The debt rose from £75 million in 1755 to £140 million in 1763. During the Seven Years' War, England's military expense and its policy of underwriting Prussian armies against France and Austria cost nearly £53 million sterling from 1759 to 1762.[19]

The end of heavy fighting with the Capitulation of Montreal quickly reduced the flow of funds from Britain to the colonies. With the beginning of peace negotiations in 1762, attempts were made to reduce expenses. The military expenditures by the Empire dropped from more than £15 million sterling in 1762 to £6,849,000 in 1763. The cost of supporting the army in America and purchasing presents to pacify the Indians was opposed in Parliament because the Seven Years' War had left England with a large debt and heavy taxes. By the end of 1763, the funded debt of Great Britain was £129.5 million with an annual interest charge of £4,688,000 sterling. Politically, Parliament could not assume an additional sum for defense in North America.[20]

The sudden end to large-scale wartime purchasing by Britain in Europe created a major economic depression, leaving a large number of unsecured bills of exchange in circulation in Europe that had been used to make wartime purchases. The Dutch bankers, who had financed much of Britain's debt, could not meet their obligations and declared bankruptcy, spreading the crisis to Germany and England. From July to November 1763, there was an acute financial panic in Europe. A heavy flow of specie from London to Amsterdam began in August 1763 as the Dutch demanded repayment of loans, creating a demand for gold and silver. The Bank of England was forced to suspend payment of its own bills as did many English merchants.[21] This chain of events increased the price of silver and stripped the colonies of specie that had been plentiful since 1759.

Merchants were quick to buy gold and silver at comparatively low prices in America and ship it to England. Baynton and Wharton, a Philadelphia mercantile house, sent more than eight thousand Spanish silver dollars from Canada, Havana, and Philadelphia.[22] By September 1763, William Darlington, Sir William Johnson's agent in New York City, was complaining of the shortage of dollars.[23]

The Currency Act of 1764 limited the supply of paper money that could be issued by the colonies, while military spending dropped to below £400,000. The steep rise in prices, that had been a symptom of the earlier, prosperous year of 1762 and the first months of 1763, gave way to a sharp decline in 1764 and 1765. Henry Cruger, a Bristol agent, reported in 1765 to Aaron Lopez, a noted Rhode Island merchant, that there were no cargoes for the ships because of the depression. Earlier, he had written that "Money is so scarce in the Kingdom and the trade of all sorts is so dull, and the English Markets over done with North American produce, especially Lumber."[24]

The end of the war brought economic distress to the colonial merchants who blamed the British government for their problems. The merchants did not believe that the sacrifices endured by Britain during the war had been of benefit to the colonies, and therefore the colonies should not be asked to assume the burden of defending the new lands.

The depression in the trade with America caused economic distress in England as well, as fewer orders were placed by American merchants in England. The principle manufacturing centers for Indian goods were Whitney, Oxfordshire (blankets), Yorkshire (wool cloth), Manchester (cotton), and Birmingham (beads, drugs, tinware, guns, and other hardware).[25] British manufacturers sold their wares via agents in London and Bristol, or directly to wholesale merchants in America. For example, in 1762, Thomas and John Hurst & Co., manufacturers of hosiery at Hinckley in Leicestershire, received an order from Baynton & Wharton through Hurst's representative on Woods Street in London. The stockings were delivered to London and then shipped to Baynton & Wharton in Philadelphia, who in turn sent the hosiery to their agents on the frontier.[26] Many of the London and Bristol merchants acted as agents, factors, or correspondents who assembled merchandise from the Continent and England for shipment to the New World.

Personal relationships were basic to good business among the factors and the manufacturers and their customers in America. Distances in the eighteenth century posed difficulties because variations in measurements and quality were much greater than in the twentieth century, and one did not always receive the exact item ordered. Indirect commercial relationships based on written specifications were unsatisfactory, and even presentation of samples did not guarantee satisfaction because of the uncertainty of the actual product delivered. The tremendous possibilities for fraud made the buyer, the producer, and the agent extremely wary. Therefore, direct personal relationships among the producer, agent, and buyer established over a long period of time were essential.[27]

Often, commercial and financial transactions between two countries would be handled by a comparatively small group of firms, most of whom were linked by ties of blood, marriage, religion, race, or at least personal acquaintance. Business was often organized on a family basis with the younger brother or son overseas to supervise a branch. Dutch firms sent relatives to London to manage their affairs just as English firms sent younger members to the American colonies to supervise family businesses. Personal recommendation was extremely important because international trade was on credit, so the wealthy merchants in New York and Philadelphia had direct ties with agents in London and Bristol.[28] Of course, this need for personal relationships gave the older, established merchants the upper hand.

Merchandise for America crossed the Atlantic Ocean from England to the commercial centers including Quebec, Montreal, New York, and Philadelphia. The trip across the Atlantic lasted up to three weeks or more. John Welles considered a twenty-six day passage from England to Quebec as "very good."[29] London was the major port, but Glasgow, Whitehaven, and Bristol were also important.[30] An example of the agent–merchant relationship and transatlantic shipment was the interaction between Anthony Merry in London and Baynton & Wharton in Philadelphia regarding a shipment of brandy in 1763. Merry had four hundred tons of brandy (more than one hundred thousand gallons) in Quebec and could not sell it. On the advice of Baynton & Wharton, Merry diverted a large shipment of brandy to Philadelphia to be sold at 20p per gallon rather than sending it to Quebec where prices were lower at the time.[31]

The need for a good agent was illustrated by the experience of Christopher Champlin in 1765. Champlin received a shipment including some defective brass kettles and his agent, John Powell, had forced the person who had supplied the kettles to compensate Champlin. Powell commented in his letter that "the tradesmen now in London require a strict scrutiny into their wares for exportation."[32]

Most of the traders on the frontier purchased their supplies in Quebec, Montreal, New York, Philadelphia, or Albany, although a substantial merchant would order directly from England on credit. The major trading houses acted as wholesalers; they obtained merchandise from England, assembled it into packs and engaged wagons, ships, or canoes to forward the cargoes to Mackinac, Detroit, Albany, and Fort Pitt, where they were sold to local traders. These services were sometimes performed for a commission charged against the receiving traders. The wealthy businessmen also acted as bankers for the others, meeting obligations, paying wages, acting as sales agencies, receiving furs and other goods from the frontier, and either selling them in America or consigning them to a London agent for sale on the London market for a commission.[33]

A markup of one hundred percent or more would provide a good margin to pay for handling costs and for the credit charges that were quite steep. The cost of credit varied with the length of time before repayment. In addition to the burden of high fixed charges, the trader on the frontier suffered when the flow of goods and furs was disturbed, because his overhead expenses continued—wages and provisions for employees, depreciation on the canoes, and interest on capital investment.

The potential for mishaps continued even after the furs were sent east to pay debts as related by Isaac Todd, a merchant in Mackinac. A canoe sent from Mackinac to Montreal in 1767 came into the hands of people who refused to pay for the furs. Another misfortune occurred in 1768 when a canoe with £800 worth of select peltry was sent to Montreal to be shipped to England, but before Todd arrived to arrange for sale or consignment, the pelts had been sent to England, and Todd could not obtain immediate credits. In 1769, bad luck plagued Todd again when he brought down a load of muskrat that could not be sold because the ships had already departed for Britain and the river had frozen. These three experiences placed Todd in such an embarrassing financial situation in 1769 that he could pay nothing to William Edgar, a Detroit merchant who supplied Todd with provisions and other supplies.[34]

Repayment of credit was generally slow. A member of the Baby family of Detroit was trusted for more than six years with a loan without paying additional interest.[35] Edgar's orders placed in 1766 were not paid until 1773, with no added interest.[36] In a poor year, the merchants had to exert an extra effort to collect debts to remain solvent. When a debtor defected to Illinois or was feared near death, the pressure for collection increased. For example, Thomas Shipboy, a New York merchant, hearing of his debtor's illness, instructed Edgar to seize all his furs and property in Detroit to apply against a debt of about £1,200 sterling.[37]

The long delay between an original order for goods and collection of cash for the furs that were sold resulted not only from the complexity in obtaining and selling the goods, but also from the lengthy process of disposing of the peltry that took both time and money.

In some years, profits were better. In 1764, Edgar and William Bruce, trading partners in Detroit, received £389 for sixteen packs of beaver and three miscellaneous packs.[38] Mr. Vigo, a Mackinac trader, who used John Askin as an agent, cleared about £700 sterling for one hundred packs, most of which were deer, along with some beaver, otter, and bear.[39]

In 1765, John Leotard and Giles Godin, two London traders, sold beaver, raccoon, otter, bobcats, and other furs as a lot for about £85 sterling, incurring charges of only about eight percent of the sale.[40] Two sales by Daniel Vialars in London in 1765 of furs worth £560 and £310, respectively, listed charges of £38.9.2 for the two lots, equal to less than five percent of the sale.[41] Alexander Henry, an early trader in the Lake Superior area, in 1766, after spending a winter trading with the Indians, sold furs for £1,875 and still had twenty-five packs of otter and marten worth approximately £450. He had a return of £2,325 on an investment of £1,462.10, a profit of more than fifty percent.[42] In all these examples, a considerable profit was made.

Some transactions involved not only the Indians but also French inhabitants, the army, the Indian Department, and other merchants. An example of these complex transactions was merchandise brought to Detroit in 1763 (see Table 1.2, p. 19). Apparently involved, although not specifically mentioned, were Edward Cole, a Detroit merchant who later became the commissary for the Indian Department in Illinois; Major Robert Rogers; Cezar Cormick, an Albany trader; and a man named Butler (probably John or Thomas Butler both of whom were associated with Sir William Johnson). The profit was more than one hundred percent. Not indicated was who paid for the original cargo, but each of the partners shared equally, receiving one-fourth of the net of £626.[43] More than one-half of the goods were sold to the army and Indian Department, and about one-fifth of the cargo was sold to British merchants. Less than one-fourth was exchanged for pelts, most likely with the French traders in the Detroit area

Table 1.2

Analysis of a Trading Venture in 1763

Purchase of trade goods in Albany	£1,400.0.0
Purchase of additional goods in Detroit	344.0.0
Purchase of furs in Detroit	295.6.8
Transportation from New York to Detroit and return	162.16.8
Interest	11.12.6
Total expense	£2,213.15.10
Sale of cargo to the army and the Indian Department in Detroit and Niagara	£2,356.3.2
Sales to British merchants in Detroit	914.4.0
Sales to French merchants in Detroit	283.9.3
Sales to others	44.18.4
Total sales	3,598.14.9
Cash for the furs purchased	£1,118.12.7
Total revenue	£4,717.7.4
Net profit	£2,503.11.6

rather than with the Indians. The French also purchased a small portion of the goods. This business venture was primarily concerned with the profitable sale of liquor to the army and Indian Department, using the influence of Major Rogers, an officer in the 80th Regiment stationed in the area, who shared in the profits. Furs were used primarily as a medium of exchange, although additional profit may have resulted from their resale.

The examples given here show the great profits, but the trade involved financial risks even for the more wealthy merchants. A period of two years or more could elapse from the time of the decision to order a cargo until information was received as to the final outcome of the venture. During that period, prices changed, boats were lost, and unforseen delays created problems in selling the goods or returning the furs to England. There is little wonder that only a few of the hundreds who tried their hand were able to make and hold large profits.

Table 1.3

Transaction of Blanket and Beaver Pelt Exchange

Cost of manufacturing the blanket	3/-
Profit of London agent on sale of blanket	1/-
Transportation costs of blanket	1/-
Profit to American wholesaler	2/-
Profit to American retailer	1/-
Transportation costs of two beaver	1/-
London agent for sales charges on fur	1/-
Sale price of beaver	10/-

American merchants conducted business at a greater risk than their English agents who, although operating on a lower margin, made fortunes because of the large volume of business. Whereas a markup of one hundred percent was usual for the American merchant, the commission extracted by the London agent was only twenty-five percent or less. However, the English merchants performed many essential steps in the transaction, and without their help, the American merchant would have had difficulty in obtaining goods. An hypothetical transaction of a blanket exchanged for two beaver pelts is shown in Table 1.3. The London agent earned a thirty-three percent profit on his 3/- purchase of the blanket. The American wholesaler earned less than fifty percent after paying the London agent 4/- and part of the transportation. The trader made only eleven percent after all the charges were deducted from the sale price of the beaver.

The frontier merchants obtained merchandise on credit in Montreal, Albany, Schenectady, Philadelphia, Detroit, Mackinac, Fort Pitt, or Niagara from large concerns such as Baynton, Wharton & Morgan or Phyn & Ellice, and dealt directly with the Indians, *voyageurs*, or winterers. The winterers usually would return because the undesirable alternatives were remaining with the natives or going off to Illinois. Unless a man returned to pay his debts, he became an outlaw, so custom favored the man who came back, even if he could not pay his complete debt. Returning to repay credit was encouraged because the rule was that the most recent debt was paid first, and all previous creditors could only share in the remaining assets. Therefore, it would be possible for a creditor to obtain credit for the next year even though he was unable to pay everything.

This practice varied from the standard form of bankruptcy where all creditors received a percentage of their debt from the assets of the creditor. The more lenient rule made it possible for a winterer, who had the misfortune to lose everything, to obtain a full outfit on credit based on the merchant's confidence in the creditor's ability to deal profitably with the Indians, and on the assurance of priority repayment, regardless of any other outstanding debts. The theory behind this lenient custom was that if the trader could obtain additional credit, he eventually would repay his old creditors at least in part.[44] In addition, this custom reflected the great demand for men skilled in the Indian trade. Many years were required to learn the language of the tribes and their customs, and a man who was known and trusted by the natives could deal far more advantageously than a stranger not knowing the rules or the language. An experienced hand, regardless of his credit standing, was far more likely than a beginner with a good credit record to return with a large shipment of furs.

For the winterer, the fur business was not always profitable because of the tremendous risks. The goods that he purchased had passed through many hands, and because of the high cost of transportation and markup to cover losses by others, these products had become very expensive. Furs obtained from the Indians were sold at a low price because, again, the cost of movement had to be added to the price paid before the pelts were sold in London.[45] On the other hand, with little or no capital, an adventurous young man could, with luck, net £100 sterling in one summer, far more than a skilled tradesman could earn in a year. Such opportunity enticed many to risk their lives in the woods. Colonel John Bradstreet, the British quartermaster in Albany, in 1764, thought that the fur trade was of value only to the bateau men, meaning the *voyageurs*.[46] Even the men who simply paddled the canoes were well paid, in Canada £6 sterling ($1,200) or more for the summer, in Pennsylvania £16 sterling ($3,200) for four months plus rations, and in New York over £12 sterling per season in addition to food and clothing.[47] Many took a trip or two to obtain ready cash and then returned to other employment, but these men were merely hired hands of the traders who risked not only their lives but their money as well.

The last step in the transaction was the exchange of merchandise between the petty traders and the Indians, and even at this level, sales were made on a credit basis. When the Indians visited a post they needed credit to obtain supplies of ammunition, clothing, weapons, traps, and other necessities for the coming year. Often they did not have enough furs to exchange, and the trader would extend credit to the individual native, hoping to be repaid in pelts during the coming year. The missionary, Zeisberger, commented that the Indians were fond of buying on credit, promising to pay when they returned from hunting. Some traders took the risk, hoping to receive all the furs when the Indians returned. However, if the Indians found other unscrupulous traders, they would sell the fur to them and ignore their debts. Traders learned to give very little on credit as a result.[48]

Indians seldom broke their word because that would cut off the supply of guns, ammunition, and clothes. Therefore, the Indians were forced to maintain the trust of those traders who would supply them.[49] The tribes were eager to restore a faith and credit operation in the exchange of furs when the British replaced the French. In September 1761, Sir William Johnson was asked by the Indians across the river from Detroit to grant credit as the French had done. Although Johnson claimed that he could not force the British traders to sell their goods on credit, and that it was up to the Indians to establish a credit relationship, he did instruct the traders to grant credit.[50] At Fort Pitt the extension of credit was an important factor in obtaining the peltry. Levy, Trent & Co. and George Croghan extended considerable credit to the Indians, but when they did not pay, there was dissatisfaction on both sides.[51]

In May 1763, Fred Hambuck, an agent of William Edgar of Detroit, reported that a canoe had come in from wintering with very little fur and the greater part of the goods unsold. "The trade is all over here and there is still a great deal of goods left in this Fort. Other traders being still worse off than myself having made considerable credits to the Indians last fall and but few of them paying their debts."[52] Despite these examples of nonpayment, the Indians continued to obtain credit, as a margin could be charged to cover bad debts. The need for supplies and the lure of rum were incentive enough to bring the Indians back to the posts, and given a minimum of enlightened self-interest among the merchants, the hunter would be obliged to make some payment before he obtained additional merchandise.

The fur trade was based on a sophisticated long-term credit system that extended from the agents in London to the hunter in the forest. The extension of credit greatly intensified the financial risk involved because of the volatility of the price of fur. Although handling charges on the imported goods and exported peltry were relatively inflexible, fur prices in Philadelphia, New York, and London were subject to wide variation depending on the supply of pelts. A shipment could produce a large profit or could be sold at a loss depending on the market. There were few available options to sale at the current price. Agents in London could delay the sale of furs until the price rose if the colonial merchant did not demand immediate returns. The merchant with substantial capital and credit had several other alternatives. The New York and Pennsylvania merchants could sell the fur locally if the price were high or the demand for repayment urgent. The Canadians could send peltry to New York and Philadelphia when the price was advantageous. In Illinois, there was an opportunity to sell the furs to the French and Spaniards in New Orleans for shipment to the Continent rather than to England.

The fortunes in frontier business were made or lost by the great merchants such as Phyn & Ellice of Schenectady, Michael & Bernard Gratz of Lancaster, and Baynton, Wharton & Morgan of Philadelphia. To remain in business demanded good management, a large reserve of capital or credit, and good luck.

Many merchants resorted to smuggling to evade restrictions on the sale of fur to foreign countries or to import foreign products. Fur was an enumerated article and could be exported legally only to England, but there was a good market for the pelts in Holland. The enormous impact of smuggling on the rum business was described earlier. Governor James Murray of Canada objected to a heavy tax on the fur trade in the Plan of 1764 because smuggling of furs would be encouraged. A significant illicit trade between Holland and New York existed in the 1760s, sending furs that were legally restricted to England to the Dutch in exchange for tea, canvas, gunpowder, guns, and linen. The smugglers anchored their ships at Sandy Hook outside of the New York harbor and transferred the cargo to small boats that landed in Newport, Providence, Stanford, or Norwalk. The ship then entered the New York harbor empty or went to a Connecticut port. False clearances and flags of truce that permitted a ship to enter a French port during the Seven Years' War were sold openly in Connecticut and Rhode Island.[53] If a ship captain could obtain a single French prisoner of war eligible to return to France, he would be able to take a cargo of American lumber and foodstuffs to the French West Indies where he would pick up a cargo of molasses under a flag of truce.

Lieutenant Governor Calwallader Colden of New York defended the illegal trade, pointing out that it was advantageous to trade with the Spanish colonies because they provided a market for colonial agricultural products, and the cash received was used to buy British manufactured goods. The only legal market for colonial farm produce were the British West Indies, but they required only a small part of the quantity available. The slaves in the West Indies consumed few British manufactures; the Indians consumed more manufactured goods per capita than did the slaves. Because the amount of British goods purchased was directly related to the ability to pay for the goods, Colden believed that it was good business to sell farm produce to the Spaniards and use the cash to buy British goods.[54]

In 1763, the Earl of Egremont, the British secretary of state, again requested that Colden take steps to suppress the illegal trade with Holland, but Colden could not think of another method besides placing men from the Royal Navy on board every ship suspected of coming from a foreign port to ensure that the cargo was unloaded at a proper port, ending the practice of unloading at Sandy Hook. A year later, the illegal trade of tea and gunpowder from Holland and Hamburg continued despite the presence of the Royal Navy.[55] Another method of evasion was the double cargo technique—part of the ship's cargo of foreign goods was declared and subjected to duty, and the remainder was declared to be destined for foreign ports, but actually was smuggled into New England ports where regulations were not enforced.[56] The New York merchants complained of the lack of customs control on the Delaware River, including Philadelphia, while the New York City illegal trade was harassed by the Royal Navy. The New York merchants complained that the Philadelphia merchants were able to undersell them because of the less effective control of illegal trade from

Holland. The British improved enforcement on the Delaware and in 1764 Daniel Roberdeau complained to Myler & Hall that a strict watch was being maintained in Philadelphia by the customs officers and the Royal Navy, making it "almost impossible" to smuggle, especially exports. A customs officer inspected the hold of a schooner being loaded by Roberdeau, even though he had never been suspected of smuggling.[57]

There were ample references to smuggling in the business accounts of the Philadelphia merchants of trade with Holland. In 1760, John Kidd objected to the high insurance rates for trade with Holland in a letter to the Cliffords, one of the more important firms in the Anglo-Dutch trade in Amsterdam. The Cliffords were also involved in a shipment of sugar valued at £1,380 Pennsylvania with Daniel Mildred of London. John and Peter Chevalier shipped sugar to Amsterdam in 1760, and also sent a cargo from Monti Christi to Sargent, Aufrere & Company of Amsterdam worth £800 sterling insured at forty percent, an extremely high rate in 1762. Later in the year, a ship from Hanover returned a cargo insured at the rate of only ten percent. In 1764, the Chevaliers had a credit balance (payment in excess of amount owed) with George Clifford & Sons indicating that the Chevaliers were sending more products than they were receiving in the colonies.[58]

William Morris and Scott & Michael were partners in the brig *Molly* that had been lost while transporting a cargo from Holland to the colonies.[59] In 1760, John Noble reported to Baynton & Wharton of trade between Hamburg and Monti Christi and other places, along with news of a large number of Dutch ships that would arrive in Philadelphia with cargoes obtained in Bristol. The large shipment glutted the markets in the northern colonies and lowered the prices.[60] Although the evidence is not conclusive, there were ample hints that an enormous illegal trade was carried on with Holland.

In conclusion, the opening of the frontier in 1760 marked the beginning of a major economic enterprise that would provide up to ten percent of American exports to England, helping to pay for the English goods imported to America. Military expenditures in America also contributed much to balancing accounts with England. The exchange of Indian goods for furs entailed a vast network of suppliers of manufactured goods and liquor throughout Europe and the colonies. The English suppliers funneled their products through London, Bristol, and a few other ports to Quebec, New York, Philadelphia, and West Florida. Through an intricate web of routes, these goods made their way to the consumers, the Indians, the British garrisons in the western posts, the French habitants, and a few American frontiersmen. Once the merchandise reached the consumer, the return payment in the form of furs, farm produce, or other products of the frontier usually used the same routes. At other times, returns would pass through an entirely different route, for example merchandise that came down the Ohio River would be paid for with furs and other products that went down the Mississippi River. Geographic factors, the direction of the flow of rivers, mountain ranges, unfavorable climate, or other physical features determined the flow of commerce.

The supplies that went to the consumers were many and varied and payment was just as complex. Practically the entire transaction was on credit, beginning with the manufactured goods from England to the credit extended to the Indian hunter over the winter. Eventual payment occurred because if one did not pay, it would be impossible to obtain more goods. The house of cards built on trust was destroyed by the French-instigated rebellion in 1763, and the colonial traders were driven out of frontier business.

NOTES

1. Daniel Clark to William Neale, October 16, 1760, Clark Accounts, Historical Society of Pennsylvania, Philadelphia.

2. Sanders to Champion & Hayley, May 10 and 11, 1760, John Sanders Letter Book, New York Historical Society, New York City; Sanders to Bonbonous, May 9, 1760, ibid.

3. Lawrence H. Gipson, *The Coming of the Revolution, 1759-1766* (New York: Harper, 1954), 11–12.

4. John J. McCusker, *Rum and the American Revolution, The Rum Trade and the Balance of Payments of the Thirteen Colonies*, (New York: Garland Publishing, 1989), 2:552, 584; Merrill Jensen, *The Founding of a Nation* (New York: Oxford University Press, 1968), 9; Walter L. Dorn, *Competition for Empire, 1740-1763* (New York: Harper Torchbooks, 1940), 254, 284; B. R. Mitchell, *European Historical Statistics 1750-1970* (London: MacMillan Press, 1978), 8. The American estimate is based on the 1790 census of 3,929,000, the growth rate of thirty-three percent from 1790 to 1800, and the assumption that the population would have doubled in the thirty years from 1760 to 1790, thirty-three percent for each decade. U.S. Bureau of the Census, *Historical Statistics of the United States, Colonial Times to 1957* (Washington, DC, U.S. Government Printing Office, 1960), 8–9.

5. *Historical Statistics*, 756; Edmund B. O'Callaghan, ed., *The Documentary History of the State of New York*, 4 vols. (Albany: Weed, Parsons & Co., 1849–1851), 1:473; McCusker, *Rum and the American Revolution*, 2:563–68.

6. Dorn, *Competition for Empire*, 183.

7. W. O. Henderson, *Britain and Industrial Europe, 1750-1870* (Leicester: Leicester University Press, 1972), 1–2; Dorn, *Competition for Empire*, 254, 256.

8. Dorn, *Competition for Empire*, 261, 272, 274.

9. Ibid., 255–56; M. Jensen, *The Founding of a Nation*, 18.

10. M. Jensen, *The Founding of a Nation*, 9, 12.

11. Ibid., 17, 19, 44.

12. Arthur L. Jensen, *The Maritime Commerce of Colonial Philadelphia* (Madison: The State Historical Society of Wisconsin, 1963), 118.

13. Chevalier Daybook, September 10 and 28, 1761, Historical Society of Pennsylvania, Philadelphia; A. Jensen, *The Maritime Commerce*, 120.

14. Marc Egnal, *A Mighty Empire, The Origins of the American Revolution* (Ithaca, NY: Cornell University Press, 1988), 126, 132.

15. A. Jensen, *The Maritime Commerce*, 60; Robert W. Tucker and David C. Hendrickson, *The Fall of the First British Empire, Origins of the War of American Independence* (Baltimore: The Johns Hopkins University Press, 1982), 94, 96; see Table 1 on p. xxx.

16. Egnal, *A Mighty Empire*, 128.

17. Ibid., 128.

18. Ibid., 128–29.

19. Erick Eyck, *Pitt versus Fox, Father and Son* (London: G. Bell & Sons Ltd., 1950), 136; Gipson, *The Coming of the Revolution*, 47.

20. M. Jensen, *The Founding of a Nation*, 60; Tucker, *The Fall of the First British Empire*, 87.

21. Charles H. Wilson, *Anglo-Dutch Commerce and Finance in the Eighteenth Century* (Cambridge: The Cambridge University Press, 1966), 167–69.

22. Collins and Govet to Baynton and Wharton, February 23 and March 16, 1763, Baynton, Wharton & Morgan (BWM) Papers, Microfilm F2, original in Pennsylvania Historical Commission; Baynton, Wharton & Morgan Journal A, July 12, 1763, BWM Microfilm Roll F7.

23. William Darlington to Johnson, September 7, 1763, Sir William Johnson, *The Papers of Sir Williams Johnson*, 14 vols. (Albany: The State University of New York, 1921–1965), 4:200.

24. Henry Cruger, Jr. to Aaron Lopez, October 4, 1765 and September 13, 1765, *Commerce of Rhode Island, Massachusetts Historical Collections*, 7th ser., 9, 69:124.

25. Harold A. Innis, *The Fur Trade in Canada* (New Haven, CT: Yale University Press, 1930), 166–67.

26. Memo Book, January 5, 1762, BWM Microfilm, F10, 509; Wayne E. Stevens, "The Organization of the British Fur Trade, 1760-1800," *Mississippi Valley Historical Review*, 3 (1916), 180.

27. Wilson, *Anglo-Dutch Commerce*, 12.

28. Ibid., xiii, 18–29.

29. John Welles to Johnson, May 29, 1766, *Johnson MSS*, 5:231.

30. Miles S. Malone, "Falmouth and the Shenandoah: Trade Before the Revolution," *American Historical Review*, 40 (July, 1935), 695.

31. Anthony Merry to Baynton & Wharton, May 20, 1763, BWM Microfilm F3.

32. John Powell to Christopher Champlin, October 28, 1765, *Commerce of Rhode Island*, 1:130.

33. Johnson to Lords of Trade, October 8, 1764, in Clarence W. Alvord and Clarence E. Carter, eds., *The Critical Period, 1763-1765, Illinois Historical Collections* (Springfield: Illinois State Historical Library, 1915), 10:323; Virginia D. Harrington, *The New York Merchant on the Eve of the Revolution* (New York: Columbia University Press, 1935), 71; Wayne E. Stevens, *The Northwest Fur Trade, 1763-1800* (Urbana: University of Illinois, 1928), 126.

34. Todd to Edgar, February 18, 1769, Edgar Papers, Burton Historical Collection, 15.

35. Baby to Guy, August 13, 1772, Baby Papers, Burton Historical Collection.

36. Edgar Papers, R 2, 63, 382; Todd to Edgar, June 20, and July 8, 1768, Burton Historical Collection, 15.

37. Thomas Shipboy to Edgar, August 2, 1766, Edgar Papers.

38. Ibid., R 2, 53.

39. Paul C. Phillips, "The Fur Trade in the Maumee-Wabash Country," in *Studies in American History Inscribed to James Albert Woodburn... By His Former Students* (Bloomington: Indiana University Press, 1926), 98.

40. Fees included brokerage at one percent [17/2]; duty and bill money [7/10]; landing, loading, lighterage, wharfage, landwaiters, cooper and so forth [6p]; freight primage and pierage [£2.1.6]; housing, cartage and warehouse rent [11/6]; unpacking, lotting, showing, and so forth [5/4]; sales charges and postage on letters [5/6]; and commission at two and one-half percent [£2.3.0], totaling £6.12.6, *Johnson Papers*, 4:794.

41. Fees included entries, bundling, wharfage [8p]; porters and weighers [6p]; wharfage and housing, primage [2/- and 7/6]; Dover pier [1/- and 3/9]; insurance at two and one-half percent [£14.4.6]; commissions at one-half percent [£2.16.0] for a total of £29.5.2. The second lot had charges for sorting, lotting, telling, and so forth [£1.7.6]; bundling and weighing [8/-]; sale charges [12/-]; brokerage at one percent [£3.2.1]; warehouse rent and fire insurance for twenty-five weeks [£3.15.0]; commission at both transactions were £38.9.2 for £870 worth of fur or less than five percent of the final sale, *Johnson Papers*, 4:796.

42. Marjory G. Jackson, "The Beginning of British Trade at Michilimackinac," *Minnesota History,* 11 (1930), 245.

43. Account of Merchandise, March 11, 1763, Robert Rogers Papers, 1766–1769, State Historical Society of Wisconsin.

44. Stevens, *Northwest Fur Trade*, 156; Innis, *The Fur Trade in Canada*, 217.

45. Stevens, *Northwest Fur Trade*, 154.

46. John Bradstreet, *Statement on Indian Affairs* in Franklin B. Hough, *Diary of the Siege of Detroit...* (Albany, NY: J. Munsell, 1860), 145.

47. John Lees, *Journal of [John Lees] a Quebec Merchant* (Detroit: Society of the Colonial Wars of the State of Michigan, 1911), 43; *Illinois Historical Collections* (hereafter cited as *IHC*), 10:403.

48. George A. Cribbs, *The Frontier Policy of Pennsylvania* (Pittsburgh: [n. p.], 1919), 26.

49. Paul C. Phillips, *The Fur Trade*, 2 vols. (Norman: University of Oklahoma Press, 1961), 1:509.

50. Congress at Huron Village near Detroit, September 17, 1761, *Johnson MSS*, 3:498.

51. July 20, 1762, James Kenny, "Journal of James Kenny, 1761-1763," *The Pennsylvania Magazine of History and Biography*, 37 (1913), 163.

52. Hambuck to Edgar, May 13, 1763, Edgar Papers, 15.

53. R. A. Humphries, "Governor Murray's Views on the Plan of 1764 for the Management of Indian Affairs," *Canadian Historical Review*, 16 (1935), 166; Harrington, *The New York Merchant*, 255.

54. Colden to Pitt, December 27, 1760, Colden Papers, Historical Society of New York.

55. Colden to Egremont, September 14, 1763, Edmund B. O'Callaghan and Fernow Berthold, eds., *Documents Relative to the Colonial History of the State of New York*, 15 vols. (Albany, NY: Weed, Parsons & Co., 1853–1887), 7:548; Colden to Halifax, October 9, 1764, 7:666.

56. Colden to the Lords of Trade, December 7, 1763, *NYCD*, 7:585.

57. Daniel Roberdeau to Myler & Hall, July 23, 1764, Roberdeau Letter Book, Historical Society of Pennsylvania.

58. John and Peter Chevalier Daybook, May 24, 1762, September 24, 1762, and January 1764, Historical Society of Pennsylvania.

59. John Kidd to William Neale, May 12, 1760, Kidd Letter Book, Historical Society of Pennsylvania.

60. John Noble to Baynton & Wharton, July 12, 1760, BWM Microfilm F3.

2

The Regulation of the Fur Trade, 1760–1761

Military victory over the French in 1760 assured the British foothold in America, and because the intensity of the war slowed and no longer required their full attention and complete energies, the British government was able to consider the future of the British Empire in North America. Parliament, the British government, and Lord Jeffery Amherst, the British commander-in-chief in North America, were forced to reduce expenses and advocated a firm policy toward the Indians, reducing the gifts and threatening reprisal if they misbehaved. Sir William Johnson advocated a generous policy toward the Indians, believing that it was cheaper to bribe them than to fight them. The Indians wanted an open trade, including rum, and expected lavish gifts as a reward for supporting the British and for trading furs. The colonial traders wanted free use of rum and to confine trading to the posts to compete with the French, whereas the French favored restrictions on alcohol and freedom to trade in the forests. In the beginning, the British policy favored the colonists, but later changed.

The need to reduce expenses was paramount as the high cost of the army continued in 1760, as nineteen regiments at war strength remained on the frontiers and in the St. Lawrence Valley, and nine more in other colonies costing the Empire £1,181,000 sterling annually (see Table 1.1, p. 8). After the French surrendered, they ceased supplying the Indians, who turned to the British, demanding supplies in the form of presents. The expanded market for Indian goods presented new business opportunities for colonial merchants, but created additional expense for the government.

The war was still in high gear at the beginning of 1760. On January 7, 1760, William Pitt, the British prime minister, ordered Lord Amherst to resume the attack on Canada on May 1, 1760, with the objective of capturing Montreal. The colonial governors were ordered to provide the same or a greater number of men than they had in 1759. To reduce expenses, Pitt ordered Amherst to investigate the use of available muskets in America rather than to order more from England.[1]   On February 1, 1760, Amherst wrote to the governor of Pennsylvania asking that the provincial levies bring their own arms, offering to pay twenty-five shillings for each musket damaged in service.[2]

Amherst had serious problems in carrying out Pitt's general directive. Not only was the completion of the goals of the war against the French forces in the Great Lakes a major undertaking, but also there remained the problem of garrisoning the posts that had already been taken. The uncooperative colonial governments of Maryland, Virginia, and Pennsylvania were reluctant to provide garrison troops for long periods. Closely related to the military problem was the policy toward the Indians. Whichever side supplied the Indians received their support in the war, and it was extremely difficult to conduct warfare on the frontier without their support.[3]   Amherst had opposed the extensive use of Indians in the war, and late in 1759 he ordered Johnson not to gather any further Indian allies for use by the British army in Canada. Amherst had been disappointed by the lack of Indian allies the previous year at Crown Point when they were needed and would have extended some return for the substantial expense in equipping and feeding them. General Thomas Gage, the commander in New York, seeing no need for Indian fighters on the New York frontier, ordered Johnson not to gather any more and to disband those with him.[4]

The combination of the military defeats experienced by the French removing their ability to supply the Indians on the one hand, and the reduction in the amount of presents from the British in return for Indian military support on the other, created a strain on the Indian population on the frontier. The Indians had grown to rely on firearms, brass kettles, clothing, and other goods available only from the Europeans, and they were no longer content to live as they had before.[5] In the event of a corn crop failure, as had occurred in New York, the Indians were dependent on the colonists for provisions.[6]

Although Amherst's policy reduced the amount of supplies for the Indians in 1760, there were more Indians to feed as they changed sides in the first three months of 1760. In January 1760, fifty Ottawa and Chippewa came to Fort Pitt to trade, having deserted the French cause.[7] George Croghan told Johnson in January that a British prisoner, who had escaped from the French, reported that after the fall of Fort Niagara, the Indians were convinced that the French had been defeated, and the more sensible Indians were advising neutrality. Johnson urged Croghan to continue the work of winning over the Indians to the British side, and instructed him to write Amherst requesting goods needed for the Indians. An example of the growing cost of Indian support was one of Croghan's bills for £2,000 sterling ($400,000) for the Indian Department, submitted for payment by Francis Wade, a merchant of Philadelphia.[8] The Indian expense did pay dividends as indicated in March 1760 when spies sent by Croghan to Detroit returned to Fort Pitt with information that the natives would no longer support the French cause.[9]

In March 1760, Governor James Hamilton of Pennsylvania proposed a treaty be held with the Indians on the Ohio River to make peace and transfer land. Amherst expressed the official policy—not to take land from the Indians, but to protect them as long as they behaved. If the Indians did not behave, the British would punish them.[10] Regardless of this harsh policy, many Indians came to Fort Pitt to negotiate. At a conference held between April 6 and 12, 1760, at Fort Pitt, representatives of the Six Nations, Delaware, Shawnee, Twightwees, and Mohicans, totaling about three hundred Indians, offered to renew their friendship with the British, and pleaded for supplies. The Indians urged that traders be permitted to come to their towns to provide merchandise in return for skins and furs. In response to their dire need, Croghan asked Fort Pitt's commanding officer to permit this breach of the rule prohibiting traders going to the Indian villages. The commandant at Fort Pitt agreed because of the Indian pledge to safeguard the traders. A list of prices was established, and the Indians were given a supply of rum.[11] On April 22, 1760, Lieutenant Governor James Hamilton of Pennsylvania issued passports to Frederick Bost, John Hayes, Moses Tettany, and Isaac Stille to accompany the Indians down the Ohio River to hold treaties with the various tribes. In early May 1760, more Indians appeared in Fort Pitt asking for weapons and rum, and for merchandise to be sent to their towns.[12]

By May 1760, Lord Amherst apparently had a change of heart because he ordered General Robert Monckton, who was to command Fort Pitt, to purchase an assortment of Indian articles and take them to Fort Pitt. He also approved payment to Croghan for any expenses already incurred for the Indian service. The Indians were to accompany the army in a campaign to be launched from Fort Pitt, and with their aid to capture all of Canada that summer.[13]

Although events were moving swiftly in favor of the British in the Fort Pitt area, French resistance continued along the St. Lawrence Valley. The French used Indians to spy on the British under the guise of trade. Furs taken from the French government stores were given to Indians presumably to trade in Oswego, a New York trading post located on Lake Ontario, but really to obtain information about the troops there. Because of the spying, Johnson thought the Indians from Canada should not be permitted to go to Oswego and then return to Canada with information.[14] Nevertheless, Johnson sent to Oswego a boat load of ammunition and goods for the Indians and another load to Fort Niagara for presents to the Indians. Henry Nellus, the Indian agent in Fort Niagara, reported to Johnson that rum, ammunition, and provisions had been given to the Indians during April 1760. Six boat loads of Missisago Indians arrived at Fort Niagara to trade, and Nellis provided gifts including two tomahawks borrowed from Gershon Levi, a Jewish trader at the post.[15]

In May 1760, a decided change occurred in Indians relations, as the Indians apparently deserted the French who could no longer provide supplies. Amherst sent twelve *batteaus* (a generic term for both canoes on the Great Lakes and flat bottom boats on the Mohawk, Ohio, and Mississippi rivers) of merchandise for the Indians, but Johnson had difficulty finding men to move the boats west. Settlers and merchants were paying high wages to boat men because of the rapidly expanding trade. On June 4, 1760, Johnson reported that the trade at Niagara had opened, and already nearly three hundred Indians in thirty canoes had arrived with furs. So far there had been few complaints from the Indians.

At the end of June 1760, General Robert Monckton, the new commander of the British Army in the west, arrived at Fort Pitt with reinforcements. Colonel Henry Bouquet, with an army including the Royal American Regiment and some Virginia militia, left Fort Pitt on July 7, 1760, accompanied by Croghan, to establish garrisons on the way to Lake Erie. On July 15, 1760, Croghan held a conference near French Creek, north of Fort Pitt, with Indians who promised to support the British troops, and on July 18 the army reached Presque Isle on Lake Erie.[16] Croghan returned to Fort Pitt on July 26 with a large pack train from Lake Erie.

On August 3, 1760, the conference at Fort Pitt, planned in March by Amherst, was opened by Monckton repeating Amherst's firm message of March 30, 1760, regarding the just treatment of the Indians. Johnson had objected to having this meeting because it would divert the Indians away from military service and, by placing Indian relations in other hands, would make Indian management unnecessarily complicated. Nearly one thousand Indians attended the Fort Pitt conference including Twightwees, Potawatomis, and Kickapoo. The major concern expressed by the Indians was to have a fair trade restored because they could not live without European goods.[17] The Indians were well behaved at the conference despite the generous flow of liquor, and after the conference Monckton's present of rum made them drunk for days.[18]

The amount of rum available in Fort Pitt during this period was indicated by the forty-four horse loads that accompanied the army when it set out from Fort Pitt in 1760. The troops were so drunk that they had to make camp after marching only six miles, and all of the Indian guides were drunk as well. Amherst had relented on his gift policy during this period, and in August 1760 sent a large shipment of Indian presents.[19] However, this was but a temporary respite in the general policy of reducing presents. In October 1760, General Monckton ordered Colonel Henry Bouquet to cease giving presents to the Indians in the coming year because they had already received so many. He also prohibited the sale of rum to the Indians.[20] The feeding of the Indians was to be placed on the same basis as the troops. On December 31, 1760, Bouquet prohibited the sale of any strong liquors in the garrison in Fort Pitt.[21]

Amherst's policy of cutting Indian Department expenses resulted in the dropping of some Indian officers, including John Butler, Jelles Fonda, William Hair, Henry Nellus, and Dr. Shuckburgh. The half-year accounts for the Indian Department totaled £2,724 sterling (more than $500,000) which Amherst considered rather high, but approved.[22]

In September 22, 1760, General Amherst declared the fur trade open. "Trade will be free to everyone without duty, but merchants will be obliged to take out passports from the governors, which will be furnished to them gratis."[23]   In December 1760, Rogers at Detroit promised the Indians, "you may depend on heaving a free open Trade with your Brethren the English . . . and you may depend that He (Captain Donald Campbell, commander at Detroit) will . . . see that Justice is done you in Trade."[24]   Trade was freed of all the restrictions ordered by the French and traders could go where they pleased as all monopolies were removed.

Some measure of regulation was intended for the future, and the first step was the requirement of a passport from Amherst.[25]   Johnson proposed that no trader or pretended trader should go among any of the Indian nations, or to Niagara, Oswego, or other areas to trade without a passport issued by him. Amherst refused to increase Johnson's power for fear of setting a precedent, and because the succeeding superintendent might not be as capable as Johnson. Amherst passed the recommendation to London and waited for the decision to be made there.[26]

The winter weather brought most activity on the frontier to a standstill, but 1761 was to be a year of major economic shift on the western frontier. After years of active warfare in the St. Lawrence Valley and on the frontier, military activity dropped sharply after the Capitulation of Montreal in September 1760. However, colonial enthusiasm for the war had cooled beginning in the fall of 1759, and in the spring of 1761, Amherst claimed that there was no support from the colonial legislatures. Amherst called for only two-thirds of the number of volunteers in 1761 compared to 1760, and although voted by the assemblies, the troops were slow to arrive. By July 15, 1761, none of Massachusetts' allotment of 1,637 men had arrived at Crown Point for duty.[27]

The impact of the movement of the army from North America to fight Spain in the West Indies was crucial. In January 1761, there were twenty regiments in Canada (including two in Fort Pitt), five in the Province of New York, and two in South Carolina. In May 1761, two thousand men were sent to Dominica, and in November eleven regiments totaling seven thousand men went to Martinique. By the end of 1761, only ten or eleven regiments remained in Canada and one in the Province of New York. Many of the regiments that were sent from North America to the West Indies passed through the port of New York bringing commercial activity to the port. The transfer of nine thousand men in fourteen regiments was a loss to the colonial economy of up to £200,000 sterling, and the dispersal of troops left only a few army supply contracts to be settled. The move to the West Indies was a major loss to the colonial rum trade and other commerce with the army.[28]

At the same time, the attitude of Amherst toward reducing presents to the tribes resulted in a sharp decline in the amount of money for Indian Department expenses and resulted in further loss of business for those interested in western commerce. Some of the merchants who had been involved in supplying the army and the Indian Department turned to direct dealing with the Indians.

Early in 1761, British officials expected a good trade with the Indians but considered further regulations necessary because they feared too many traders would interfere with one another and if problems arose, the British government would have to step in and suffer the consequences.[29]   Amherst wrote to Johnson that he would appoint a governor for Detroit with orders to open a fair trade between the Indians and the British, making it mutually beneficial to trade honestly and to reap reasonable profits. Amherst asked Johnson for suggestions on rules, for lists of goods appropriate for the Indians, and what profit the traders should make without imposing on the Indians. Amherst wrote that as long as the Indians behaved they would not be abused and would receive a just return for their furs.[30]

Johnson's reply on February 12, 1761, was that nothing would do more to maintain good relations with the Indians than a well-regulated trade "by a Law to be passed for that purpose, which Law should be put into Execution by proper officers or Intendants against all Delinquents." Johnson accompanied his reply with a complete list of regulations, a list of goods and prices, and recommended a profit of fifty percent at Oswego and one hundred percent at Detroit.[31]   Amherst used these suggestions as the basis of his temporary instructions to the post commanders, but agreed that a basic law needed to be made by Parliament.[32]

The Indians were disturbed by the British changes that took place in 1761. The Indians in the Montreal area were surprised at not being permitted to go to Albany as had been their habit. The Iroquois complained of the higher prices for Indian goods, the ill treatment and cheating of the traders, and the restrictions on the sale of powder.[33]

In the west, garrisons had been sent under Amherst's instruction to the various smaller outposts. On September 8, 1761, Johnson had given his instructions to the post commanders to maintain good understanding with the Indians, to keep in touch with other posts, to employ an interpreter, to see that traders followed regulations, and to repair Indian guns at royal expense. No mention was made of presents.[34]   Furthermore, all traders needed a pass, and if they did not obey regulations, they would be banished from the posts.

Commerce had been permitted late in the navigation season in 1760, but few merchants had been able to take advantage of the new areas until 1761. Amherst saw the opening of trade as reason to eliminate free presents because the Indians would not bring furs to trade if they received merchandise without paying. Furthermore, as long as the Indians were busy hunting, they would not have time to plot against the British. Amherst complained of Croghan's generosity with the Indians in Fort Pitt and cautioned that Johnson's deputy in Montreal, Daniel Claus, be told not to spend too much there.[35]

To reduce the expense of the presents, Amherst suggested to Johnson that he purchase his goods directly from merchants in England undercutting the merchants in the colonies. Amherst passed the information to Johnson that Thomas Harris, a merchant in New York City, had a large stock of Indian goods available for purchase by Johnson. Harris was returning to England and would place orders for Johnson.[36]

The enormous amount of money spent for gifts in 1761 was indicated by the requisitions for payment of more than £3,000 New York (nearly $400,000) for the presents given to the Indians in Detroit in the fall of 1760, and for £1,000 New York received by Johnson for a conference and some miscellaneous supplies in Canada. Croghan, in July 1761, had spent £400 Pennsylvania currency in one month for gifts. Croghan believed strongly in presents to the Indians, which he provided from his own stock as long as he could afford it, knowing that Indian friendship was necessary for trade and that the Indians considered the presents as part payment for the furs.

Traders were spreading out rapidly despite Colonel Bouquet's rule that no trade was to take place beyond the posts. In early 1761, William Trent, one of Croghan's agents, gave a cargo to a French trader on credit to take to the Miami River at the request of the post commander.[37] In June 1761, Captain Donald Campbell sent fifty men from Detroit to rescue some Pennsylvania traders at Sandusky who, ignoring Bouquet's orders, were threatened by the Indians.[38] In July 1761, a trader presented a general pass to Bouquet claiming that it was for any Indian settlement and therefore he need not remain at Fort Pitt.[39] Although Bouquet refused to honor the pass, in November 1761 James Kenny, the agent for the Pennsylvania Commission, noted that many traders had gone to the Indian towns.[40] The effect of the post-only rule was to confine the legitimate traders to the posts while the vagabonds from all areas, especially Illinois, took over the trade. The colonial traders complained bitterly of this in 1761, yet General Thomas Gage in 1762 remained convinced with Johnson that the five posts—Kanamistigoua on Lake Huron, Mackinac, Green Bay, Detroit, and Ouiatanon—were adequate to carry on all trade.[41] The result of the post-only rule was a great loss of trade for the Quebec, Albany, and Fort Pitt merchants, and allowed inroads into the northern trade by the Illinois traders.

The Indians were also unhappy with the changes in 1761. Johnson wrote to Richard Peters in March 1761, relating the improvement in the behavior of the Indians in Pennsylvania in the past two years, believing that if the Indians were managed well according to a uniform plan, they would become friends rather than enemies.[42] At a meeting with the Senecas, Onondagas, and Mohawks at Fort Johnson, the Indians complained that the British had failed to open the trade freely and that goods were sold at a very high price at the posts. Furthermore, because the reluctance of the British to provide ammunition limited their hunting, the Indians had fewer skins and furs to trade. Johnson reminded them that they had been outfitted by the British in 1760 at great cost, and that in response, they had deserted the British troops, an action that angered General Amherst.[43] In fact, Amherst hated the Indians and considered their dissatisfaction of little concern.[44]

Johnson believed that the Indian traders would be very difficult to control, and the post commanders should have the authority to give presents, especially ammunition that the traders were not permitted to provide. Supplies of ammunition were very short in the Albany area, and Johnson urged that government stores be made available to him as the traders had no powder.[45] Amherst surprisingly made a generous order in April for supplies (twenty quarter-barrels of powder, 10 cwt. of musket shot, and two thousand flints) to Johnson for use by the Indians.[46] On May 30, 1761, Amherst made another 300 cwts. of powder available to be delivered as Johnson ordered.[47]

Apparently, even these gifts were not enough. By June 1761, the Indians were upset over the shortage of powder. Johnson reported that the Indians feared the British coldness and that the refusal of ammunition confirmed the French stories that the English would destroy the Indians. As a result, the Indians had not come down to the posts to trade as usual, and Johnson feared that something was brewing among them. Amherst's position was that he was sorry about reports of an Indian uprising, but if they did "it will fall on their own heads with a powerful and heavy hand."[48]

Johnson believed that a personal tour of the upper lakes, meeting with the tribes and giving presents, would alleviate their fears.[49] On June 7, Johnson wrote to Amherst concerning the proposed tour of the lakes, and presented his estimate of £1,845 for presents, which would include four hundred shirts, blankets, stockings, vermillion, looking glasses, knives, hats, pipes, kettles, but no guns or ammunition.[50] Amherst replied that although it was a large sum, Johnson was the best judge. He asked Johnson to limit the expenses and asked for a second list of absolute necessities, for example, to eliminate strouds and to require that ammunition come from the posts. The Indians already had plenty of weapons, and Amherst was against increasing that amount. Amherst advanced Johnson £1,000 sterling to pay bills for the Indian Department, but wanted an accounting, including the amount used for presents in Detroit.[51] On June 12, 1761, Johnson replied that he could not cut the list of presents because less would have no effect. He felt that the Indians must be provided with ammunition, which could not be purchased from the traders. If the tribes did not receive any weapons, then smiths must be provided to repair the ones already in use. Amherst agreed to provide the complete list of presents, and Johnson urged Amherst to provide a warrant for £1,250 sterling so that Ferrall Wade, a Philadelphia merchant, could pay for the goods before Johnson left for Detroit. Johnson referred to this large present as a mere trifle with which to impress the western Indians of the generosity of the British government.[52] In addition to presents worth more than £3,000 New York ($378,000) made by Croghan and Rogers in Detroit in 1760, Johnson's proposed gift of a further £1,845 New York ($232,000) in 1761 was generous, but only equaled the cost of maintaining a British regiment on the frontier for about a month and a half.

In July 1761, Johnson held a congress with the Oneida and the Tuscarora who complained that the trade promised during the war was being denied, and they were being mistreated by the British officers. Furthermore, powder was not available for hunting, and all of the trade goods were priced high. Another congress was held at Oswego on July 21, 1761, with the Onondaga Indians who also complained of the mistreatment by the traders, despite promises of regulated trade and low prices.[53]

Concerning complaints of high prices, Amherst believed the traders were at fault, and supported Johnson's intent to regulate prices. Amherst believed that the traders to whom Johnson gave passes "misused the liberty you gave them of carrying off small quantities of rum and that they take nothing else." Amherst's belief was reinforced by Captain Donald Campbell of Detroit who complained that the Niagara traders came from Oswego with rum and little else. Nevertheless, Amherst remained firm that limited quantities of powder were to be given to the Indians.[54] In Montreal, General Thomas Gage insisted on his right to give passes to trade, despite Johnson's objection that all passes were his prerequisite under Amherst's orders.[55]

During the summer of 1761, the threat of Indian uprisings spread across the frontier. On July 5, 1761, the first rumor of the intent of the Six Nations to rise against the British was reported to Colonel Bouquet. The Delaware Indians warned that they had been approached to join the uprising.[56] Amherst considered the reports "to be so very wild that I cannot give credit to them."[57] After making inquiries at Oswego and elsewhere, Johnson reported that the Indians denied any knowledge of the plot. His naive attitude was that if there was a plot, the impending conference in Detroit would bring it to an end.[58] Governor James Hamilton of Pennsylvania joined in the warning of the impending Indian uprising, but Amherst's reply in September was that there was no need for alarm.[59] Despite Amherst's refusal to admit fear, Johnson took two companies of reinforcements to Detroit in September 1761.

When Johnson reached Niagara in late July 1761, he received a letter from Amherst prohibiting further presents to the Indians and to keep ammunition scarce, fearing that rebellion might occur. Amherst viewed the presents as bribes and felt that the proper way to supply the Indians was through regulated trade, so that the Indians would be busy hunting rather than plotting.[60]

The great council at Detroit took place from September 4 to 16, 1761. During this council, Johnson attempted to conciliate the Lake tribes: the Chippewa, Ottawa, Wyandot, Potawatomi, Kickapoo, Twightwees, Delaware, Shawnee, Mohicans, Mohawks, Oneidas, and Senecas. He also attempted to establish regulations for the trade. The military officers were to maintain a good understanding with the Indians, and a good interpreter was to be placed at each post. Officers were to regulate the trade that was to take place only at the posts, and the trader must have a pass from Johnson or Croghan. A smith was to be assigned to each post to repair weapons. If a trader broke these regulations, he was to be banished from the post by the commanding officer. His license was to be taken from him, and he would be prohibited from trading at any post in the future.

The complaints of the Indians at the Detroit conference were that the cost of merchandise was too high and that very little powder was being provided.

Johnson complained that the Indians were stealing horses from both the British government and the traders. Uprising rumors persisted, and Johnson believed that the Indians had agreed on a plan by September 1761.[61] Johnson tried to reassure the Indians and to alleviate abuse from the traders by restricting trading to the posts, as was customary in New York prior to the war. By doing so, British and colonial merchants could compete with the French Canadians, but this system would work only if the furs were not intercepted by traders who went among the Indians in their towns.

Another conference was held at Mackinac. A British army detachment reached Mackinac on September 28, 1761, and on the next day, Henry Balfour, the commander of the garrison, held a conference with the Indians, who pleaded for ammunition for hunting. Balfour accused them of trading their fur at Niagara for rum and being drunk with no thought of their family and therefore were responsible for their own misfortune. Despite this tongue-lashing, Balfour relented and gave the Indians ammunition and other supplies. He also requested traders to extend credit, although the French merchants claimed Indians would not repay their debts.[62]

The British occupied Green Bay in October 1761 and left a garrison of eighteen men and two English traders. The French traders working for licensed English traders in Montreal remained active, passing through Green Bay on their way to trade with the Sioux Indians to the west.[63] However, although the Indians liked the cheaper prices offered by the British in Green Bay, they preferred to have the traders come to their villages during the winter, not allowed by the British rules, but that rule would have given the furs to the French traders from Illinois. In 1761, Lieutenant James Gorrell, the commander at Green Bay, made no attempt to prevent the Canadians from going to the villages. Gorrell permitted the French to winter with the Wisconsin and Sioux Indians regardless of rules restricting trade to the posts.[64]

In October 1761, Johnson optimistically reported to the Lords of Trade that the western Indians were well disposed toward the British and that unless greatly irritated, the tribes would not break the peace. For a meeting with the Six Nations in New York, Johnson asked Amherst for additional ammunition and provisions.[65] Amherst agreed to pay an absolutely necessary amount, but hoped that it would be very small. Amherst also complained of the large claims of Captain Campbell, the commandant in Detroit, and hoped that more economy would be practiced in dealing with the Indians.[66] In December 1761, Amherst provided £3,000 New York ($400,000) to purchase a present for the Six Nations conference and for Captain Daniel Claus, Johnson's agent in Canada. Johnson wanted more money for Oswego, Detroit, and Niagara on the grounds that presents should be discontinued gradually.[67] Amherst agreed to supply £1,000 while urging Johnson to be as sparing as possible. He also approved of Campbell's accounts, but refused to provide the additional request for presents at Detroit because the traders should provide for the Indian needs.[68] This occasion was the first time Amherst refused a large request for presents.

Amherst continued to complain of the money demands for gifts in December 1761, writing that he was amazed that the amount claimed for Indian presents almost doubled the initial request, and ordered Johnson to be sparing in the future. Because of the peaceful state of the country and the good regulation of trade, Amherst wrote, "I can see very little reason for bribing the Indians." However, he did send Johnson a warrant for an additional £1,000 sterling and another warrant for the balance of the Indian Department account.[69]

In the meantime, in December 1761, Amherst had received instructions from the Earl of Egremont, the secretary of state in England, who approved of Amherst's policy, but stressed that the Indians were to be treated humanely. Many people in England believed that the Indians were alienated from the British by the malicious traders who had cheated them, in contrast to the French, and Egremont ordered Amherst to end the abuse.[70]

While Johnson was touring the Great Lakes and spending a fortune for presents in the summer of 1761, Colonel Bouquet in Fort Pitt was experiencing severe problems with the Pennsylvania traders. In July 1761, Colonel Bouquet wrote to Captain Campbell in Detroit telling him of the conflicts. At first the traders in Fort Pitt refused to obey orders, but after six months of strict discipline, Bouquet thought he had brought them in order.[71] However, Bouquet continued to have trouble with the traders and the Indians throughout the remainder of 1761.

General Monckton, in August 1761, informed Bouquet that traders were not to go where they pleased, and that passes allowed them to go only where the commanding officer of the post (Colonel Bouquet) saw fit. Bouquet was responsible for the conduct of the settlers and traders and therefore must validate the licenses. Bouquet had challenged William Crawford's general pass that Crawford claimed gave him the right to trade at any Indian settlement and therefore was not confined to Fort Pitt.[72] Monckton supported Bouquet's position that no traders were to go to the Indian towns, only to the places deemed proper by the commanders of the advanced posts.[73]

Besides the traders, the Indians were giving Bouquet considerable trouble at Fort Pitt. Horse stealing was a very serious problem, and on July 10, 1761, Bouquet cut off all trade with the Shawnee until they promised to stop stealing the horses and also returned the White prisoners that they held.[74] Croghan reported that even though the Shawnee and Delaware had no grievances, the Senecas complained that the Six Nations had aided the English during the war and later their offer of help had been refused by Amherst in Canada, and there was no reason to cut off their trade.[75] The Indians asked that the price of goods be established at lower rates than the French, as had been promised. Croghan's two assistant agents took turns traveling among the Delaware, Shawnee, Miami, and Sandusky.[76] Following the council with the Indians in Detroit, Johnson sent the trade regulations to Fort Pitt.[77] In October, James Kenny, the clerk of the Pennsylvania Indian Commission, noted that Johnson's rules for trading had been posted, including price regulation and the requirement that everyone have a pass from Johnson or Croghan.[78] However, rather than lowering the price of goods for the Indians, Johnson's regulations increased prices. In November 1761, Kenny reported that the regulations prohibited the sale of rum or liquor to the Indians, that no more than five pounds of powder or lead were to be sold to the Indians at one time, and that no trade was to be conducted after the evening gun at sundown. The penalty for disobeying was that the trader's house would be pulled down.[79] Despite these orders, traders and settlers were both giving and selling rum to the Indians in order to attract business. On August 3, 1761, Kenny reported that one of the Indian families obtained rum in Fort Pitt by pawning their clothes, wampum, and everything they had. One Mohawk Indian had killed another during a drunken spree.[80]

By October 1761, the Delaware and the Shawnee had released some of their White captives and were given presents in return. Bouquet agreed to the Indians' request that traders be sent to their towns. However, Amherst's policy of limiting presents was inaugurated in the fall of 1761. On October 17, 1761, seventy-five Senecas stopped in Fort Pitt on their way to fight the Cherokee in the south. Instead of the expected bountiful supply of ammunition as usual, they were very disappointed to receive only fifty pounds of lead and fifty pounds of powder for the entire war party.[81]

The Philadelphia merchants had little regard for the ability of Johnson to regulate the trade. Daniel Clark, a prominent Philadelphia merchant in the frontier business, was glad to hear that the Indian trade had been regulated, but he doubted Johnson's authority to do so. Clark believed that only the Pennsylvania legislature or Parliament could pass regulations for trade, and therefore it was not necessary to obey Johnson's rules.[82]

Indian regulation was still in a flux at the end of 1761. In November 1761, Johnson wrote Claus, his agent in Canada, that he looked forward to Claus' visit that winter to discuss matters relative to the management of the Indians in Canada. Johnson felt that he had more power to settle Indian affairs on a uniform plan than ever before, as a result of his tour of the western posts.[83] Claus replied that the problem of the mistreatment of the Indians by the officers and soldiers in Montreal remained even though the army attempted to stifle any knowledge of this. The Indians added to the problem with their drunkenness.[84]

The most significant phrase in the instructions to the post commanders was limiting the trade to the posts. The British had not occupied all of the minor posts that the French had maintained, and these posts became fur markets with no official representatives. Before 1760, the Indian trade had been carried on in New York at posts such as Oswego and Schenectady where the Iroquois had acted as middlemen, obtaining furs from the western Indians, and bringing the furs to the New York posts and trading for merchandise. The system worked well for the New Yorkers as long as energetic traders did not venture out illegally and take the furs before the Indians arrived at the forts. The Indians could not be cheated as easily under the eyes of officials as in the woods, and therefore, unskilled traders could do as well as the more experienced. Traders had less fear of loss of life or property if trading was done in the posts, while the Indians were guaranteed a better share if bargaining was under supervision.

For these reasons, Johnson sought to extend the restriction of trading to the posts throughout the Northern Department for Indian Affairs. The Indians did not favor the restriction that meant traveling long distances to the forts, because they were accustomed to having the goods brought to them. The existence of the unlicensed French traders from Illinois made the regulation impossible to enforce. The Quebec merchants realized that they would be surrendering the trade to Illinois if they did not send their *voyageurs* to the Indian villages to spend the winter. Even partial enforcement of the restriction resulted in a great loss of trade for the Quebec, Albany, and Fort Pitt merchants, and serious inroads into the northern trade by the Illinois traders. However, the post-only rule was to be continued under future plans being made by the British for regulation of the trade.

NOTES

1. Pitt to Amherst, January 7, 1760, *Documents Relating to the Colonial History of the State of New York*, eds. Edmund B. and Fernow Berthold, 15 vols. (Albany, NY: Weed, Parsons, & Co., 1853–87), 8:422.

2. Amherst to Governor of Pennsylvania, February 21, 1760, *Pennsylvania Colonial Records,* 16 vols. (Philadelphia: J. Severns & Co., 1851-52), 8:454; Daniel Clarke to William Neale, October 16, 1760, Clark Accounts, Historical Society of Pennsylvania.

3. Jack M. Sosin, *Whitehall and the Wilderness: The Middle West in British Colonial Policy, 1760-1775* (Lincoln: University of Nebraska Press, 1961), 28, 36.

4. Amherst to Johnson, October 2, 1759, Sir William Johnson, *The Papers of Sir William Johnson*, 14 vols. (Albany: State University of New York Press, 1921–65), 10:126.

5. Sosin, *Whitehall and the Wilderness*, 28.

6. Johnson to Amherst, March 7, 1760, *Johnson MSS*, 3:197.

7. Sewell E. Slick, *William Trent and the West* (Harrisburg: Archives Publishing Company of Pennsylvania, 1947), 86.

8. Johnson to Croghan, February 16, 1760, *Johnson MSS*, 10:137–39.

9. Croghan to Johnson, January 26, 1760, ibid., 10:136.

10. Amherst to Governor Hamilton, March 30, 1760, *Pennsylvania Archives*, 1st ser., 12 vols. (Philadelphia: Joseph Severns & Co., 1851-56), 3:715 (hereafter cited as *PA*).

11. Conference at Fort Pitt, April 6-12, 1760, *Johnson MSS*, 3:208–09, 216–17.

12. Slick, *William Trent*, 88; Passport, April 22, 1760, *PA*, 1st ser., 3:720.

13. Johnson to Croghan, May 14, 1760, *Johnson MSS*, 10:149–50.

14. Johnson to Gage, April 25, 1760, ibid., 3:227.

15. Johnson to John Lottridge, May 7, 1760, ibid., 10:143–44.

16. Slick, *William Trent*, 89–90.

17. Johnson to Board of Trade, June 5, 1760, *The Documentary History of the State of New York*, ed. Edmund B. O'Callaghan, 4 vols. (Albany, NY: Weed, Parsons & Co., 1849–51), 2:459-60; Nicholas B. Wainwright, *George Croghan, Wilderness Diplomat*

(Chapel Hill: University of North Carolina Press, 1959), 172; Slick, *William Trent*, 91; Council at Fort Pitt, August 12, 1760, *PA*, 1st ser., 3:745–47.

18. Croghan to Johnson, September 6, 1760, *Johnson MSS*, 10:178–79.

19. Amherst to Eyre Massey, 46th Regiment, August 27, 1760, *Johnson MSS*, 10:176; Gates to Bouquet, July 6, 1760, *Transcripts of Bouquet Papers, Canadian Archives Report* (1889), (Ottawa: Canadian Archives, 1890), 45.

20. Order of General Monckton, October 8, 1760, ibid., 332.

21. Monckton to Bouquet, October 26, 1760, ibid., 50; Bouquet Order, ibid., 298.

22. Amherst to Johnson, November 8, 1760, *Johnson MSS*, 3:277; Amherst to Johnson, November 13, 1760, ibid., 10:195.

23. Adam Shortt and Arthur G. Doughty, *Documents Relating to the Constitutional History of Canada, 1759–1791* (revised edition), 2 vols. (Ottawa: J de L. Tache, 1918), 1:41.

24. Indian Conference, December 3–5, 1760, *Johnson MSS*, 10:199.

25. Gage Report, March 20, 1762, Shortt and Doughty, 1:91–93; Johnson to Amherst, November 15, 1760, *Johnson MSS*, 10:197.

26. Amherst to Johnson, November 19, 1760, *Johnson MSS*, 10:198.

27. John Shy, *Toward Lexington, The Role of the British Army in the Coming of the American Revolution* (Princeton, NJ: Princeton University Press, 1965), 100–01.

28. Shy, *Toward Lexington*, 96–101; Sosin, *Whitehall and the Wilderness*, 35; Account of Merchandise, March 11, 1763, Robert Rogers Papers, State Historical Society of Wisconsin.

29. Croghan to Johnson, January 13, 1761, *Johnson MSS*, 3:303.

30. Amherst to Johnson, February 1, 1761, ibid., 3:316–17.

31. Johnson to Amherst, February 12, 1761, ibid., 3:330–31.

32. Amherst to Johnson, February 22, 1761, ibid., 3:343–45.

33. Johnson to Amherst, April 23, 1761, ibid., 3:443, 436; 10:237–38, 256–57.

34. Instructions for the Officers Commanding at Mackinac, St. Joseph, etc., September 8, 1761, ibid., 3:473.

35. Amherst to Johnson, February 22, 1761, ibid., 3:343–45.

36. Amherst to Johnson, March 14, 1761, ibid., 10:235.

37. Croghan to Gates, May 20, 1760, *Massachusetts Historical Collection,* 4th ser. (Boston: Massachusetts Historical Society, 1871), 9:248; Bouquet to Monckton, February 24, 1761, ibid., 391 (hereafter referred to as *MassHC*).

38. Campbell to Amherst, June 17, 1761, ibid., 3:439.

39. Bouquet to Monckton, July 24, 1761, *MassHC*, 4th ser., 9:435.

40. James Kenny, "Journal of James Kenny, 1761-1763," *The Pennsylvania Magazine of History and Biography*, 37 (1913), 26.

41. Gage Report, March 20, 1762, Shortt and Doughty, 1:94.

42. Johnson to Peters, March 4, 1761, *PA*, 1st ser., 4:44.

43. Indian Conference, March 8, 1761, *Johnson MSS*, 10:238–39.

44. Johnson to Claus, March 10, 1761, ibid., 3:354; Johnson to Claus, May 1, 1761, ibid., 10:259.

45. Johnson to Amherst, March 21, 1761, ibid., 10:244–45.

46. Amherst Order, April 20, 1761, ibid., 10:256.

47. Amherst to Johnson, May 30, 1761, ibid., 10:275.

48. Johnson to Amherst, June 21, 1761, ibid., 10:291; Amherst to Johnson, June 24, 1761, ibid., 3:421.

49. Captain Donald Campbell to William Walters, June 17, 1761, ibid., 3:405; Slick, *William Trent*, 100.

50. Johnson to Amherst, June 7, 1761, *Johnson MSS*, 10:277–79.

51. Amherst to Johnson, June 11, 1761, ibid., 10:284–85.

52. Johnson to Amherst, June 12, 16, and 28, 1761, ibid., 10:286–87, 290, 306; Amherst to Johnson, June 15, 1761, ibid., 10:288–89.

53. Johnson to Amherst, July 7, 1761, ibid., 10:312; Indian Congress, German Flats, July 7, 1761, ibid., 3:430–33; Amherst to Johnson, July 11, 1761, ibid., 3:506–07; Congress at Oswego, July 21, 1761, ibid., 3:443.

54. Amherst to Johnson, July 11, 1761, ibid., 3:506–07.

55. Johnson to Claus, November 14, 1761, ibid., 3:566.

56. Slick, *William Trent*, 98.

57. Amherst to Johnson, July 8, 1761, *Johnson MSS*, 3:505.

58. Johnson to Amherst, July 24, 1761, ibid., 3:510–12.

59. Hamilton to Amherst, August 31, 1761 and Amherst to Hamilton, September 6, 1761, *PA*, 1st ser., 4:68–69.

60. Amherst to Johnson, August 9, 1761, *Johnson MSS*, 3:515.

61. Indian Conference at Detroit, September 8–10, 1761, ibid., 3:473–75, 486–87.

62. Henry Balfour's Conference with the Indians, Mackinac, September 29, 1761, ibid., 3:544–45.

63. James Gorrell, "Journal of Proceedings from October 14, 1761, to June 1763," *Wisconsin Historical Collections*, 1 (1916):26.

64. Journal of James Gorrell, March 25, 1763, *Johnson MSS*, 10:711–14.

65. Johnson to Amherst, November 5, 1761, ibid., 10:330–31.

66. Amherst to Johnson, November 22, 1761, ibid., 3:571.

67. Johnson to Amherst, December 6, 1761, ibid., 3:581.

68. Amherst to Johnson, December 20, 1761, ibid., 3:594.

69. Amherst to Johnson, December 26, 1761, ibid., 10:347–48.

70. Egremont to Amherst, December 12, 1761, ibid., 3:588.

71. Bouquet to Campbell, July 7, 1761, *Michigan Pioneer and Historical Collections*, 40 vols. (Lansing: Wynkoop, Hallenbeck, Crawford Co., 1874–1929), 19:90 (hereafter cited as *MPHC*).

72. Monckton to Bouquet, August 24, 1761, *CA*, 1889, 59.

73. Bouquet to Monckton, July 24, 1761, *MPHC*, 19:97.

74. Bouquet to Monckton, July 10, 1761, *CA*, 1889, 59.

75. Croghan to Johnson, July 25, 1761, *Johnson MSS*, 10:316.

76. Croghan to Johnson, October 12, 1761, ibid., 3:551.

77. Johnson to Bouquet, September 18, 1761, *CA*, 1889, 208.

78. Kenny, October 8, 1761, 24.

79. Kenny, November 21, 1761, 28.

80. Ibid., 16.

81. Slick, *William Trent*, 101.

82. Clark to John Ormsby, October 24, 1761, Clark Account, Historical Society of Pennsylvania.

83. Johnson to Claus, November 22, 1761, *Johnson MSS*, 10:333–34.

84. Claus to Johnson, December 3, 1761, ibid., 3:575.

3

Canada

The major source of furs and the most profitable area for frontier commerce surrounded the Great Lakes that had been part of French Canada. In 1760 this land was opened to British and colonial merchants who perceived a golden opportunity to profit from a trade previously closed to them.

The routes used to the Great Lakes were the Ottawa River leading to Lake Huron, the St. Lawrence River to Lake Ontario and Lake Erie, and the Mohawk River from Albany to Oswego on Lake Ontario. The second area opened for trade was the Ohio River valley and Illinois, reached via the Ohio River down to the Mississippi River and up the Mississippi River from New Orleans. The major seaports of Quebec, New York, Philadelphia, and New Orleans tied Europe with America.

Climate influenced the relative value of the routes. Montreal and Quebec had average temperatures below freezing from November to March, and during that time, ice blocked the waterways. Along the Mohawk River leading from Albany to the lower lakes, the average low temperatures were below freezing in January, February, and March, blocking the river. On the Ohio River route, the average temperature was only two or three degrees below freezing in December, January, and February with little threat of the river freezing.[1] The longer winters and tedious navigation on the St. Lawrence and Ottawa rivers hindered the Canadians. The Lake Erie route was blocked by ice for nearly six months. When the Lake Erie ice melted in the early spring, large quantities of broken ice floated down the Niagara River, blocking the river and melting very slowly. On the other hand, the extreme warm weather in New Orleans caused furs shipped down the Mississippi to rot, and shippers had to make arrangements for immediate transportation out of the port.

Weather also affected the water level of rivers and lakes and made commerce in the west a seasonal business. Letters from that time comment on the weather and its effect on business. Prompt action paid dividends, whereas delay could mean financial disaster; therefore all activity had to be planned with an eye on the calendar and the map.

Each route was exploited by a different mixture of merchants and traders with varying ethnic and religious backgrounds, giving each route unique characteristics. The northernmost, the Ottawa River, was used in the beginning of the seventeenth century by French explorers, followed quickly by French fur traders bringing European goods to the Indians.

Among the French population in 1760, there were 130 *seigneurs*, 100 gentlemen and bourgeoisie, 125 notable merchants, and about 50 legal and medical professionals. This rather small group of Frenchmen controlled Canada, and established business relationships with the incoming British and colonial merchants. The French *seigneurs* and the former British military officers established ties, and intermarriages were common between the officers and the French women of this class. The British had the capital and the contacts in London necessary to obtain credit, whereas the French had the means of moving merchandise to the Indians and obtaining furs in return, making the two groups interdependent.[2]

The French, however, were not eager to accept the British as full partners in the fur trade, even though they were forced to deal with the British when cut off from French suppliers. Later on, the more astute Frenchmen sought connections in London; for example, the Baby brothers, prominent merchants in Detroit and Montreal in 1764, were ordering direct from Joseph Henry Guinand of London. One of the Baby brothers wrote a merchant, Valade, in New York City in the same year referring to Guinand and Hankey of London as associates.[3]

Not only did the French try to eliminate the British middlemen in Quebec by dealing directly with London suppliers, they were cool to attempts to share in the retail trade at the western posts where they were reluctant to accept the British as partners. Of more than one thousand ventures recorded in the fur trade license records, only forty show a French–British partnership or indicate a British merchant providing the bond or security for a French trader. In 1767, Governor Guy Carleton claimed that the French were willing to take the English with them, but the records show little evidence of such cooperation in the earlier years.[4]

Despite determined French opposition, the British and colonial mercantile community grew in Canada during the early years. Many of the British and American merchants who came to Canada in 1760 had gained experience on the frontier in Pennsylvania or New York, and moved to Quebec and Montreal to compete with the French merchants. Only a few Albany merchants moved to Montreal, preferring to operate from Albany and Schenectady, moving goods to Canada on Lake Champlain during both summer and winter, and using the Mohawk River to Oswego in the summer. Two other groups were Jewish merchants and discharged army officers, many of them Scots, from both the British army and the provincial regiments.

There were about two hundred British and colonial merchants in Quebec and Montreal in 1764, dropping in 1765 to about thirty merchants from New York, Pennsylvania, and other colonies.[5] The merchants who survived had learned that the fur business required discipline, and many of the early British and colonial entrepreneurs who would not or could not adjust to conditions left Canada.[6]

In the early 1760s, the French remained numerically superior to the British merchants in Quebec and Montreal, and much of the actual conduct of the trading venture remained in French hands. The French handled their dealings with the Indians more skillfully, and, in addition, they had knowledge of the territory and a well-established system of exchange with the Indians. However, the British soon began encroaching on the French as they, too, learned to deal with the tribes. The British, with their greater supply of capital, better business organization, better London contacts, and greater government protection, were then able to obtain a larger share of the wholesale trade than the French. Beyond Montreal, however, the French continued to dominate numerically. In 1767, the French in Mackinac still outnumbered the British by four to one, but the British sent more in value, £22,000 worth compared to only £16,000 by forty French traders.[7]

Geography was taking its toll on the French domination of frontier commerce. As traders ventured farther into the northwest from Lake Superior, more capital was needed because the cycle from purchase of supplies to return of cash from the sale of pelts covered more than three years. As a result, the British who had capital were successful, whereas those without capital or long-term credit failed in the northwest area. The trade at Detroit, Green Bay, and Mackinac, on the other hand, required less capital as rather quick returns were possible, and in these areas competition continued between the British and petty French merchants.[8]

Among the British merchants who came to Canada from Britain were many with Scottish names. The majority of the Scots had originally come to Canada as soldiers, as did some of the other British merchants. The preponderance of Scots were discharged from the Scottish regiments that fought in North America because of British ministerial policy dating back to 1756. After the Jacobite Uprising was overcome in 1745, the Highlanders who had spent their lives training to be soldiers were without an occupation.[9] Many of them turned to service in the British army beginning in 1749 with the 42nd Regiment (the Black Watch) originally formed in 1743 from Scottish militia companies.

In 1756, the Black Watch was sent to America, and in 1757, William Pitt, Britain's wartime leader, ordered the creation of two additional Scottish regiments, the 77th and 78th, each to consist of one thousand men. Fearing the Scots would not be loyal, the Duke of Argyle, the leading political figure of Scotland, was asked to recommend reliable officers to recruit these regiments.

The 77th was raised by the Honorable Archibald Montgomerie who recruited thirteen companies for a total of some fourteen hundred men, well over the number requested. Most of the men enrolled were from the Fraser, MacDonald, Cameron, and Maclean clans, although some were brought in from other areas. The 78th was raised by the Honorable Simon Fraser, son of Simon, Lord Lovat, a prominent Jacobite rebel executed in 1745. The Fraser, McTavish, and McGillivrary clans from Lord Lovat's estate provided many recruits. By July 1757, both regiments had been sent to America. An additional one thousand men were recruited later to provide replacements for the three Highland regiments in America, the 42nd, 77th and 78th.[10] In a slightly more than two years between four thousand and five thousand Scottish fighting men had been recruited into the three regiments. Despite official rules to the contrary, many English regiments stationed either in Scotland or in the northern counties of England, recruited Highlanders to fill their ranks during the early years of the Seven Years' War. Scots made up more than one-sixth of the thirty thousand British troops in America.

The Scottish regiments had outstanding military records during the Seven Years' War, and all three regiments suffered heavy casualties during the campaigns in the West Indies. After 1763, the British disbanded these regiments in America, the 77th in Pennsylvania in 1764, and the 78th in Canada in 1763. The 42nd Regiment, like many other British regiments, had two battalions, each with an authorized strength of one thousand men. The Second Battalion of the 42nd was disbanded in Canada in 1763, whereas many soldiers of the First Battalion of the 42nd were released in America at the end of their enlistment; nevertheless the regiment continued to exist.

The men discharged from the three regiments were given three alternatives: accept land and remain in America, re-enlist in the 42nd Regiment, or return home. Many soldiers of the 77th and the First Battalion of the 42nd remained in Pennsylvania, whereas many from the 78th and the Second Battalion of the 42nd elected to remain in Canada.[11]   These discharged soldiers and their relatives, whom they encouraged to come to Canada in later years, formed the nucleus of the band of Scots in the fur trade, as well as in land development.[12]

Many of the "British Canadians" in the period from 1760 to 1774 had clan names linking them to the 42nd, 77th, and 78th Regiments. Sir William Johnson wrote to Governor Calwallader Colden of New York in 1765 concerning Hugh Fraser, formerly a lieutenant in Colonel Simon Fraser's regiment (78th), who had been discharged in Canada. Hugh Fraser had brought some industrious people from Scotland in 1764 and had asked for one hundred acres for each of his people plus an additional grant for himself. If Colden were to grant this land, Fraser promised to bring more Scots, a move that Johnson supported.[13]

Regardless of the deep-seated prejudice of the English against the Scots, which distorted some of the documents, evidence indicates that the Scots did have some weaknesses. Guy Carleton wrote to the Earl of Shelburne that most of the British inhabitants in Canada were either disbanded officers and soldiers who had settled in Canada when they were discharged, or "adventurers" in trade who could not remain in England and came to Canada to make their fortune.[14] On the other hand, many accounts describe the hardy character of the Scots who gained their fortunes not by political connections, but by hard work.

Although there was competition between the British and French at the merchant level, both groups relied on French canoe men. The *voyageurs* or *engages* who actually paddled the canoes remained almost entirely French on the Ottawa River route and were primarily French on the Great Lakes. The only non-French personnel mentioned in the records were a few Indians.

I have preserved and tabulated the names and employment of over two thousand individual *engages* during the period from 1760 to 1774. Considering that only about six hundred men operated a hundred canoes in a single year, this data is ample for statistical purposes. Of the two thousand, less than ten percent took four or more voyages during the fifteen years between 1760 and 1774, leading to the conclusion that the great majority of the *engages* were not professional, and did not make the fur trade a lifetime occupation. The *engages* were sons of farm families, taking the job for one or two years in order to obtain cash for the family, and nearly every Canadian family had at least one member in the fur trade.[15] Planting and harvesting could be done before and after the summer's voyage. A farm family in Canada had little opportunity to sell produce, and employment in the fur trade was the only significant source of cash. The cash was used to buy luxuries such as sugar and coffee, as well as metal tools and other essentials that could not be produced on the farm. This assumption is confirmed by a statement in the petition of the Montreal merchants in 1766 complaining that the restraint of the Indians to the posts would result in forfeiture of more than £2,000 sterling by the "country people in this district who usually make the voyage between spring and harvest."[16]

The new *engage* was called a *mangeur de lard*, or one who ate fat because he was not accustomed to the rigorous diet made necessary by the small amount of provisions carried in canoes on long trips to the west.[17] The young country boys were illiterate and had little time for debauchery because hard work filled their lives.

The *winterers*, men who would spend the winter with the Indians, were quite different in character. They were an essential link in the trade, spending the cold months in the hunting grounds trading with the Indians and coming into the posts at the beginning and end of winter to dispose of furs and to obtain more merchandise. An example was Gerrit Griverat who, in April, May, October, and November of each year from 1768 to 1773, obtained supplies from Rinkin & Edgar in Detroit. Experienced men were scarce, and men who had not previously wintered among the Indians were not successful.[18]

The merchants worried a great deal about the winterers. Isaac Todd in Mackinac in 1768 received news that M. Robins, a winterer, had collected seven packs of fur during the season, but had not come in by the end of June. Fearing that Robins and his men had drunk all the liquor, Todd sent another trader to collect whatever pelts Robins still had. Unfortunately, Robins was already in debt £1,360 sterling to another merchant who had first call on any pelts that came in. Furthermore, there was fear that Robins would trade the furs to Askin who had gone out with liquor and goods during the spring.[19]

The life of a winterer was not easy because it was continually beset by the hardships of cold weather, insufficient food, and hard work and was in constant danger from the Indians who robbed and killed. The correspondence of the period was filled with incidents of robbery.[20] Winterers often had Indian wives, whose families would provide some protection.

The *coureur de bois*, the unlicensed trader, was a problem before the British came to Canada. He, too, wintered with the tribes, often living with an Indian woman and adopting the native way of life. Occasionally, he would come back to the settled area of Canada and recklessly spend his accumulated profits. There were several hundred of these unlicensed traders, called *vagabonds* by the British, among the Indians in 1762.[21] Croghan, the Indian agent, described them as "an idle lazy set, a parcel of renegades from Canada much worse than the Indians."[22]   General Thomas Gage, the British commander-in-chief, described Mackinac in the months of June and July as being inhabited by several hundred vagabonds, "many of whom have inhabited the Indian country from twelve to thirty years, differing little from the Natives except in colour, and being more addicted to vice."[23]

The Indians relied on the winterers and vagabonds as the only sources of European merchandise between the annual visits to the posts. Each year during the late summer or fall, the vagabonds and winterers would obtain their goods in Detroit, Mackinac, or at other posts, then proceed into the Indian country, erect shelters, and open trade. Although the British objected to this method and attempted to concentrate all trade to the post, they never succeeded. Johnson reported to the Board of Trade that vagabonds were still dealing with the Indians even during the Pontiac Rebellion.[24]

The French vagabonds continued to be a menace to the legal trade, obtaining supplies in Illinois after the British occupied the posts on the Great Lakes in 1761. The Illinois-based vagabonds competed with the traders from the St. Lawrence and Ohio rivers and destroyed Sir William Johnson's plans for creating a well-regulated trade centered around the garrisoned posts.

The Indians were the major players in the fur trade. Without them there would be no one to hunt the animals and take the pelts to the traders. The Indians were the ultimate source of most of the peltry, and the number of Indians was a determinate factor in the availability of pelts. More Indians meant more hunters and more fur, and too few Indian hunters allowed a rapid expansion in the animal population followed by a great abundance of furs a few years later. Given a sharp reduction in hunting and several mild winters, a deer herd would double in number within a few years, whereas overgrazing would reduce the herd during the first severe winter. Therefore, the number of Indians determined the availability of fur and ultimately the market for goods.

The number of natives in the area north of the Ohio River cannot be determined precisely. The original numbers were probably much higher than in 1492 as disease, starvation from interrupted food supply, and killing could have reduced the population by at least ninety percent, leaving about one hundred thousand in North America.[25] Sir William Johnson estimated that there were ten thousand hunters in his Northern Department.[26] Assuming an average of three dependents for each hunter would give forty thousand in Canada, the northern colonies, and the area between the Mississippi and the Allegheny Mountains, which was nearly one-half of the estimated total for North America. Following his tour north of the Ohio River in 1761, Thomas Hutchins estimated that there were more than four thousand warriors in twenty tribes excluding the Iroquois, the Sioux, and western Canadian Indians.[27] Although Hutchin's estimate was less than half of Johnson's, it excluded some tribes that he included.

The reduction of the Indian population was related to the destruction of Indian culture. Three elements destroyed the Indian culture: disease destroyed their faith in traditions; Christianity replaced the old traditions; and the fur trade provided a motive for unrestricted hunting and the end of peaceful coexistence with nature.

The impact of diseases brought by the Whites had a devastating effect on the Indian population. The major killers were smallpox and the plague. Epidemics would strike villages and tribes causing the death of as much as ninety percent of the population. Horrible descriptions have been recorded by people who visited villages struck by disease where no living souls remained and the lodges were filled with corpses. Lacking any knowledge of how to cure the sick, the healthy Indians deserted and left them to starve, as they knew that to remain would expose them to the same horror.[28] Given the catastrophic loss of hunters, the remaining women and children would die of starvation. Several generations passed before the population increase was made easier by the greater abundance of game.

The epidemics struck certain areas and then moved on as infected individuals fled to neighboring areas. As a result, disease often preceded direct contact with the Europeans.[29] In 1734, a smallpox epidemic struck the lower Mississippi valley and extended as far north as the French villages in southern Illinois.[30] Other smallpox epidemics struck in 1738 and 1752, often killing ninety percent of a tribe.[31] Epidemics had an impact on the fur trade in 1760 because fewer hunters meant a rapid increase in the number of animals.

Disease broke traditional Indian customs and beliefs. Prior to contact with the Europeans and their insatiable demand for fur, the bond between the Indian and the animals prohibited excessive killing. Because the old traditions could not cope with the devastation of disease, Indian conduct lost its spiritual control.

If the old ways could not cure the sick, why should the hunters be prevented from killing as many animals as they wished?

The impact of disease and alcohol on the fur trade is difficult to quantify in the trade statistics because of other trade-disrupting factors, including the cutting of the French trade route by the Royal Navy during the Seven Years' War, which left a large quantity of fur in the Great Lakes area in 1760. Pontiac's Rebellion severely disrupted the fur trade in 1763 and 1764, and the illegal activities diverted a sizable portion of furs to Illinois and elsewhere.

Fewer hunters in the twenty years preceding the end of French control resulted in a marked increase in the number of animals. In the 1760s, the hunters found ample numbers of deer, beaver, and other game. From 1760 to 1764, there was an unusually large supply of beaver pelts and deerskins traded north of the Ohio River largely due to the increasing number of Indian hunters reducing the overabundance of animals that resulted from fewer hunters in the preceding two decades. However, this surplus was quickly eliminated, and the Iroquois and Algonquin had almost exhausted the beaver in their areas by the late eighteenth century.[32]

Contact with the White man had completely changed the Indian way of life and encouraged them to become full-time hunters. Alcohol provided by the Europeans had a demoralizing impact at a time when the Indians needed to cope with changing conditions. Although Indian reliance on European goods may have been overstated, the metal utensils, tools, and firearms had made life easier.[33] As full-time hunters, they relocated to obtain a better supply of pelts for trading. Customarily, during the late fall the Indians left their summer camps for the hunting grounds, but in the spring, instead of going directly to their summer camps, they stopped at the trading post to exchange their pelts for merchandise and liquor.

Restrictions on hunting disappeared in the face of European demand for pelts as well as the new tools they provided which made hunting easier, and the luxuries provided in exchange for the furs. Had the Indians wanted to kill more animals in the past, they lacked the technology that the Europeans provided, as well as an unlimited market.[34]

Another view was that the Indians were acquisitive before White contact; furs were being used as a medium of exchange with other tribes. One study indicated that an Indian in the eighteenth century could survive by hunting, fishing, and trapping for twenty-eight hours a week, and traveling fifteen hours a week. The Indians had the technology to kill more animals before the availability of European goods, but chose not to because there was a limit on what they could consume, preserve for later use, and carry. Rather than living a wretched life, Indians happily lived off the abundance of the land. The tools of the White man were mere improvements on existing handmade tools.[35]

The Indians were not as dependent on European technology as assumed. Most Indians visited a trading post only once a year, although the *voyageurs* who spent the winter in Indian villages provided additional goods. The

transition from handmade implements to metal tools from the Europeans was
slow. There was little demand for metal traps, and the handmade traps and
snares continued in use well into the nineteenth century.

However, the Indian was not altogether a hapless victim of the rapacious
trader. Kenny, at the Pennsylvania Commission trading store in Fort Pitt,
mentioned a Delaware Indian who could total the value of his peltry in his head
when he came in with £100 worth of peltry. Kenny related the stratagem of one
Indian diverting the attention of the storekeeper while another stole. Traders
took advantage of this trait by placing needles and other small items in easy-to-
steal locations, thereby encouraging the Indians to return to their stores. The
natives were not above trying to cheat an unskilled trader. They would bring in
wet peltry and refuse to make allowance for the added weight of the water.
Kenny's solution was to make a reasonable allowance and not tell them.[36]

The Indians' desire for European merchandise, greater traveling time, and
intermingling with the White man, as well as with other tribes, changed their
customs and habits. Ever present was the fact that the British were the
forerunners of permanent occupation, whereas the French had not seriously
infringed on their territory in more than a century.

In conclusion, the five major groups in the Canadian trade were the British
merchants, the colonial traders, the French merchants, the French canoe men,
and the Indians. The Jewish merchants were less important in Canada and are
described later. All of these groups were eager to resume trade in 1760.

On September 13, 1760, after the capitulation of Montreal, General Jeffery
Amherst invited colonial traders to Canada. Most of them went to Quebec and
Montreal either by sea or by way of Lake Champlain. The French accepted the
conquest and were pleased that the English had cash to buy local produce.[37]
On October 22, 1760, Governor James Murray of Canada opened trade with the
Indians to everyone with no restrictions except that the Indians were not to be
cheated and no liquor was to be sold.[38] At least twelve canoes were sent to the
upper posts from Montreal with goods for the Indians.

Anticipating the opening of trade to British and colonial merchants, many
sent cargoes of goods to be traded; for example, John Noble of Bristol, England
sent a cargo of captured French goods worth more than £2,600 sterling
($520,000) to Montreal in 1760, and he advised the firm of Baynton & Wharton
of Philadelphia to do the same.[39] Many Philadelphia merchants, realizing the
potential of the Canadian markets, sent cargoes of dry goods and rum for sale
to the army, the French, and the Indians.[40]

Typical of these early colonial traders was Hans Leger from Albany, who
received a pass in October 1760 from General Gage at Montreal to trade with
the Indians in dry goods only (no rum!). However, Daniel Claus, Sir William
Johnson's Indian agent in Montreal, had advised Gage that Leger was a petty
trader who seldom dealt honestly and would be a disgrace to the British.[41]

Another trader, Wilson (probably William Wilson who traded on the
Pennsylvania frontier from 1768 to 1774), went to Montreal in 1760 to

investigate business possibilities, and Johnson asked Claus to advise Wilson concerning trade with the Indians.[42] Claus responded in November 1960 that Wilson was satisfied and intended to remain in Montreal over the winter. Wilson had sold nearly £400 Quebec on his first day of business and hoped to sell his entire stock to French merchants within several months. Claus feared that Wilson would have nothing left when the Indians came from hunting.[43]

Another merchant, Daniel Clark of Philadelphia, on October 2, 1760, sent cloth and other goods valued at £30 on board the Brig *Boscowen* to Quebec.[44] John Collins reached Quebec with a cargo from Baynton & Wharton by November 1960.[45] John Day also went to Quebec with another stock of goods for Baynton & Wharton. However, only a few vessels reached Montreal from Quebec before winter set in, and liquor and dry goods were selling at a premium. Although the winter was mild and the river had not frozen by December 27, 1760, few goods arrived from Europe, and therefore prices remained high all winter. On the other hand, it was feared that prices would drop in the spring, because goods worth £80,000 sterling ($16 million) were on ships at Halifax and Louisburg waiting to go upstream when the ice melted on the St. Lawrence.[46]

In February 1761, Collins, in Quebec, analyzed the trade in Canada for his employers, Baynton & Wharton. The dry goods previously sent for sale to the army had not been sold because the troops were supplied directly from London and the French refused to buy English goods because French styles were preferred. The British merchants were not eager to purchase goods, because they believed that peace would come in 1761, at which time many British firms would ship goods to Canada causing a drop in prices.

Because of the mild winter, the river to Montreal would open for ships early in 1761, so Collins urged Baynton & Wharton to move their cargoes to Canada early, and asked them to fill the orders he had received from Montreal merchants with shipments directly from London. The merchandise had to arrive by September 1761, as the Montreal merchants came to Quebec in September and October to buy goods.[47]

The great prize was the fur accumulated by the French during the war when trade between Canada and France had been severed. The value of this fur was estimated at more than £100,000 sterling ($20 million).[48] More than one hundred thousand pounds of beaver skins were held by four French merchants in Quebec who purchased the fur with the intent of shipping it to France under an article of the Capitulation of Montreal that provided for the free transport of furs belonging to the French South Sea Company. Collins had protested that this article did not allow the British merchants an equal chance.[49] General Murray believed that the article was illegal and held all furs at Quebec in the fall of 1760. Claus, the Indian agent in Montreal, wrote to Johnson in March 1761 saying that the abundance of South Sea Company fur in the upper posts, if diverted to English channels, would be a fine haul. However, most of the fur apparently was sent to France in the following years.

Some Montreal merchants tried to use the Philadelphia merchants to bypass the British. Collins was asked to go to Montreal with dry goods and rum, but was told his activity must be secret from the English merchants in Quebec. In return, Collins was promised that he would be the sole supplier of the fur traders in Montreal. Collins, expecting a profit of more than one hundred percent, sent the merchandise to Montreal on sleighs from Quebec in February.[50] Although Collins reported that trade was slow, by early spring 1761, he had sent nearly £1,000 sterling ($200,000) in bills of exchange and silver dollars to Baynton & Wharton, and had placed another order for goods for the French merchants at Quebec and for the British garrison.[51] Collins believed that trade would increase once the French were convinced that there would be no immediate peace and that Canada would not be returned to France. However, as a result of the slow start, many British merchants returned to England discouraged.[52]

In March 1761, Collins went to Montreal expecting to find a good market, but instead found that it was well stocked with English goods that had been brought by sleigh from Albany during the winter. More than two hundred sleigh loads had come up the Lake Champlain route from Albany.[53] This route, the scene of illegal commerce for many decades, became a major source of supply in 1761, a great blow to Collins. Two Philadelphia merchants, Ferral Wade and John Welles, reached Montreal on May 24, 1761, with a cargo in one of the first vessels to make the trip over Lake Champlain.[54]

During the spring of 1761, forty-seven canoes went from Montreal to the interior, thirty-seven to Mackinac, and ten to Detroit. By cooperating with the French, Collins hoped to acquire most of the furs for Baynton & Wharton. By the end of March 1761, Collins still had not sold the dry goods brought from Quebec to Montreal in February, so he transferred the stock to another merchant to sell to the Indians in the ensuing months.[55] Returning to Quebec in April 1761, Collins found the French still reluctant to purchase from the British and colonial merchants, who were forced to sell their goods at public auction at low prices. Merchandise was growing cheaper every day because several ships from London had arrived, and prices were less than at New York.[56]

John Day's cargo from Baynton & Wharton arrived in Quebec on May 20, 1761. Not finding a market in Quebec, he took his cargo to Montreal where he opened a store. Neither the soldiers nor the French had cash, so he traded for beaver. More beaver was available, but the French were reluctant to sell because they hoped to send the fur to France.[57] Still, by June 22, 1761, Day had obtained fifteen hundred pounds of beaver and £100 worth of other furs and hoped that by September he would be able to ship a large quantity to England.

The importance of being the first ship to arrive in Quebec at the beginning of the season was symbolized by Day's misfortune in waiting at Halifax for the convoy, rather than sending his ship ahead on its own. As a result, other ships arrived before his, and by the time Day's shipment, worth £3,200 Pennsylvania ($368,000) arrived, the market was glutted with goods and sales were slow.[58]

Of the £3,200 Pennsylvania that he had taken to Canada, Day sold most for £3,197 New York ($403,000) and the remaining goods worth £568 ($65,000) had been left in the hands of William Govet, also an agent of Baynton & Wharton.[59] Both Collins and Day had orders from Baynton & Wharton to buy all the peltry available and ship it to Richard Neave in London.[60] By July, Day had shipped furs worth £3,800 sterling ($760,000) to London, of which £3,000 Halifax were to the credit of Baynton & Wharton.[61]

Meanwhile, in Quebec, John Collins unhappily reported the departure of six regular army regiments at the end of June. With their departure went the purchasing power that had previously provided bills of exchange in sterling.[62] In August 1761, Collins was in Montreal packing fur worth £1,300 Halifax into bales to be shipped to Richard Neave in the same ship that would carry the £3,000 Halifax shipment from John Day.[63] To buy his furs, Collins drew up two bills of exchange on July 29, 1764, for £2,048 to be paid by Thomas Wharton.[64] By November 1761, Collins had used all his cash and could buy no more furs because the French would not pay for the merchandise purchased on credit. In dealing with the British and colonial merchants, the French merchants insisted on buying goods on credit but refused to sell furs for anything but cash.[65]

Collins proposed to Baynton & Wharton that they enter into direct trading with the Indians rather than selling goods to the French merchants. By going directly to the source, they would eliminate the middlemen at both ends of the transaction. Much of the merchandise on hand was suitable for direct trade, including coarse blue cloth, calico, calamanco (a glossy checked woolen cloth), and checks that were designed to sell to the Indians. Collins could hire a trustworthy French trader, the canoe men, canoes, and other equipment. The canoes would be ready to leave Montreal by May 20, 1762.

Collins asked that future shipments to Quebec be made to appear as French merchandise using French marks and made in styles similar to the French, which were more desirable to the Canadian buyers.[66] Baynton & Wharton did better than imitating; they smuggled a cargo of French goods from St. Lucia by obtaining for their ship in Louisburg false papers from the customs collector, Gregory Townsend, a friend of Collins. Governor Murray boarded the ship in Quebec to inspect for smuggled goods, but released the ship, assuming, on the basis of the false documents, that the goods had been captured from the French. Collins and Day sent additional smaller lots of fur to Richard Neave later in 1761, but one of the fur shipments was damaged when the vessel ran into a storm. The furs had to be sold for the insurance.[67] Baynton & Wharton did not do well in Canada and were fortunate that an order for Indian goods in the fall of 1761 had not been filled because many ships had come direct from Europe and the surplus of available merchandise drove down prices.

Baynton & Wharton hoped to obtain both furs and bills of exchange drawn by the army that could be used to pay Richard Neave in London and balance their account. In this three-way trade, merchandise (some from the colonies and some purchased in England), was shipped to Canada and sold to the army, the Indian Department, and the French. The bills of exchange and furs received in Canada were then used to pay the English suppliers for goods sent to both Canada and Philadelphia. In 1761, Baynton & Wharton shipped goods worth more than £5,000 Pennsylvania ($575,000) to Canada in two cargoes. Collins and Day then sold these goods for more than £5,600 Halifax ($896,000) in furs and bills of exchange that were sent to Neave. These transactions played a major role in balancing Baynton & Wharton's account with Neave.

The transactions of Baynton & Wharton represented a sizable percentage of the entire western trade from Montreal. The merchandise sold to the French in Montreal and Quebec was then traded to the Indians. The average value of merchandise in a single canoe in the Canadian trade was about £400 Quebec ($56,000) and fewer than fifty canoes went west in 1761, for an estimated value of £20,000 Quebec ($2.8 million). Baynton & Wharton sent merchandise to Canada equal to about one-third of that total. Collins reported that other merchants were returning £5,000 to £6,000 in sales during 1761, indicating a brisk trade, for furs were included that had been saved while trade with France was cut off.

Other Philadelphia merchants were trading with Quebec and Montreal in 1761. John and Peter Chevalier, in early 1761, sent two cargoes to Quebec, one worth more than £200 Pennsylvania and the other more than £400 Pennsylvania.[68] On August 17, 1761, the Chevaliers received £242 Pennsylvania for skins returned from Quebec resulting from their trading efforts in Canada. However, the enterprise was not a total success, as one trunk of dry goods worth £148 was returned unsold with other goods worth £60, about one-third of the merchandise dispatched.[69]

Daniel Clark of Philadelphia sent two cargoes worth £600 Pennsylvania including calico, cotton, dishes, spoons, basins, tankards, mugs, teapots, buttons, buckles, cutteau knives, pistol caps, knives, razors, scissors, iron, candles, and wine to Quebec in March 1761.[70] Fishwick and Pentlington, also from Philadelphia, went to Quebec with several tons of merchandise in the spring of 1761.[71] In February 1761, Bernard Gratz of Philadelphia had his agent, Preston Paine, in Quebec selling wine, leather breeches, and shoes to the garrison. Paine reported that he had become acquainted with the French merchants and expected to do better in the future. His plans were to remain in Quebec until the fall of 1761 when he would return to Philadelphia.[72]

The British and colonial merchants who came to Montreal and survived were in general an able group of men. There was a heavy turnover in the first few years because of inexperience. Carleton informed the Earl of Shelburne, first lord of trade in London, that "Experience has taught almost all of them, that This Trade requires a Strict Frugality, they are Strangers to, or to which they will not submit." Many left Canada, and Carleton expected more would leave within in a few years.[73] The traders who went to Canada in 1761 were classified as the dregs of the British colonies by Johnson. These traders included discharged provincial soldiers and canoe men. This classification was an over simplification because the business was in the hands of the most respectable names in the colonies.

After the burst of prosperity in 1761 created by the accumulated furs of the previous few years, a period of quiet set in. Only twenty-four canoes were sent west during 1762, eleven going to Mackinac and eight to Detroit. However, furs worth about £94,000 sterling (nearly $19 million) were exported to England in that year as the opportunity to ship to France had ended.

The French inhabitants in Canada were in a lamentable state, according to John Welles, a merchant from New York. The French had lost their country and were receiving letters from home telling them to return to France because Canada would remain English. Others had been ruined by the loss of the value of French paper money. To add to their financial difficulties, the merchants of LaRochelle, the port to which the Canadians had sent their furs and remittances in the form of bills, would not accept any Canadian bills of exchange drawn on the French Royal Treasury after October 15, 1759. This refusal meant that any payments from Royal officials to Canadians in bills of exchange in the final year of hostilities in the St. Lawrence valley were worthless. F. Baby wrote to his relative Duperon Baby from LaRochelle that the French Minister of Finance, Choiseul, would take action, but that meanwhile there was no solution, and the bills were worthless.[74]

During the following month, a letter, again from F. Baby to Duperon Baby, expressed the bitterness of the French inhabitants: "I see with a heart full of bitterness the sacrifice of our youth passed in a barbarous country and our hard work brought to nothing by a stroke of fortune." F. Baby had praise for the British treatment of the Canadians, but the Indians were still afraid of the strange new government.[75]

The Philadelphia merchants continued to do business with Canada in 1762. Daniel Clark corresponded with White & Caldwell of Quebec, acknowledging receipt of a draft. However, Clark's experience was not good as he wrote: "Since I have the misfortune of sending anything to Quebec due with all my soul wish I was done with it."[76] John and Peter Chevalier were still active in Montreal in 1762 and received a bill of exchange on John Day, apparently the result of selling merchandise to Day, one of Baynton & Wharton's agents.[77] The latter were concerned with the activities of their agents in Quebec and sent Samuel Eldridge and William Long to investigate. John Collins, another of Baynton & Wharton's agents, formed a partnership with William Govet in Quebec during 1762. Collins had also left a cargo in Montreal in the hands of other Canadian merchants in 1761. In July 1762, Collins was in Montreal attempting to buy peltry to send to England.[78] Eldridge and Long reported that unwise management and poor estimates of conditions, combined with a bad market, had caused Collins to lose a great deal of money in his dealings.[79] By September 1762, Collins sent to London pelts and miscellaneous goods valued at only £1,419 Halifax ($227,000) and had to borrow £500 in order to purchase the pelts.[80] Collins asked that the cargo for the next year arrive on the first vessel in the spring to enable him to sell within a month when prices were high.

Neave, Baynton & Wharton's agent in London, had trouble filling orders expressed in French terms; therefore Collins collected samples of his needs and planned to go to England to select on the basis of these samples. This method was the only one that Collins could devise to get a well-assorted cargo of goods. Collins warned Baynton & Wharton from Montreal that there were new customs officers, "so be cautious, as a new broom sweeps clean."[81] This comment was a clear indication that Baynton & Wharton were continuing to smuggle French goods into Canada.

In general, the colonial merchants had done quite well during 1762 in the Canadian market, despite problems with poor management, lack of knowledge of the trade, and the massive transfer of troops from Canada during 1762 which must have cut sharply into their military trade. The future was bleak, however, because when peace came, trade was expected to drop off sharply.[82]

The news that Canada was to be annexed by England was known in America by February 1763. Collins and Govet were already deep in a scheme to ship furs direct from Quebec to France. They were trying to locate where to ship pelts in France, as well as determining the prices that the furs would bring at those places. The French merchants attempted to keep the prices secret, but Collins did obtain a record of a small sale at LaRochelle, the best port.[83]

Baynton & Wharton were involved in a variety of enterprises in Quebec early in 1763. They had plans for exporting wheat from Canada, but their agents, Collins and Govet, could not locate a vessel in Quebec. Therefore, a ship with a load of goods was sent from Philadelphia to remove the wheat in the spring. Collins cautioned Baynton & Wharton to state that the ship from Philadelphia was bound for Salem (not Canada), as the lemons and claret on board were being illegally imported. Baynton & Wharton were to get a cocket (a royal seal from the custom officials) or ship the illegal products as prize goods (merchandise captured from the French).[84] Meanwhile, in Quebec, Collins and Govet were buying large quantities of wheat that was produced on the small family farms along the St. Lawrence River. These farmers still harvested the grain with hand scythes. Collins and Govet purchased eleven thousand bushels of wheat at 3/9p and 4/- Quebec per bushel ($308,000) from Thomas Story, Joseph Horton, Jr., John White, and others who had obtained the wheat from French merchants.[85] In February 1763, Baynton & Wharton sent £1,100 in goods on the *Postilion* from Philadelphia to Quebec and a £6,680 cargo on the *Boscawen*.[86] The *Leopard* arrived in Quebec in June 1763 with £2,000 in brandy and 1,200 bushels of salt for a value of all the shipments in early 1763 of more than £10,000 Pennsylvania (more than $1,150,000, including $230,000 worth of brandy).[87]

A good deal of fur was expected in Montreal in 1763 at the end of the season when the canoes came down the rivers from the west. Forty canoes loaded with Indian goods had been sent west (probably worth $2.2 million).

These included canoes to Illinois, Lake Superior, and Lake Michigan, areas that had seen few canoes since the war. To supply the goods for the canoes, the French made major purchases from Collins and Govet, leaving them with only a few goods from the cargo that Day had taken up in 1761. The leftovers could not be sold because they were not suited to the market. The articles that had been ordered from Neave in London in 1762 did not arrive with the ships from England in June 1763 at the beginning of the season, leaving Collins without new merchandise to sell.[88]

Despite the turmoil caused by Pontiac's Rebellion, the canoes began to return to Montreal in August 1763. Govet reported that twenty-five canoes with forty tons of furs had arrived in Montreal from Mackinac, sent down after the Indians took the fort. The Indians had taken much of the peltry from the colonial traders and then sold it to the French. However, this shipment was much smaller than would have normally come down from the Great Lakes, and Govet believed that beaver would probably sell at the very high price of 8/- ($80 per pelt).[89]

Faced with heavy losses and delays in payment as a result of the Indian uprising and its effect on the Pennsylvania trade, Baynton & Wharton ordered Collins and Govet to resort to other means of obtaining remittances for Neave in London. In July, they were ordered to purchase £3,000 sterling in whalebone to be shipped to Neave. If available, they were to purchase whalebone and spermaceti (the head matter of whales used in making high quality candles) using bills with delayed payment dates because there were already too many demands on Baynton & Wharton for immediate cash. Collins and Govet were able to ship one ton of spermaceti oil and a bundle of whalebone to London consigned to Sargent Aufrere & Co. in September on board the *Eltham* and the *Quebec Packet*.[90] Despite some opposition from the French, Collins and Govet were able to get 4,388 bushels of wheat on board the *Leopard* destined for Lamar, Hill & Bissett, merchants at Madeira, in August 1763 and an additional 3,165 bushels on board another vessel that was also sent to Madeira. The value of these two cargoes was nearly £1,200 Halifax ($192,000) a major remittance to Madeira to pay for the wines that found a ready market in Philadelphia.[91]

Baynton & Wharton were also able to ship various products valued at £1,834 Pennsylvania in December 1763, from Quebec to London. This shipment may have been either furs or the whalebone and oil that Collins and Govet had been purchasing.[92] The shipments and remittances from Quebec in 1763 to Neave, including £1,000 Pennsylvania in silver dollars, were valued at less than £8,000 Pennsylvania, compared to the £10,000 Pennsylvania in goods shipped to Quebec. In addition, Collins had drawn bills of exchange for £3,000 sterling to buy the whalebone and spermaceti, for a total investment of more than £15,000 Pennsylvania, compared to shipments of less than £8,000 Pennsylvania for an apparent loss of about £7,000 Pennsylvania (more than $800,000). This severe loss to Baynton & Wharton was directly attributable to Pontiac's Rebellion.

The trade on the upper lakes was very risky for the British and colonial traders. The experience of Edmund Moran in Green Bay was an example of the hardships experienced.[93] In 1763, the partnership of Evans Shelby, Edmund Moran, and Samuel Postlewaite conducted an extensive trade at Green Bay. On May 16, 1763, Moran wrote to Joseph Spear & Co., the prominent Pennsylvania merchants, that the Indians were trading well, but because the Canadians were arousing the tribes against the British, trading at Green Bay would not be worthwhile until the French were stopped.[94] However, Moran was doing quite well and reported that Dennis Croghan had come in with seventy packs of beaver, "each to weigh 30 French wt."[95] Moran sold most of his merchandise to Louis Constant, a merchant from Detroit, but also dealt with John Lottridge, a former New York militia officer and trader at Oswego who later replaced Claus as Johnson's Indian agent in Canada. After collecting furs from his winterers among the Indians, Moran planned to take the skins to Detroit. His partner, Evan Shelby, ordered Moran to sell his merchandise, valued between £2,000 and £3,000 to the French at wholesale prices, expecting to collect furs in return. Moran and Shelby were to meet in Detroit in June 1763, to discuss the cargo of merchandise that Shelby would bring in, and to decide whether to sell their goods in Detroit or Green Bay. Selling the choice items in Detroit and leaving the less desirable ones for sale in Green Bay was to be avoided.[96] Moran also provided merchandise for the army, receiving a bill of exchange for £259 New York (payable by Alexander Stedman and Taylor) which he used to pay his other partner, Samuel Postlewaite. Postlewaite, in turn, sent the bill to Jeremiah Warder in Philadelphia.[97] Stedman, a Philadelphia merchant, was also dealing with Daniel Roberdeau, another Philadelphia merchant active in Quebec exporting rice and importing Madeira wine. There were several Taylors active on the Pennsylvania frontier. Warder had dealings with many frontier merchants and was one of the "suffering traders" who claimed losses from Pontiac's Rebellion.

Moran was fortunate to leave Green Bay without harm and with a cargo of furs that sold for £2,000 sterling in New York, but he owed a considerable amount of money to his suppliers.[98] Stephen West was waiting to be paid £722 sterling in Philadelphia in September 1763, and in December 1763, Baynton & Wharton were owed £168 Pennsylvania by Moran, Shelby, William McClellan, and Andrew Blair for a note given originally to Robert McCrea. The partnership of Shelby, Moran, and Postlewaite lost £1,440 at Green Bay in 1763 as a result of the Indian uprising, £420 at Fort Bird on the Monongahela River in Pennsylvania, and eight horses taken by the Indians valued at £80; for a total loss of £1,940 and of that, only £89 was reimbursed.[99] On the basis of the various transactions, Moran and his partners turned over more than £4,200 Pennsylvania in 1763, one of the major operations in the west that year.[100]

During Pontiac's Rebellion, Lieutenant Gorrell, the British commander at Green Bay, returned his garrison to rescue the traders and soldiers captured at Mackinac, all of whom were made prisoners and robbed. One trader, Tracy, was killed along with twenty soldiers. The French were not bothered by the Indians, and after the massacre, Charles Langlade obtained the release of the garrison. When the Ottawas arrived, they took the prisoners from the Chippewa, and later the garrison was escorted back to Montreal by the Indians. The uprising brought all trade to a halt on the Great Lakes.

The exchange of goods with the Indians was still prohibited in 1764. No licenses were issued for the upper country for 1764, yet eight ships (*Ranger, General Murray, Canada, London, Nancy, Little William, Eltham,* and *Royal George*) left Quebec for London during 1764 carrying more than eighty-five thousand beaver skins that had been accumulated during the previous winter and were shipped when the ice cleared.[101]

In October 1764, Ralph Burton (who replaced Gage as commander at Montreal in October 1763) informed Johnson that no goods for the Indians had gone up either the Great Lakes or the Ottawa River during the summer of 1764.[102] The effect in Canada was severe. Samuel Eldridge reported to Baynton & Wharton in November 1764, that dry goods were in the hands of the public auctioneers and that auctions were even postponed because no cash was available. Everyone was having trouble collecting debts.[103] Welles & Wade wrote to Johnson asking, on behalf of the Canadian merchants, whether the New York and Philadelphia traders would be allowed to go west in the spring and on what footing the trade was likely to be established.[104]

The following year brought disaster to most of the British and colonial merchants in Canada, with debts increasing and no furs coming from the Indians. The problems that the colonial merchants were facing in Quebec and Montreal in 1764 were not as serious to Baynton & Wharton, who may have, in fact, profited by the distress of the other merchants. Their agents, Collins and Govet, were able to sell the firm's goods for £5,000 Quebec payable in the spring of 1765 at a 40 percent to 50 percent advance over the Philadelphia price. There was great hope of selling the remainder in the spring and of sending large remittances to Neave in London. Baynton & Wharton recommended to Collins that spermaceti oil be sent rather than furs, as the price of skins was down in England.[105]

However, Baynton & Wharton were worried about Collins' activities. In London, Neave was demanding remittances because of the large outstanding balance. In May 1764, Collins shipped to Neave in the name of Baynton & Wharton a parcel of furs valued at only £1,317 Quebec, whereas Day, Baynton & Wharton's other agent in Quebec, sent a large parcel of furs in the same sloop for the account of Lauchlin McLean and Baynton & Wharton in the amount of £6,663 Quebec.[106]

Despite the ordinance for the prohibition of liquor to the Indians, Baynton & Wharton, on April 13, 1764, dispatched 167 hogsheads of rum and other spirits (10,521 gallons, worth a minimum of $250,000 wholesale) on the brig, *Lark*, to Eldridge and Long (the agents Baynton & Wharton had sent to check on Collins and Govet). Included in the cost was £99 paid to Joseph Coleman for 521 kegs and the cost of filling them, at about twenty gallons per keg. The rum carried in canoes for the Indians was usually carried in twenty gallon kegs weighing about 160 pounds. Therefore, the liquor probably was to be sold to the Indians rather than intended for the consumption of the French inhabitants of Quebec. The cargo was valued at £2,150 Pennsylvania (nearly $250,000) including expenses, and was sent in partnership with Wishart and Edwards, John and Peter Chevalier, Latham and Jackson, Reese Meredith, Joseph Wharton, Jr., and Joseph Coleman.[107] Baynton & Wharton, and their partners, were in a large-scale liquor business intended for the Indians despite the prohibition by the British army.

Another valuable cargo of miscellaneous merchandise on board the sloop, *General Gage*, was lost, and Baynton & Wharton recovered £6,743 Pennsylvania in insurance for their two-thirds share of the £10,115 Pennsylvania (£5,950 sterling or nearly $1.2 million). McLeane & Stewart owned the other one-third.[108] The contents of the cargo were not indicated, but Baynton & Wharton's share was worth three times the value of the previous cargo, and the two shipments were worth about $1,450,000!

Even though trade was closed, Baynton & Wharton continued to do business. Collins and Govet ordered a shipment of merchandise from Neave valued at £1,553 Pennsylvania (£914 sterling) from England, but because the Indian trade was closed legally, Baynton & Wharton ordered these Indian goods sent from Quebec to Philadelphia where the products could be sold to Johnson for Indian presents. Baynton & Wharton had already sold £2,600 worth to Johnson for cash, and he would need more in the fall of 1764. The Philadelphia partners admonished their Quebec agents for failing to make payments, even though they had promised to do so. Collins and Govet were urged to buy spermaceti oil and furs on ninety days credit to be sent to Neave to help balance Baynton & Wharton's account.[109] In December 1764, the Quebec agents responded sending a cargo from Quebec to Philadelphia valued at £2,350 Pennsylvania on the sloop, *Tristram*, and merchandise worth £1,100 to London on the brig *Canada*.[110]

Eldridge, another agent of Baynton & Wharton in Canada, complained in November 1764, that spermaceti oil could not be obtained and that furs could be purchased and shipped only at a disadvantage. Furs could be purchased solely in small lots at auction.[111] Eldridge was somewhat successful in picking up small bills of exchange. For example, from William Brymer, the victualler (the agent who supplied food for the army) in Quebec, Eldridge obtained a bill for £185 sterling and from Apollo Morris, the paymaster, a bill for £14.7 sterling.[112] Eldridge was also able to send off a shipment worth more than £1,200 to London in November 1764.[113] During that year, the company sent £4,500 Pennsylvania in goods to Quebec and possibly £9,000 Quebec, had been sent to England. However, these shipments did not balance the £7,000 Pennsylvania deficit of 1763 and deficits resulting from the problems in Pennsylvania.

The failure of the British and colonial merchants to build a major inroad into western commerce by way of Quebec resulted primarily from the refusal of the French to exchange peltry for goods. Because the market was glutted, the British and colonial merchants were forced to sell on credit and at unfavorable terms to the French who sent their pelts to France in 1760 and 1761 and sold them for cash in later years at high prices. Pontiac's Rebellion destroyed the British and colonial traders who had ventured west in search of furs. While they were robbed and killed, the French were unscathed and able to ship eighty-five thousand beaver pelts in 1764. The French had used the Indians to destroy the colonial traders and remove them from western commerce. In the peace that followed, the British government would confirm the victory of the French who formed alliances with the Scottish merchants in Montreal and Quebec.

One result of this situation was the enterprising decision by Baynton & Wharton to recoup their losses in two dramatic moves, an attempt to gain compensation in land from the Indians and to venture an enormous sum of money in Illinois. Both the attempt to open the Illinois market and the efforts of the "Suffering Traders" would have major political consequences.

NOTES

1. U.S. Bureau of the Census, *Historical Statistics of the United States, Colonial Times to 1957* (Washington, DC: U.S. Government Printing Office, 1960), 246.

2. Douglas Dunham, *The French Element in the American Fur Trade* (Ann Arbor, MI: University Microfilms, 1950), 107-108.

3. F. Baby to ____, February 25, 1762, Baby Papers, Burton Historical Collection.

4. Dunham, *French Element*, 114.

5. Walter S. Dunn, Jr., *Western Commerce, 1760-1774* (Ann Arbor, MI: University Microfilms, 1971), Chart E; Gustave Lanctot, *Les Canadians Francais et Leurs Voisins du Sud* (Montreal: Bernard Valiquettes, 1941), 93.

6. Carleton to Shelburne, November 25, 1767, in *Canadian Archives Report*, 1889 (Ottawa: Canadian Archives, 1890), 42–43.

7. Dunham, *French Element*, 42, 105–06, 116–17.

8. Louise P. Kellogg, *The British Regime in Wisconsin and the Northwest* (Madison, WI: State Historical Society, 1935), 103–104; Harold Innis, *The Fur Trade in Canada* (New Haven, CT: Yale University Press, 1930), 390.

9. The Jacobites were Scottish supporters of the Stuart claimant to the throne of England. In 1745, they formed an army and attempted to overthrow George II, but were defeated.

10. Charles H. Steward., comp., *The Service of British Regiments in Canada and North America. A Resume* (Ottawa: Department of National Defense Library, 1962), 322; Frank Adam, *The Clans, Septs and Regiments of the Scottish Highlands* (Edinburgh: W. & A. K. Johnston & G. W. Bacon, 1965), 448; John W. Fortescue, *A History of the British Army,* 13 vols. (London: MacMillan and Co., 1899), 2:300; Frederick Watson, *The Story of the Highland Regiments* (London: A & C Block Ltd., 1925), 17–22, 33–34; C. R. Middleton, "A Reinforcement for North America" in *Bulletin of the Institute of*

Historical Research, 41 (1968), 58–71; William S. Wallace, ed., *Documents Relating to the North West Company* (Toronto: Champlain Society, 1934), 35.

11. Captain George Clark to Bouquet, August 11, 1763, *CA Report*, 1889, 237.

12. Amherst to Bouquet, August 7, 1763, ibid., 27; William S. Wallace, ed., *Maseres Letters, 1766-1768* (Toronto: The University Library, 1919), 60.

13. Johnson to Colden, August 15, 1765, Sir William Johnson, *The Papers of Sir William Johnson*, 14 vols. (Albany: The University of New York, 1921), 4:824.

14. Carleton to Shelburne, November 25, 1767, *CA Report,* 1888, 42–43.

15. Kellogg, *British Regime*, 25-26.

16. Montreal Merchant Petition, March 30, 1766, *Johnson MSS*, 5:130–33.

17. Dunham, *French Element*, 17–18.

18. William Edgar Papers, 1750-1775, Burton Historical Collection, R 2, 129, 144.

19. Todd to Rinkin & Edgar, June 28, 1769, Edgar Papers.

20. Thomas Anburey, *Travels Through the Interior Parts of America*, 2 vols. (London: Printed for W. Lane, 1791), 1:112; Marjory G. Jackson, "The Beginning of British Trade at Michilimackinac," *Minnesota History*, 11 (1930), 240; Maxwell to Rinkin, May 16, 1769, Edgar Papers, 15; Johnson to the Colonial Secretary, August 26, 1769, *Wisconsin Historical Collections*, 18 (1908), 297–98; Captain John Vattas to Haldimand, June 16, 1773, ibid., 310–11.

21. Gage Report, March 20, 1762 in Adam Shortt and Arthur G. Doughty, *Documents Relating to the Constitutional History of Canada, 1759-1791*, 2 vols. (Ottawa: J de L. Tache, 1918), 1:284.

22. Croghan, Letters and Journals, p. 141, quoted in Paul C. Phillips, 2 vols., *The Fur Trade* (Norman: University of Oklahoma Press, 1961), 1:587.

23. Louise P. Kellogg, "A Footnote to the Quebec Act," *Canadian Historical Review*, 13 (1932), 153.

24. Johnson to Board of Trade, October 8, 1764, *Johnson MSS*, 4:557.

25. Calvin Martin, *Keepers of the Game* (Berkley: University of California Press, 1978), 44–46.

26. Johnson to Board of Trade, October 8, 1764, *Illinois State Historical Collections*, 10:322.

27. *Johnson MSS*, 10:544–46.

28. Martin, *Keepers of the Game*, 64–65, 99–100; Arthur J. Ray, *Indians in the Fur Trade: Their Role as Trappers, Hunters, and Middlemen in the Lands Southwest of Hudson Bay, 1660-1870* (Toronto: University of Toronto Press, 1974), 105–06.

29. Alan D. McMillan, *Native Peoples and Culture in Canada* (Vancouver: Douglas & McIntyre, 1988), 109.

30. Jennifer S. H. Brown, W. J. Eccles, and Donald P. Heldman, eds., *The Fur Trade Revisited, Selected Papers of the Sixth North American Fur Trade Conference, Mackinac Island, Michigan, 1991* (East Lansing: Michigan State University Press, 1994), 175.

31. Martin, *Keepers of the Game*, 99–100.

32. Diamond Jenness, *The Indians of Canada* (Toronto: University of Toronto Press, 1977), 254–55; McMillan, *Native Peoples*, 108.

33. Jenness, *Indians of Canada*, 254.

34. McMillan, *Native Peoples*, 109; Martin, *Keepers of the Game*, 13.

35. Ibid., 13, 16–17.

36. December 18 and 20, 1761, February 4, 1762, James Kenny, "Journal of James Kenny, 1761–1763," *The Pennsylvania Magazine of History and Biography*, 37 (1913), 30, 32, 40.

37. Daniel Claus to Johnson, November 6, 1760, *Johnson MSS*, 10:193.

38. Murray Proclamation, October 22, 1760, Phillips, 1:540–41.

39. John Noble to Baynton & Wharton, July 12, 1760, Baynton, Wharton & Morgan Collection, Microfilm F3.

40. Arthur L. Jensen, *The Maritime Commerce of Colonial Philadelphia* (Madison: State Historical Society of Wisconsin, 1963), 74–75.

41. Daniel Claus to Johnson, October 27, 1760, *Johnson MSS*, 10:191.

42. Johnson to Claus, October 10, 1760, ibid., 3:268.

43. Claus to Johnson, November 20, 1760, ibid., 3:283.

44. Journal, October 2, 1760, Daniel Clark Papers, Historical Society of Pennsylvania.

45. John Collins to Baynton & Wharton, November 12, 1760, BWM Microfilm, F2.

46. Daniel Claus to Johnson, October 27, 1760, *Johnson MSS*, 10:189.

47. John Collins to Baynton & Wharton, February 17, 1761, BWM Microfilm, F2.

48. Claus to Johnson, June 10, 1761, *Johnson MSS*, 3:403.

49. John Collins to Baynton & Wharton, February 17, 1761, BWM Microfilm, F2.

50. John Collins to Baynton & Wharton, February 17, 1761, ibid.

51. John Collins to Baynton & Wharton, January 30, 1761, ibid.

52. Ibid., March 7, 1761.

53. Ibid., March 7, 1761.

54. Claus to Johnson, May 24, 1761, *Johnson MSS*, 3:396.

55. Claus to Johnson, February 25, 1761, ibid., 3:348.

56. Claus to Johnson, June 10, 1761, ibid., 3:403.

57. John Day to Baynton & Wharton, June 6, 1761, BWM Microfilm, F2.

58. John Collins to Baynton & Wharton, May 23, 1761, ibid.

59. John Day to Baynton & Wharton, August 18, 1761, ibid.

60. John Collins to Baynton & Wharton, July 20, 1761, ibid.

61. John Day to Baynton & Morgan, July 14, 1761, ibid.

62. John Day to Baynton & Wharton, June 22, 1761, ibid.

63. John Collins, to Baynton & Wharton, August 15, 1761, ibid.

64. John Collins to Baynton & Wharton, July 29, 1761, ibid.

65. John Collins to Baynton & Wharton, November 12, 1761, ibid.

66. Collins to Baynton & Wharton, November 15, 1761, ibid.

67. John Collins to Baynton & Wharton, November 26, 1761, ibid.

68. John and Peter Chevalier Daybook, February 27, 1761 and March 30, 1761, Historical Society of Pennsylvania.

69. John and Peter Chevalier Daybook, August 17, 1761.

70. Journal, March and April, 1761, Clark Papers.

71. John Kennedy Certificate, July 19, 1764, BWM Microfilm, F4.

72. Preston Paine to Bernard Gratz, February 23, 1761, William V. Byars, ed., *B[ernard] and M. Gratz* (Jefferson City, MO: The Hugh Stevens Printing Co., 1916), 53.

73. Carleton to Shelburne, November 25, 1767, Shortt and Doughty, 1:284.

74. F. Baby to Duperon Baby, March 22, 1762, Baby Papers.

75. F. Baby to Duperon Baby, March 18, 1762, Baby Papers.

76. Daniel Clark to White & Caldwell, April 15, 1762, Clark Papers.

77. John and Peter Chevalier Daybook, October 28, 1762.

78. John Collins to Baynton & Wharton, July 3, 1762, BWM Microfilm, F2.

79. Samuel Eldridge and William Long to Baynton & Morgan, June 27, 1762, ibid.

80. Collins to Baynton & Wharton, September 9, 1762, ibid.

81. Collins and Govet to Baynton & Wharton, October 27, 1762, ibid.

82. Collins to Baynton & Wharton, November 9, 1762, ibid.

83. Collins & Govet to Baynton & Morgan, February 23, 1763 and March 14, 1763, ibid.

84. Collins & Govet, February 23, 1763, ibid.

85. Collins & Govet to Baynton & Morgan, March 14, 1763, ibid. Thomas Story was a British merchant in Quebec who signed the petition against Governor Murray in 1765. A merchant named White provided bond for a Frenchman taking a canoe to Mackinac in 1767.

86. Accounts, February 1763, BWM Microfilm, F7.

87. Accounts, June 1763, ibid.

88. Collins & Govet to Baynton & Morgan, March 14 and June 25, 1763, ibid, F2.

89. Govet to Baynton & Wharton, August 13, 1763, ibid.

90. Baynton & Wharton to Collins & Govet, July 4, 1763, ibid; Journal A, 1762-1765, September 12, 1763, ibid, F7.

91. Collins & Govet to Baynton & Morgan, August 11, 1763, ibid., F2; Journal A, 1762-1765, September 12, 1763, ibid., F7; John Collins to Baynton & Wharton, September 13, 1763, ibid., F2.

92. Journal A, 1762-1765, December 10, 1763, ibid., F7.

93. Note, 1763 in Lyman C. Draper's handwriting, Edmund Moran Papers, 1763-66, State Historical Society of Wisconsin.

94. Edmund Moran to Joseph Spear & Co., May 16, 1763, *Johnson MSS*, 10:669-71.

95. Edmund Moran to Captain Shelby, May 14, 1763, Moran Papers.

96. Moran to Shelby, May 14, 1763, ibid.

97. Bill of Exchange, June 18, 1763, Shelby, Moran, & Postlewaite, ibid.

98. Stephen West to Evan Shelby, September 30, 1763, ibid.

99. Account of Losses of Evan Shelby in 1763, ibid.

100. Stephen West to Evan Shelby, September 30, 1763, ibid; Bill of Exchange, Shelby, Moran, & Postlewaite, June 18, 1763, ibid.

101. BWM Microfilm, 1764, F6:577-81.

102. Claus to Johnson, August 30, 1764, *Johnson MSS*, 4:516.

103. Samuel Eldridge to Baynton, Wharton & Morgan, November 12, 1764, BWM Microfilm, F4.

104. Welles & Wade to Johnson, November 21, 1764, *Johnson MSS*, 4:598.

105. Baynton, Wharton, & Morgan to Collins & Govet, March 28, 1764, BWM Microfilm, F3.

106. Baynton, Wharton, & Morgan to John Fell, May 27, 1764, ibid., F1.

107. Journal A, 1762-1765, April 13, 1764, ibid., F7.

108. Journal A, 1762-1765, May 7, 1764, ibid.

109. Baynton, Wharton, & Morgan to Collins & Govet, July 27, 1764, ibid., F3.

110. Journal A, December 24, 1764, ibid., F8.

111. Samuel Eldridge to Baynton, Wharton & Morgan, November 12, 1764, ibid., F4.

112. Samuel Eldridge to Baynton, Wharton & Morgan, December 3, 1764, ibid.

113. Journal A, November 5, 1764, ibid., F8.

4

New York

New York City and Philadelphia were the financial capitals of the thirteen colonies. Beginning in 1760, about one dozen major merchants sent agents to Quebec and Montreal (the capitals of the fur trade in Canada) to sell dry goods and rum to the French merchants who supplied the fur traders. Although the merchants from New York City did not deal directly with the Indians, about one hundred petty traders, the Albany Dutch, went to Fort Niagara and Detroit by way of the Mohawk River with cargoes mostly of rum for direct sale to the Indians. Despite resistance from the French, both classes of merchants did well until the uprising in 1763, when many of the Albany traders were murdered. After the fighting ended, the petty traders were limited to the forts. Even the large merchants lost out after 1763, because the French bypassed the colonials and dealt with the opportunistic Scottish officers discharged in 1763. In 1764, the rules prohibiting rum and restricting trade to the posts were enforced effectively, driving the New Yorkers out of the fur trade and turning the merchants against Britain.

The Dutch in Albany had competed for furs with the French in Montreal in the seventeenth century, and after New Amsterdam became English, Albany enjoyed the advantage of cheap West Indian rum, superior English cloth and kettles, and lower prices than the French were able to offer the Indians. The Iroquois of New York became middlemen, purchasing goods from the Dutch and English and in turn supplying the tribes farther west.[1]

An intense internal rivalry developed in New York between descendants of old Dutch families (called the Albany traders, although many lived in Schenectady and elsewhere along the Mohawk and Hudson Rivers) and the recently arrived British merchants.[2] The antagonism between the Dutch and the British was apparent in a letter by Sir William Johnson: "The Dutch are grown so imperious since ye present administration, that in short there's scarce any

bearing with them, . . . the mean low lived rascals."[3] Elsewhere, Johnson
described Oswego traders as Dutch from Albany, Schenectady, and the Mohawk
River who in general were very ignorant, and practiced parsimony in diet,
clothing, and all other expenses. They were content to deal with small cargoes
that could be traded within three or four months enabling them to live in
idleness the remainder of the year.[4]

The Albany Dutch sold goods to both the White settlers in the Mohawk
Valley and the Indians who lived in close proximity to the White settlements.
Johnson complained of the unscrupulous storekeepers who provided cheap rum
to get the Indians drunk, and then made enormous profits from the remainder
of their goods.[5] The Albany merchants were often criticized for the fact that
a much higher percentage of their trade was in rum, as compared with the
merchants from the other areas. The Albany traders "intent upon gain, right or
wrong, sell them spirituous liquors; and after making them drunk, cheat defraud
and overreach them in bargains. any wonder the Indians fight back?"[6] In
Detroit, Captain James Stephenson commented that the traders, most of whom
were from New York, "were a sad set, for they would cut out each other's
throat for a raccoon skin."[7] In the face of such damning contemporary
comment, little more can be said. Trading with the Indians was an extremely
dangerous and risky method of gaining a livelihood, and only adventuresome or
desperate men dared involve themselves.

Farmers of Dutch descent also served in the roles of canoe men and
teamsters, just as the farm boys from the St. Lawrence Valley served the French
merchants. Transporting merchandise from the Hudson Valley to the West was
carried on by canoe men and wagon masters who usually had Dutch names.[8]
In addition to filling the roles of petty merchants, boatmen, and teamsters, the
Albany Dutch were also merchants. Many had reputations extending across the
Atlantic, and family connections among the merchants in Albany, New York,
and London were as important to the Dutch as to the British.

Unlike the French in Canada, the Albany merchants had good connections
with England. They had ties with New York correspondents, with English
agents, or directly with the English suppliers.[9] The Sanders family of Albany
obtained merchandise in London, Amsterdam, and the West Indies as well as
from Lawrence Vander Spiegel, their agent in New York City, and sold many
supplies to the British army in the New York campaigns during the late 1750s.
John Sanders of Schenectady, the most active member of the family during the
period from 1760 to 1774, imported fabrics, tools, gloves, hats, nails, household
utensils, and many other items from London, while returning ginseng, furs, and
specie in payment. His correspondents in London were Champion & Hayley,
James Bonbonous, Moses Franks, John Steel, Champion & Dickinson, and
Henry Jordice. Sanders traded with customers in Schenectady and along the
Mohawk River Valley, many of whom described themselves as fur traders on
various petitions during this period.[10]

David Vander Heyden of New York dealt with his brother, Dirk, in London. Gerrard G. Beeckman of New York had his younger brother, William in Liverpool as his correspondent, whereas Jacob and John Beeckman were merchants in Albany.[11] Perhaps the most prominent Dutch merchant was Jelles Fonda, a former agent of Sir William Johnson. Fonda's headquarters were in the Mohawk Valley and supplied many of the canoes that carried merchandise from Albany to Detroit.

In addition to the Dutch, the Irish, Scottish, and English were active in New York, along with men whose families had been in America for one or more generations. John Askin, an Irishman who later succeeded in the Mackinac trade, had his beginnings in Albany in the 1760s. Daniel Campbell, a Scot, was a prominent Schenectady merchant who established a sizeable business in Niagara and Detroit. John Macomb, an Albany merchant who later gained prominence in Detroit, was active in Niagara from 1761 to 1766. James Phyn, a Scot, entered a partnership with John Duncan and Peter VanBrugh Livingston in 1763, that had employed James Sterling in 1762 to take over dealings in Detroit. John Porteus of Detroit and James Sterling were added to the partnership in 1765 to open business in Mackinac when Livingston and Rutherford dropped out. Phyn & Ellice subsequently became one of the major trading companies on the frontier.

The major customers of Phyn & Ellice were not the Indians, but the army, the Indian Department, and traders who dealt with the tribes and the inhabitants of the posts in the West. Through the firm's agents, such as James Sterling and John Porteus, their trade extended not only to Detroit, but also to Mackinac, the Mississippi, and into the area northwest of Grand Portage. Phyn & Ellice even cooperated with their rivals from Montreal by supplying them with heavy goods in Mackinac.[12] Their major advantages in developing their thriving business were the capital provided by Alexander Ellice and the convenient transportation system on the Hudson River and the Mohawk River-Oswego-Lake Erie route.

In contrast to the upcountry merchants, the wholesalers in New York City did not specialize in frontier commerce. Many undoubtedly had a far greater interest in the local New York City trade. Robert Adams supplied Johnson with presents for the Indian Department, but had other customers too. William Darlington conducted Johnson's business in the 1760s, supplying items not only for his own household, but also for the Indian Department. Pigou & Booth supplied goods for several Indian traders. Peter Hasenclever and Thomas Shipboy supplied merchants on the frontier. The traffic up the Hudson River affected practically every merchant in New York City either directly or indirectly.

A fifth group were the Jewish merchants. Whereas location determined the affiliation of most of the groups in frontier commerce, the Jewish merchants overlapped all of the geographical divisions and, based on religion and mutual trust, conducted business with one another and all of the other groups in all areas. Centuries of persecution had created closer ties among the Jews than place of residence or national background. During the eighteenth century, personal relationships and confidence between buyer and seller were essential to all transactions, as there was no guarantee of quality, shipment dates, or date of payment. Jews in America and Europe dealt among themselves, just as the Scots in Montreal turned to their relatives, Phyn & Ellice, to supply them from Schenectady when profitable; and as the Quaker merchant, John Reynell of Philadelphia, turned to William Redwood, a merchant of Newport, Rhode Island, because of religious and business ties. Trusting the person with whom business was transacted was essential, and the strong religious and family ties among the Jews made their success possible. Nevertheless, Jewish firms also dealt extensively with the Scots and others in the fur trade, often acting as agents for the sale of furs.

The international ties of the Jewish community strengthened their position in frontier commerce because the trustworthy network provided the capital, assembled the merchandise in Europe, moved it to American and Canadian ports, and transported the cargoes up the rivers and lakes to the frontier. The furs obtained in exchange and the credits received from the army in return for provisions returned through the same chain.

Amsterdam was the greatest center of Jewish financiers, Portuguese Jews of the Sephardic community who had emigrated to Holland in the eighteenth century. Of forty-one persons settling accounts of shares in 1764 on the Amsterdam bourse, thirty-seven were Portuguese Jews. These financiers had their representatives in London, one of whom was Samson Gideon, who raised several million pounds sterling for the British government during the period from 1740 to 1760.[13] Because of the close links of the Jewish bankers with financial officials of the British government through numerous loans, and also because the Jews were able to raise the necessary capital to carry on large-scale enterprise, they were able to bid successfully for the government contract to supply the army in America during the Seven Years' War.

New York City was the first center of the Jewish community in America, and from there they moved to Newport, Charleston, and Philadelphia during the eighteenth century. The New York City community began as a Sephardic one, although by the end of the eighteenth century, Ashkenazin Jews from Germany, Poland, and eastern Europe, had arrived in increasing numbers.[14] Among the families in America were Franks, Levy, Seixas, Isaacs, Gomez, de Lucena, Hendricks, Hayes, Myers, Simson, Judah, and Pinto.[15] Hayman Levy was the most prominent individual in western commerce, and at one time, he claimed to be the largest fur dealer in the colonies.[16] Although this claim was open to question, Hayman Levy was the agent for Phyn & Ellice, one of the largest partnerships in the fur trade, and received most of their furs, acting in turn as their agent in obtaining supplies from Europe and other colonies. With these connections, Levy's relative share of the peltry coming down the Hudson River must have been far greater than any other merchant in New York City.

Between 1730 and 1750, many Jews, most of whom were Sephardic, came to Philadelphia. Some had come from Portugal by way of Holland and England where their relatives and associations had formed good business connections. David Franks and his brother, Moses, had moved from New York City to Philadelphia in 1740 and during the following year formed a short-lived partnership. David Franks later formed a partnership with Nathan Levy and entered western business employing Joseph Simon, the leading merchant of Lancaster, as their agent. Jacob Henry also entered the partnership before 1754. Through their London influence, David Franks and his father, Joseph, of New York City, became the provisions contractors for the British army, and during the Seven Years' War, they handled more than £750,000 (about $150 million) in provision contracts.[17]

Among the Jews arriving in Philadelphia during the war was Michael Gratz, who came as a clerk to his brother, Bernard Gratz. The eight Jews who signed a nonimportation agreement in Philadelphia in 1765 included Bernard and Michael Gratz, Benjamin Levy, David Franks, Samson Levy, Haymen Levy, Jr., Mathias Bush, and Moses Mordecai.[18] The firm of Simon, Trent, Levy & Franks, along with Baynton, Wharton & Morgan, were the two major companies supplying the frontier during the 1760s. Joseph Simon and Andrew Levy from Lancaster and Isaac Levy and David Franks from Philadelphia claimed losses to the Indians of £28,000 in 1763, indicating a sizable investment in western commerce.[19] There was some resentment of the Jews. Beeckman, one of the Dutch traders, complained of the competition of both Quakers and Jews in the Irish flax seed trade. This prejudice was not limited to New York City.[20] The French *seigneurs* of Quebec, in their petition supporting Governor Murray, referred to the Jews who "exalt themselves among the king's new subjects [i.e., the French]." The *seigneurs* claimed that unwary Frenchmen had previously not known of "this kind of men and had ruined themselves."[21] Prior to 1760, Jews had been excluded from Canada, but after 1760, many came from other colonies. These included David Lazarus, Uriel Moresco, Samuel Jacobs, Simon Levy, Fernandez da Fonesca, Abraham Franks, Andrew Hays, Jacob de Maurera, Joseph Bindona, Levy Solomons, and Uriah Judah. Others commuted between New York and Canada.[22] By 1768, a Jewish congregation was established in Montreal. The congregation was made up of the Portuguese--Dutch-English Jews of the Sephardic community.[23]

In 1760, the Jews were engaged in the frontier trade with the Indians, the British army, and the French settlers. The Jews were interested chiefly in Mackinac, Illinois, and western Pennsylvania, representing approximately ten percent of those involved in these areas, but their per person capital was higher than the French Canadians and many of the western Pennsylvanian merchants. Ezekial Solomon, a Jewish merchant, reached Mackinac in 1760, preceding Alexander Henry and the army. The combined pressure of the French and the British army must have had some impact because many Jews left Canada after 1763, and from a total of thirty identified in 1760, there were only fourteen to nineteen from 1763 to 1774. From 1769 on, the Jewish merchants in Montreal obtained licenses for only about five canoes a year, a small part of the total, indicating that they had more or less been driven out of the direct trade with the Indians in Canada.

The groups in New York (the Albany traders, the Dutch boat men, the British traders, the New York merchants, and the Jewish merchants in New York City) used the New York routes to compete with the Canadians in 1760. The two routes followed two major breaks in the mountain barrier between the Atlantic Coast and the Great Lakes. Both routes began with the trip up the Hudson River to Albany. One continued via Lake Champlain heading north to Montreal, and the second followed a series of portages and rivers to Lake Ontario. The trip from New York to Albany was very speedy using Hudson River sloops, which were sailing vessels especially designed to navigate the Hudson River. The trip could be made in as few as three days, but, depending on winds, might take two weeks.[24]

On the northern route from Albany, quantities of goods could be sent during the winter months by sleigh over the snow and ice to and from Albany and Montreal. The water trip up from Albany via Lake George, Lake Champlain, and the Richelieu River to Montreal was about two hundred miles and could be traveled using boats and canoes in approximately nine days.[25] Before the Seven Years' War, there was a considerable contraband trade between the Albany merchants and the French using the Iroquois as middlemen. British goods were purchased by the Iroquois in Albany, transported north to Montreal, and sold to French merchants who in turn exchanged the merchandise farther west in the Great Lakes area.[26] An advantage of this route was that in the seventeenth century, merchandise was appreciably cheaper in Albany than in Montreal. For example, eight pounds of powder sold in Albany for one beaver and in Montreal for four beaver, whereas a gun sold in Albany for two beaver brought five beaver in Montreal.[27] The net result was that the Albany Dutch merchants were making a considerable amount of money supplying goods to Montreal in addition to the more direct trade with the Indians.[28]

The merchants from Albany had upstaged the Quebec merchants in the winter of 1760–1761 by shipping their goods by sleigh from Albany to Montreal. John Welles and Matthew Wade traveled from Philadelphia via Albany, stopping to see Sir William Johnson on their way.[29] Other traders traveling to Montreal from New York were Dirk Vanderheyden and Samuel Stringer. On March 17, 1761, MacKenzie and Oakes, merchants in Quebec, wrote to James and Charles Crokatt of the vast quantities of goods sent to Montreal over Lake Champlain in sleighs. The result was a glutted market that would be worse after the arrival of goods from Europe by way of Quebec.[30]

The western route to Lake Ontario from Albany began with a fourteen-mile wagon trip to Schenectady on the Mohawk River, then by canoe on the Mohawk River to Fort Stanwick followed by a four-mile portage to Wood Creek. The canoes were then paddled down Wood Creek for about twenty miles to Lake

Oneida and the Oswego River. After a short portage of a few hundred feet and a mile of rapids, the canoes moved down the Oswego River to Lake Oneida and Oswego followed by a boat trip along the southern shore of Lake Ontario to Fort Niagara. At Niagara, a portage skirted the falls and the boats resumed the trip along the southern shore of Lake Erie to Presque Isle, Sandusky, and Detroit.[31] The trip of 170 miles from Albany to Oswego on Lake Ontario could be traveled in a week, but with cargo approximately two weeks.[32] The average was eleven days, and an additional nine days on Lake Ontario brought one to Fort Niagara. To reach Toronto, one had to skirt the west shore of Lake Ontario for two or three more days.[33]

Schenectady was the first stop after Albany and developed as a trading center because of the universal rule that whenever one "broke cargo," transferred goods from one form of conveyance to another, for example from ship to wagon, that point became a center of activity and a logical place to do business. In the process of the transfer, goods often were separated into smaller lots and retailed to lesser merchants. The goods from Albany were divided and an assortment loaded on canoes for shipment farther west. The process of dividing the merchandise into canoe loads required many business transactions and many people. Most of the population of Schenectady performed related activity, working as canoe men, making canoes, or packing goods. The most numerous were the canoe men employed by the merchants.[34]

At every point where the cargo was unloaded and reloaded, trading took place. In 1758, hearing that the Indians were being treated unfairly, Johnson sent George Croghan to German Flats, located on the west end of the portage between the Mohawk River and Wood Creek, to supervise the trade.[35] Fort Stanwick, at the east end of the portage, also became a trading point. The post at Oswego on Lake Erie, built some time after 1722, was of greater importance. The French recognized the post as a threat to their relations with the Indians and in August 1756, took the post, capturing two regiments of provincial troops.[36]

Oswego was the chief trading point for the British before 1760, with about eighty traders annually dealing in goods with a value of £20,000 sterling.[37] The most prominent merchant was Henry Van Schaack. Van Schaack began trading in Oswego in 1759, importing English goods and selling in Niagara and Detroit.[38] By 1768, the Dutch settlers used horses and carriages to create a monopoly for carrying the canoes and cargo over the portage.[39] In the 1760s, the Mohawk River route continued to be significant despite the competition from Montreal and Quebec. In 1767, twenty percent of the peltry and skins from Mackinac were sent to Albany. The New York merchants preferred the Albany route and tried to avoid the Quebec route right up to 1774.[40]

Niagara, the next important post along this route, was also linked to the Montreal route by Lake Ontario. In 1726, a stone storehouse was built by the French at Niagara to compete with the British post at Oswego.[41] After Niagara's capture by the British, Edward Cole from New York and John Van

Eps from Schenectady were among the first to travel there in May 1760 to open trade with the Indians.

In 1761, Peter Van Brugh Livingston of New York City; Walter Rutherford, a former captain; and John Duncan, a former lieutenant in the 44th Regiment, formed a partnership with William Sterling and approached Sir Jeffery Amherst to obtain permission to establish a settlement on the portage at Niagara.[42] Rutherford inferred that the matter had been discussed with Johnson before communicating the proposal to Amherst, recognizing the great advantage of having forts established at both ends of the Niagara portage as the French had done.[43] In May 1761, Johnson called this plan bad policy because it would prove to the Indians that the British intended to drive them out of their country.[44]

However, by July 1761, James Sterling had received a grant for ten thousand acres at the Niagara Portage to build a storehouse. At the end of July 1761, the storehouse was completed and stocked with goods.[45] Albany merchants protested this favorable position, which was intercepting furs from the Indians using the portage road from Lake Erie to Lake Ontario. In October 1761, Johnson objected that Sterling was monopolizing the trade by intercepting the Indians on their way to Fort Niagara with his post on Navy Island, a large island in the Niagara River above the falls. Another petition in 1762 attacked the privilege given to Rutherford & Duncan.[46] In January 1762, the Albany merchants petitioned the Board of Trade in London protesting the Niagara settlement of the partnership of Rutherford, Duncan & Sterling on the grounds that they would monopolize the trade that was contrary to the promise of a free trade.[47] In February 1762, Johnson reported to Amherst that he had received a memorial signed by fifty Indian traders protesting the trading house at Niagara Falls. The traders wanted permission to trade at Little Niagara, as well, to give the Indians a greater choice and to share in the profits of the company of Rutherford, Duncan & Sterling.[48] Amherst responded that he had never granted exclusive privilege to any person to trade at Little Niagara. Everyone was free to carry on the trade there, agreeable to regulations.[49] On April 21, 1762, Johnson wrote to Captain William Walters at Niagara that no monopoly had been granted at Niagara by Amherst and that all were free to trade under the rules at the carrying place of Niagara.[50]

In October 1762, Amherst formerly rejected Rutherford & Duncan's petition for land to settle families as well as their trading privilege. Amherst stated that the permit to settle was given with no restriction on any trade. The family settlement was to be only a temporary matter.[51] Amherst revoked the grant to Sterling on October 20, 1762, on instructions from the Board of Trade.[52]

The major importance of Niagara was its portage. From the point where the boats were taken out of Lake Ontario to Fort Niagara was nine miles. From Fort Niagara to Lake Erie was another eighteen miles. The strong current in the Niagara River could be overcome only by canoes moving near the shore. Under French rule before 1760, the Senecas had carried the canoes and cargo over the portage, but when the British took over, they introduced carts. The cost of carrying the goods in carts was high, but because of the length of the portage, the cost was less than having the canoe men carry the cargo themselves. In June 1761, Cezar Cormick paid John Scott £47 New York for carrying goods at Niagara. In 1762, the rate was 4/- per pack.[53]

A more efficient method of carrying cargo around Niagara Falls was necessary to compete with the Ottawa River route. In 1763, John Stedman received a contract to widen the portage road. In the spring of 1764, Lieutenant Benjamin Roberts constructed machines for lifting boats as long as forty-five feet out of the water and up the escarpment, a steep cliff located on the river bank south of Fort Niagara. The enormity of the task can be appreciated by viewing the site. The equipment included a windlass that lifted the boats nearly one hundred feet. Once on top of the escarpment, the boats and supplies were moved by wagons drawn by oxen and horses under the control of John Stedman. Wharfs and other facilities were also completed before Colonel John Bradstreet arrived with his force on his way west.[54]

In February 1764, Bradstreet described the movement of his troops over the Niagara portage. Even with the machines, fifteen days were needed to move six thousand barrels using fifty ox carts with eight barrels each trip. Because of the length of the portage, an ox cart could make only one trip back and forth each day. The boats were moved with horses and carriages. Three weeks were necessary to move two thousand troops and their supplies around the Niagara Falls.[55] Bradstreet recommended that the system be maintained under government control and that fees be charged for use.[56] Later, a petition was sent to the Board of Trade requesting that use of the portage remain free of any restrictions.[57] However, in 1768, John Stedman still retained the monopoly at the portage and charged £3 New York for carrying a canoe with men and 3/10p New York for each pack of approximately one hundred pounds. A canoe load of twenty-five packs plus provisions could be carried in two-and-one-half cart loads for £5 New York. In addition, the charge for the canoe would bring the total to £8 New York ($1,000).[58] The profits on the portage monopoly were considerable and in later years, Stedman received £1,500 sterling ($300,000) in fees for a net profit after expenses of £1,000 sterling.[59]

The expansion of trade with the Indians in the Albany area was indicated by the increasing tempo of correspondence of John Sanders, a New York merchant. In July 1761, Sanders was corresponding with Moses Franks regarding an invoice for £125, with James Bonbonous about two invoices for nearly £85, and with Champion and Hayley about an invoice for £110. In November 1761, Sanders wrote to Champion and Hayley that he had sent them a hogshead of beaver and peltry to sell at the best advantage. The estimated value of the shipment was £186 New York currency. He also ordered a shipment of goods including cloth, muslin (a fine thin cotton cloth), garlics (a type of cloth), chintz, handkerchiefs, calico, and needles.[60] On the same day, Sanders sent a bill of exchange to Moses Franks for £104 sterling and ordered Robert and

Richard Ray of New York to buy for his account frieze, serge, suiting, taffeta, boys' stockings, and mohair suiting.[61] Also in November, Sanders paid John Bonbonous £100 sterling and ordered nails, broad axes, frying pans, and other dry goods.[62] Despite the departure of most of the army in June 1761, John Sanders was able to pay all his debts in full either in sterling bills of exchange or by shipment of furs.

In 1761, Albany traders used a high proportion of rum, and the Indians received few of the other goods normally obtained. In November 1761, the Seneca chiefs came to Niagara and asked for ammunition, clothing, and provisions. Some were provided by the commandant, Captain William Walters, who told them to use the few skins they had left to buy more supplies from the traders.

Rum continued to be a problem in 1762. The New York traders stated that they should have the same right as the Canadians to trade rum, but Amherst insisted on continuing the prohibition against its sale. Although the New York traders were not forced to return their rum from Niagara, they were prohibited

Table 4.1

Amounts of Rum Confiscated at Fort Niagara

Traders	Amount of Rum
Rutherford, Duncan & Co.	244 gallons
DeCouange and Co.	286 gallons
William Newkirk	451.5 gallons
Barret Visscher	69 gallons
Ganet Reychman	424 gallons
Collin Andrews	290 gallons
Jacobus Taller	111 gallons
Volkert Van Veghten	220.5 gallons
Henry Williams	240 gallons
John Maxwell	166 gallons
Total	2,602 gallons

from selling it to the Indians and had to dispose of the rum in any other way as best they could at Niagara.[63] Johnson made the point clear to Amherst that only total prohibition of rum would be effective because the eager Indians would travel any distance and pay any price for liquor. Therefore, the traders who offered rum would get all the furs and those without rum would get none.[64]

Captain Walters confiscated large amounts of rum from the traders at Niagara (see Table 4.1). This amount of rum was excessive for the few traders to have on hand for their own use over the winter. The average French trading canoe carried only 120 gallons, so the total was equal to the amount normally carried by twenty canoes. Some Indians begged Walters to allow the sale of rum, asking for only a two-gallon keg to carry away with them. On their insistence, Walters gave them two gallons of rum to take home, but he predicted great trouble during the coming summer.[65]

The result of these disputes was the polarization of groups in western New York somewhat echoing the factions in New York City. George Klock and Jelles Fonda, the leaders of the Dutch traders, were associated with the Livingston faction and with the group that had obtained the license to establish a trading post at Niagara, the Sterling, Duncan & Rutherford Company. On the other hand, Johnson was associated with the Schuylers, as well as Goldsbrow Banyar, Major Robert Rogers, and others. This division of merchants also was reflected in struggles over land grants along the Mohawk Valley.[66]

The summer of 1762, brought a great many Albany traders and provincial American officers to Niagara and the west. The rum problem was still not solved, and in June 1762, Jean DeCouange, the interpreter at Niagara, reported trouble among the western tribes because of the end of the rum supply. He had a report that traders from Canada with passes from Gage were selling rum at Toronto, and drawing all the Indians away from Niagara. On June 27, 1762, DeCouange sent copies of the Gage passes, complaining of the disadvantage to the post-bound traders if the others were not similarly restricted.[67] Amherst assured Johnson that he would order Gage to prohibit trade at any place other than the posts and to conduct business under regulations established by Johnson.[68]

In August 1762, Henry Van Schaak, an Albany merchant, reported that a vast quantity of rum was being sold to the Indians along the Mohawk River by the inhabitants at German Flats, located at one of the portages on the Mohawk route. Prohibiting rum at the western posts was pointless if this practice continued, as the Indians simply came farther and farther east to obtain rum. Johnson believed that the sale of liquor should be prohibited all along the Mohawk as far as Albany and Schenectady.[69] Amherst believed that the civil power should punish retailers of rum, as there was a law with a £50 fine ($10,000) against such trade.[70]

In the fall of 1762, the full story of the traders at Toronto was revealed. In the spring of 1762, some traders from Albany, including one of the Schuylers, James Stevenson, and Everart Wendel, went to Montreal and obtained a pass from Gage to trade at Toronto. On March 4, 1762, Joseph Dubois of Montreal also engaged a trader to go to Toronto with a canoe load of goods. Unknown to Gage, the traders at Toronto had a large quantity of rum with them that had an adverse effect on trading at Fort Niagara because the Indians came naked to Niagara having traded all their furs for the rum.[71] The traders sent a belt (a messenger who used the wampum beads on the belt to remind him of the segments of the message that he related orally) to Mackinac telling the Indians to come to Toronto to obtain rum.[72] Hearing of the illegal trade, the commander at Niagara sent twenty-four soldiers, but they found only a trader named Knaggs (later a partner of John Seeger) with a servant and ten gallons of rum. Knaggs was brought back to Niagara.[73] Johnson believed that the rum trade at Toronto had been the result of giving a pass to trade other than at a post and that those involved should be severely punished, but did not know how.[74]

During 1762, trade along the Mohawk route continued at a brisk pace. John Sanders dealt with two London correspondents, John Bonbonous and Moses Franks. From Bonbonous, Sanders received an invoice for £84 sterling. In his dealings with Moses Franks, Sanders made remittances in bills of exchange, including a bill for £100 sterling drawn by James Syme, a London merchant, on James Colebrook, Arnold Nesbitt, George Colebrooke, and Moses Franks, all merchants in London. At the same time, Sanders ordered additional broadcloth, drucket, lindsay, garlics, purple calico, and blankets.[75] Sanders also communicated with Dirk Vanderheyden of London, whose brother Jacob Vanderheyden was his partner dealing in furs. Dirk Vanderheyden asked John Sanders for his business on the grounds that he could serve Sanders better than any other supplier.[76]

Commerce on the Great Lakes came to an abrupt halt after Pontiac's Rebellion which began in the summer of 1763. The Indians first came to Fort Niagara demanding rum, but were refused by the commanding officer. They returned on June 2, 1763, and murdered a trader, John Wendell, and wounded his brother about a day's travel from Niagara.[77] The Wendells had supplied the Indians with rum in Toronto in 1762, and when they were attacked may have been selling rum illegally outside of the fort. Henry Van Schaak and Peter Ryckman reported to Johnson that other traders had been killed. Van Schaak, based at Oswego, had sold rum and ammunition to the Indians in 1762, as well as supplying the Indian Department with huge quantities of goods. Ryckman was also an active Albany trader.[78] To prevent any goods reaching the Indians, Amherst ordered that no traders were to leave Oswego and Niagara.

After the fighting subsided in September 1763, Johnson held a conference with the Onondagas and the Oneidas. Following the practice of giving the Indians substantial presents of goods at such conferences, Johnson ordered a supply from Gertruy Vanderheyden.[79] The Indians were warned that there would be no trade with anyone who fought the English. To demonstrate the different treatment of friends and enemies, the Indians who had not rebelled were permitted to trade.[80] Despite Johnson's efforts to quiet the Indians in

New York, the British army suffered a serous setback in September 1763 at Fort Niagara when sixty-four men from the 80th Regiment, the 55th Regiment, and the New York Provincial Regiment were killed by the Seneca Indians from the Gennesseo village.   Three hundred and ninety Indians were involved and claimed eighty scalps, with only one Indian being wounded.[81]

In October 1763, trade with the Indians was cut off at Fort Niagara. DeCouange, the interpreter, reported that the only Europeans at Niagara were settlers.[82]   At Oswego, Alexander Duncan stopped several Canadian traders carrying Indian goods and ammunition who were on their way to Detroit with passes from Gage.   Six canoes had arrived carrying seventy-five barrels of powder, all of which was seized.[83]   Duncan confiscated the trader's passes and stored their ammunition and goods in the fort.   However, other Canadian canoes were traveling up the Ottawa River, and one canoe had gone to Toronto. Duncan did give passes to Wells and Wade, based on the report that the Indians had dispersed from Detroit.

In November 1763, the Indians were eager to reopen trade, and three Genessee Indians arrived at Albany with a small supply of beaver.   No one would trade with them without permission, and they were sent under guard to Johnson by Volkert P. Douw and "J. P." (James Phyn).[84]   The Indians at Detroit and Niagara were in a peaceful mood because of the lack of ammunition and the hunting season had arrived.   Lieutenant Governor Calwallader Colden of New York advised Johnson that he should supply the Six Nations with a small amount of ammunition to remind them of their need for British goods, but cautioned that giving too much ammunition would enable the friendly Indians to supply those still at war.[85]   The Genessees, who had attacked the British troops near Fort Niagara in September, came to a conference at Johnson Hall in December 1763 and asked for peace.   Although Johnson gave to members of the Five Nations presents worth £600 New York, he gave nothing to the Genessee because they were still at war.[86]

Colden advised the Earl of Halifax, first lord of the Board of Trade, in December 1763, that peace should be made with the Indians, but that all trade from Canada be prohibited during the summer of 1764 to demonstrate to the Indians their need for goods.   Even though the Indians would be forced to accept the invitation of the French in Illinois to move west of the Mississippi into Spanish territory, Colden urged that all trade be done at posts such as Detroit and Mackinac because the Indians had robbed the traders in the woods.   He specifically singled out the Senecas (Genessees) for punishment.[87]

Letters such as Colden's to the Board of Trade had an impact and led to restrictions.   The New York and Albany traders differed from those in Pennsylvania in that most of the New York trade was transacted at posts, and the loss from the uprising had been minor compared to the losses suffered by the Pennsylvania merchants.   Therefore, there was no organization or petition from the New York merchants to recoup their losses such as the Pennsylvania merchants developed.[88]   However, there was a sharp reduction in the amount of trade by the Albany merchants because of the uprising, as indicated in the correspondence of John Sanders. In April 1763, Sanders sent a bill of exchange for £50 sterling to John Bonbonous, his agent in London, even though he had no outstanding debt, and placed a very small order for goods. In October 1763, Sanders received notice that the net proceeds of a hogshead of beaver and furs were £86 sterling from Champion and Hayley and sent them a bag of Spanish dollars along with an order for merchandise likely destined for the colonists—cambric, calico, dishes, plates, pewter, and taffeta. On May 9, 1763, Sanders sent forty "half joes" (worth nearly $400 each or $16,000) to Robert and Richard Ray, and received an invoice for goods valued at £63. He was unable to send any furs to England in 1763.[89]

However, some furs did find their way to New York from the posts on the Great Lakes. Evan Shelby and Edmund Moran were captured at Green Bay in 1763, but Moran escaped and went to New York where he sold furs worth £2,000 sterling.[90] Moran did not abandon his hopes to make a fortune in the fur trade and in September 1764, he was on his way to Fort Pitt with eighteen horse loads of goods.[91] He accompanied Bouquet's army to the Tuscarora camp in October 1764, leaving most of his goods at Fort Pitt, but by October 21, 1764, he had already sold nine horse loads to the army and expected to sell the remainder.[92]

In the early part of 1764, trade with the Indians in New York Province was very slow. In January, John Sanders in Albany sent only £50 sterling in a bill of exchange to cover his account with James Bonbonous. This amount was about one-third of the normal cash remittance.[93] However, supplying the army and the Indian Department under Johnson was a profitable alternative business. John Duncan and James Phyn at Schenectady supplied Johnson with goods for distribution to the Indians as presents and also to maintain his estate.[94] Henry Montour and John Johnson, Indian agents at Niagara, obtained clothing from the traders there to give to the Oneida Indians.[95]

The favored position of the Rutherford group, with its permission to operate the Niagara portage, ended in January 1764, when Gage ordered that the Niagara portage be opened for use by British traders without any fee or molestation from either the Indians or any other claimants.[96]

In March 1764, the main issue was the rum problem. The Albany merchants continued to use rum as the primary item in trading with the Indians and sent a petition in March 1764, protesting its prohibition on the grounds that such a policy would ruin business. The petition claimed that the Indians needed only a few furs to obtain necessities, but would hunt avidly to buy rum. The Albany merchants also protested the ignorant regulation of the post commanders, but they did favor the restriction of the trade to Fort Pitt, Niagara, Detroit, and some minor posts, believing the most profitable trade could be done at the posts making free use of rum.[97]

By spring 1764, there was a renewed interest in Indian goods, probably because of Johnson's need to provide presents at his treaties in the ensuing summer. In April, Duncan and Phynn, a partnership at Schenectady, were sending large quantities of goods to Johnson, promising that they would rival the Dutch.[98] Although there was a shortage of goods both in Albany and in New York City, and transportation was difficult, Duncan and Phynn were able to ship a large order of Indian goods, including 568 blankets, by way of Abraham Van Epps, a Dutch trader at Schenectady.[99]

John Sanders, also in Schenectady, increased his business, sending a large order to James Bonbonous along with a payment of two hundred Spanish silver dollars ($10,000). Sanders sent Champion & Hayley five hundred Spanish dollars in payment for goods, along with a small bundle of bear skins and peltry. Sanders also sent an additional five hundred silver dollars ($25,000) and sixty-five pistereens ($585) to Champion & Hayley to sell on his behalf, along with a large order for French blankets, strouds, gartering, and cloth.[100] The plentiful supply of Spanish dollars may have resulted from prize money given to the British troops who returned from Cuba.

The New Yorkers were anxious to reopen trade with the Indians and applied for licenses. In April 1764, Gage reported that he had refused passes to Duncan, Sterling, Campbell, and others on the grounds that there would be no trade until peace was restored.[101] Colden doubted that trade could be opened in 1764, but if it was, he wanted to know what limitations should be placed on licenses and asked for Johnson's advice.[102] By August 1764, Johnson advised Colden that he should grant licenses to honest men to carry on commerce with the Indians as the best method of keeping the peace. Johnson had allowed the Indians at Niagara at the treaty in early August to buy goods (except ammunition) with furs that they had. He told the Indians that the loss of trade was one of the penalties for the war. Johnson agreed with the Albany merchants that the sale of rum must be allowed because the Indians demanded it and would hunt only in return for rum.[103] In September 1764, Colden again asked Johnson about trade. Colden did not believe that Johnson would approve licenses until Bradstreet had completed his expedition to Detroit. Duncan was pressing for a license as soon as possible, and Colden was willing to give him one, believing that Johnson would not object. However, Colden wanted Johnson to set the terms of the license. Was trade to be confined to the posts and what security would be required to ensure compliance with the rules?[104] Johnson responded that no licenses should be granted until Bradstreet had completed his work and the Indians were made to feel the need for goods. Johnson stressed that the trade be confined to the posts as the safest way, even though the merchants were willing to risk going among the Indians. The trade could be made fairly only if the exchange was under the inspection of a proper officer who had the power to exclude a trader for violation of rules.[105] Failing to obtain legal permission to trade, some of the merchants attempted to get their goods on board the military vessels that supplied the troops at Niagara and Detroit. Sterling and his associates had tried every possible trick to load their goods on board with the help of the ship captains. Gage stressed that if they did succeed and were caught, they were to be punished, as all trade was at a legal stop in October 1764.[106]

In December 1764, Gage recommended that the Indian trade be reopened. Colden proclaimed its reopening on December 10, 1764, but again asked Johnson to set the rules for all the colonies. Colden did so because it was expected that the other colonies would open trade with the Indians, and he did not want the New Yorkers to be at a disadvantage.[107] Gage's only limitations were that the traders have a license from the governor of the province in which they lived and that they give a bond to trade only at the posts.[108] Johnson's response to Colden's request for rules was that the Plan of 1764 would be finalized by the spring and that this plan would form the basis for rules to be enforced.[109]

Opening the trade so late in the year meant there would be no real commerce until the spring of 1765. Even so, the decision was significant because the merchants had time to order goods and the prospect would help quiet the Indians. The traders anticipated a good season in the spring of 1765. Sanders sent a large order to Champion & Hayley in October 1764, and, in payment for his previous order, sent a bag of seventy gold half johannes ($26,000).[110]

However, the New Yorkers' renewed prosperity from sales to the Indian Department came to an abrupt halt as Johnson turned to Baynton & Wharton, obtaining a shipment worth more than £2,800 Pennsylvania ($322,000), and reducing his purchases from the Schenectady traders. Despite the offers of Duncan & Phynn to provide goods at low prices, their bill for 1764 for Indian presents including kettles, axes, vermillion, and jews-harps totaled only £47 New York.[111] This shift in buying was a major blow to the New York merchants in 1764 who relied on the army and the Indian Department to stay in business.

After Pontiac's Rebellion in 1763, the Albany merchants lost their fight to compete in the fur trade with the British and French merchants from Montreal. Both now had access to cheaper British goods formerly not available to Montreal. The Canadians were disturbed by the threat of the Albany traders who formerly had been eliminated by the French army, and therefore the French turned to the Indians to drive out the New York and Pennsylvania traders. The Canadians asked the British government for preferential treatment on the basis that Canada was dependent on the fur trade and used British manufactured goods in their trade; New York used rum made from molasses from the West Indies trade and farm produce for provisions for the army.[112]

Johnson believed that the Quebec merchants feared the New Yorkers because, for the first time, both had equal advantages. In fact, the situation had turned against the New Yorkers. The Quebec merchants still had the best routes in the Ottawa River and the Great Lakes. With the experience of the *voyageurs* at their disposal, the Quebec merchants could not be outdone in dealing in the Indian towns. Only through limiting the trade to the posts or through unchecked use of rum could the New York traders seriously infringe on the Canadians.

Practically driven out of the fur market by Pontiac's Rebellion and army restrictions, the New Yorkers turned to the dressed deer market. Deer replaced beaver in New York City exports after 1763. The cheaper transportation by way of the Great Lakes and the Hudson River made the deerskin trade profitable, while the additional care needed made wiser the plan to take the fur down the Ottawa river route and into the hands of the Quebec merchants. The New Yorkers, especially those opposed to the Livingstons, had ample reason to resent the loss of opportunity on the frontier to Montreal as a direct result of the alliance of the British army, the Indian Department, the Canadians, and the Indians.

NOTES

1. Harold A. Innis, "Interrelations Between the Fur Trade of Canada and the United States," *Mississippi Valley Historical Review*, 20 (1933), 323.

2. Sir William Johnson, *The Papers of Sir William Johnson*, 14 vols. (Albany: State University of New York Press, 1921-65), 7:1105-07.

3. Johnson to Goldsbrow Banyar, March 14, 1758, ibid., 2:781.

4. Johnson Review of Trade, September 22, 1767, *Illinois Historical Collections* (Springfield: Trustees of the Illinois State Historical Library, 1903-23), 16:25-26 (hereafter cited as *IHC*).

5. Johnson to Board of Trade, October 8, 1764, ibid., 10:322.

6. Ibid., 10:156-57.

7. Clarence M. Burton, *The City of Detroit, Michigan, 1701-1922*, 2 vols. (Detroit: The J. S. Clarke Publishing Co., 1922), 1:497.

8. Receipt, December 24, 1764, *Johnson MSS*, 11:511.

9. Virginia D. Harrington, *The New York Merchant on the Eve of the Revolution* (New York: Columbia University Press, 1935), 237.

10. Inventory, John Sanders Papers, New-York Historical Society.

11. Harrington, *New York Merchant*, 185-86.

12. R. H. Fleming, "Phyn, Ellice and Co. of Schenectady," *Contributions to Canadian Economics*, 4 (1932), 9-10, 25.

13. Charles H. Wilson, *Anglo-Dutch Commerce & Finance in the Eighteenth Century* (Cambridge: Cambridge University Press, 1941), 14, 116-17.

14. Rufus Learsi, *The Jews in America: A History* (New York: World Publishing Co., 1954), 30; Peter Wiernik, *A History of Jews in America* (New York: The Jewish History Publishing Co., 1931), 70.

15. Harrington, *New York Merchant*, 17.

16. Wiernik, *History of Jews*, 70.

17. Maxwell Whiteman, *The History of the Jews in Philadelphia from Colonial Times to the Age of Jackson* (Philadelphia: Jewish Publication Society of America, 1957), 26-29, 30-31, 38.

18. Ibid., 39, Wiernik, *History of Jews*, 76.

19. Whiteman, *History of Jews*, 66.

20. Harrington, *New York Merchant*, 229.

21. *Canadian Archives Report*, 1888, 21.

22. Jeremiah Warder to Edmund Moran, November 18, 1763, in Edmund Moran Papers, 1763-66, State Historical Society of Wisconsin; Wiernik, *History of Jews*, 432.

23. Learsi, *Jews in America*, 34.

24. Edward P. Hamilton, *The French and Indian War* (Garden City, NY: Doubleday, 1962), 19.

25. Ibid., 12.

26. Wayne E. Stevens, "The Organization of the British Fur Trade, 1760-1800," *Mississippi Valley Historical Review*, 3 (September 1916), 176.

27. Helen G. Broshar, "The First Push Westward of the Albany Traders," *Mississippi Valley Historical Review*, 7 (1921), 229.

28. Harold A Innis, *The Fur Trade in Canada* (New Haven, CT: Yale University Press, 1930), 177.

29. Johnson to Claus, June 11, 1761, *Johnson MSS*, 10:281–83.

30. Mackenzie & Oakes to James & Charles Crokatt, March 17, 1761 in Marjory G. Jackson, "The Beginning of British Trade at Michilimackinac," *Minnesota History*, 11 (September 1930), 238.

31. Journal of Peter Pond, Reuben G. Thwaites, "The British Regime in Wisconsin," *Wisconsin Historical Collections*, 18 (1908), 325.

32. Hamilton, *French and Indian War*, 16–17.

33. *Johnson MSS*, 7:723–30.

34. Burnet to Board of Trade, May 9, 1727, Edmund B. O'Callaghan, ed., *The Documentary History of the State of New York*, 4 vols. (Albany, NY: Weed, Parsons & Co., 1849-51), 1:291 (hereafter cited as *DHNY*); Paul C. Phillips, *The Fur Trade,* 2 vols. (Norman: University of Oklahoma Press, 1961), 1:397.

35. Johnson to Croghan, January 30, 1758, *Johnson MSS*, 2:778.

36. *DHNY*, 1:308.

37. Johnson to the Board of Trade, October 8, 1764, *Johnson MSS*, 4:556.

38. Frederick W. Barnes, "The Fur Traders of Early Oswego," *Proceedings of the New York Historical Association*, 13 (1914), 134.

39. Johnson to Henry Moore, September 28, 1768, *Johnson MSS*, 6:412.

40. Simon McTavish to William Edgar, December 24, 1774, William Edgar Papers, 1750-1775, vol. R 2; William S. Wallace, ed., *Documents Relating to the North West Company* (Toronto: Champlain Society, 1934), 47–48.

41. Innis, *Fur Trade*, 88.

42. Fleming, "Phyn, Ellice and Co.," 8.

43. Walter Rutherford to Johnson, May 12, 1761, *Johnson MSS*, 10:265.

44. Johnson to Claus, May 20, 1761, ibid., 10:270.

45. Henry R. Howland, "The Niagara Portage," *Buffalo Historical Society Publications*, 6 (no date), 39.

46. Edmund B. O'Callaghan and Berthold Fernow, eds., *Documents Relating to the Colonial History of New York*, 15 vols. (Albany, NY: Weed, Parsons & Co., 1853-18-87), 7:488–89, 614 (hereafter cited as *DCHNY*).

47. Petition of Albany Merchants to the Lords of Trade, January 28, 1762, *DCHNY*, 7:488–89.

48. Johnson to Amherst, February 5,1762, *Johnson MSS*, 3:620.

49. Amherst to Johnson, February 14, 1762, ibid., 10:382–83.

50. Johnson to Amherst, April 29, 1762, ibid., 3:723.

51. Amherst to Mr. Sharpe, October 20, 1762, *DCHNY*, 7:508–09.

52. Sanders Letter Book; Henry Nellis to Johnson, May 8, 1760, *Johnson MSS*, 10:145; Johnson to Haldimand, May 3, 1760, ibid., 3:234.

53. Johnson to the Board of Trade, August 30, 1764, *IHC*, 10:306; June 1, 1761, July 16, 1762, Askin Papers, B4, Burton Historical Collection.

54. Innis, *Fur Trade*, 177; Memorial of Lieutenant Benjamin Roberts to Hillsborough, Robert Rogers Papers, Minnesota Historical Society; John Lees, *Journal of [John Lees] of Quebec, Merchant* (Detroit: Society of the Colonial Wars of the State of Michigan, 1911), 26.

55. Bradstreet to Amherst, February 20, 1764, Franklin B. Hough, *Diary of the Siege of Detroit in the War with Pontiac...* (Albany, NY: J. Munsell, 1860), 245.

56. Ibid., 154–55.

57. Henry Van Schaak to Johnson, November 7, 1762, *Johnson MSS*, 3:928.

58. Lees, *Journal of [John Lees]*, 27–28.

59. Innis, *Fur Trade*, 220.

60. John Sanders to James Bonbonous, July 11, 1761, Sanders Letter Book; John Sanders to Champion & Hayley, November 4, 1761, ibid.

61. John Sanders to Moses Franks, November 4, 1761, ibid.

62. John Sanders to John Bonbonous, November 4, 1761, ibid.

63. Amherst to Johnson, February 14, 1762, *Johnson MSS*, 10:382–83.

64. Johnson to Amherst, April 1, 1762, ibid., 3:664.

65. William Walters to Johnson, April 5, 1762, ibid., 10:426–27.

66. Johnson to William Corry, March 15, 1762, ibid., 3:649.

67. DeCouange to Johnson, June 22 and 27, 1762, ibid., 3:793, 811.

68. Amherst to Johnson, May 16, 1762, ibid., 3:742.

69. Johnson to Amherst, August 1, 1762, ibid., 10:478.

70. Amherst to Johnson, August 22, 1762, ibid., 10:488–89.

71. Lottridge to Johnson, December 12, 1762, ibid., 3:969.

72. Amherst to Johnson, November 21, 1762, ibid., 3:943; Gage to Amherst, November 21, 1762, ibid., 3:943.

73. Percy J. Robinson, *Toronto during the French Regime, 1615-1793* (Toronto: University of Toronto Press, 1965), 148–49.

74. Johnson to Amherst, December 7, 1762, *Johnson MSS*, 3:962.

75. Sanders to Bonbonous, October 17, 1762, Sanders Letter Book.

76. Dirk Vanderheyden to John Sanders, June 14, 1762, John Sanders Collection, Box 13, New-York Historical Society.

77. DeCouange to Johnson, June 5, 1763, *Johnson MSS*, 4:134–35.

78. Journal of Indian Affairs, June 14, 1763, ibid., 10:723.

79. Johnson to Gertruy Vander Heyden, August 20, 1763, ibid., 10:789.

80. Journal of Indian Congress, September 5, 1763, ibid., 10:831.

81. Johnson to Amherst, October 6, 1763, ibid., 10:866.

82. De Couange to Johnson, October 22, 1763, ibid., 10:907–08.

83. Alex Duncan to Johnson, October 1, 1763, ibid., 4:212.

84. Volkert P. Douw to Johnson, November 3, 1763, Hough, *Diary of the Seige of Detroit*, 190.

85. Colden to Johnson, December 19, 1763, *Colden Papers, New-York Historical Society Collections* (1876), 267.

86. Indian Affairs, December 22, 1763, *Johnson MSS*, 10:972.

87. Colden to Halifax, December 22, 1763, *Colden Papers*, 274.

88. John Sanders to John Bonbonous, April 27, 1763, Sanders Letter Book.

89. John Sanders to Bonbonous, April 27, 1763; Sanders to Champion & Hayley, October 7, 1763; Sanders to Bonbonous, October 29, 1763, ibid.

90. Baynton & Wharton to Callendar, October 16, 1763, Baynton, Wharton, Morgan & Morgan Microfilm, F1, Pennsylvania Historical Society, 230.

91. Edmund Moran to Evan Shelby, September 12, 1764, Moran Papers, State Historical Society of Wisconsin.

92. Moran to Evan Shelby, October 21, 1764, Ibid.

93. Sanders to Bonbonous, January 18, 1764, Sanders Letter Book.

94. John Duncan to Johnson, February 23, 1764, *Johnson MSS*, 11:77.

95. Henry Montour to Johnson, May 23, 1764, ibid., 11:197–98.

96. Gage to Johnson, January 12, 1764, ibid., 4:292.

97. Albany Merchant to the Lords of Trade, March 1764, *DCHNY*, 7:613.

98. Duncan & Phyn to Johnson, May 28, 1764, *Johnson MSS*, 4:432.

99. James Phyn to Johnson, April 8, 1764, ibid., 4:395.

100. List of Goods, April 5, 1764, ibid., 11:122.

101. Gage to Bouquet, June 5, 1764, *CA Report* (1889), 67.

102. Colden to Johnson, May 25, 1764, *Colden Papers* (1876), 329.

103. Johnson to Colden, August 23, 1764, *Johnson MSS*, 4:513.

104. Colden to Johnson, September 3, 1764, *Colden Papers* (1876), 356.

105. Johnson to Colden, September 21, 1764, *Johnson MSS*, 4:541–42.

106. Gage to Bradstreet, October 15, 1764, *IHC*, 10:344.

107. Colden to Johnson, December 10, 1764, *Johnson MSS*, 4:612–13.

108. Colden to Gage, December 8, 1764, *Colden Papers* (1876), 419.

109. Colden to Board of Trade, December 12, 1764, ibid., 441; Johnson to Colden, December 18, 1764, *Johnson MSS*, 4:622–23.

110. John Sanders to Champion & Hayley, October 26, 1764, Sanders Letter Book.

111. Bill of Duncan & Phyn to Johnson, December 17, 1764, *Johnson MSS*, 11:508–09.

112. Broshar, "First Push Westward," 229; Wayne E. Stevens, *The Northwest Fur Trade 1763–1800* (Urbana: University of Illinois, 1928), 35–36; Innis, *The Fur Trade*, 174.

5

Pennsylvania

Even more than New York, the disenchantment of Pennsylvania with the British government in 1765 related closely to previously established factions in the colony. The frontier traders and the Philadelphia merchants with business interests in the west anticipated great profits once the French army was removed in 1760, and trade was opened with the Indians. Supplying the British army and the Indian Department offered additional opportunity. When these hopes were dashed, resentment followed. In contrast, the Quakers, concerned about the abuse of the Indians by the traders selling little else than rum, sided with the British in their attempts to regulate trade and prevent encroachment on Indian land. Religion was more of a factor in Pennsylvania than in Canada and New York. Commercial competition was not between nationality groups, but between religious groups, that is the Quakers, the non-Quakers, and the Jews.

The defeat in July 1755 of the expedition under General Edward Braddock designed to drive the French out of the Ohio Valley, changed the equation in Pennsylvania. The Quakers withdrew from the Assembly, and a new nonexpansionist group was willing to cooperate with the expansionists to support defense measures during the war, beginning with an appropriation of £60,000 Pennsylvania in November 1755. Among those pressing for frontier defense were William Allen, William Plumstead, Thomas Willing, and John Kidd, all of whom later were involved in the fur trade.[1] Allen was a chief justice of Pennsylvania, as well as a commissioner at the Indian Conference in 1762, and represented Baynton & Wharton in September 1762. Willing was a prominent Philadelphia merchant who sent goods to the frontier in July 1759 and complained of Croghan's rule of trade. Plumstead was an associate of David Franks and Croghan in land speculation, army provisions, and deerskins between 1761 and 1765. Kidd was the partner of William Parr and both were appointed western county officials. Daniel Roberdeau, one of the leaders of the moderate nonexpansionist group, on the other hand, was a Philadelphia merchant dealing in rice and Madeira wine in the 1760s.[2]

After the surrender of Canada in 1760, the Quakers, opposing British requests, refused to grant more money for the military. When the frontier was opened to trade in 1760, the Quakers argued that rather than using force, dealing fairly with the Indians would pacify them. When British actions after Pontiac's Rebellion forced the Pennsylvania merchants out of the trade, the expansionists opposed the British government, while the Quakers opposed any protest.[3]

The more substantial merchants in Philadelphia were wholesalers who either sold to smaller traders or hired others to deal with the tribes. The Quaker firm, Baynton & Wharton (joined in 1763 by George Morgan to form Baynton, Wharton & Morgan), and the partnerships formed by David Franks, a Jew, were the most powerful. Franks had excellent political connections in London and was a subcontractor supplying provisions to the British army. Baynton, Wharton & Morgan relied on connections with Johnson, General Gage, and Croghan, who as an experienced Indian agent, had the best knowledge of the area.[4]

Before 1760, the trade with the Indians was divided between the private merchants and a public company created on April 8, 1758, by the Pennsylvania legislature based on the Quaker conviction that the private dealer was not to be trusted with the Indians, and that a government trading agency would protect the savages. The commission received a major portion of its capital from Amos Strettel, a Philadelphia merchant with family ties in London. The commission subsequently received cash through the auction of its skins and furs by Thomas Lawrence, the public auctioneer in Philadelphia.

The Indian Commission of nine members was appointed to barter with the tribes. The commissioners, many of whom were merchants, were James Child, William West, Amos Strettell, Thomas Willing, John Reynell, Joseph Richardson, Edward Pennington, William Fisher, and Joseph Morris. As agents for the commission, John Langdale, Josiah Davenport, and Robert Burchan were appointed.[5] The profits were to be used for missionaries and teachers among the natives. The commission also operated as a wholesaler to the smaller traders who went to the Indian towns.

The major sources of merchandise for the commission were merchants in Philadelphia, including Willing and Morris, William Fisher, Edward Pennington, Francis West, and Amos Strettel. From London, John Strettel supplied gunpowder and Daniel Mildred shipped cloth and ten barrels of gunpowder valued at £357 to the Pennsylvania Indian Commission from London.[6]

The traders on the frontier were from a lower economic strata compared to the Philadelphia merchants. Before the Seven Years' War, about three hundred Pennsylvanians were dealing with the Indians of the Ohio Valley, including up to twenty-one licensed traders, each accompanied by approximately ten horse drivers.[7] Many had served in the Pennsylvania provincial regiment stationed on the frontier in 1759, where the soldiers observed easy profits being made.

Colonel Hugh Mercer, the Pennsylvania battalion commander at Fort Pitt, heard that half the officers among the Pennsylvania troops had resigned in 1759 to follow the British army during the next spring as sutlers or peddlers. Mercer believed that the quartermaster should prevent such vermin from coming west.[8] Of the 304 officers identified as serving in the Pennsylvania militia during the French and Indian War, twenty-three were later recorded in frontier business.[9]

Most of these men became petty traders dealing with the Indians on the Pennsylvania frontier. The typical fur trader from Fort Pitt has been described as being rough, bold, and as fierce as the Indians, wearing a blanket coat or deerskin, and armed with a rifle, knife, and tomahawk.[10]   A man named Strump was described as wearing a light brown cloth coat, a blue great coat, an old hat, and leather breeches. Ironcutter, presumably his Indian companion, wore a blanket coat, an old felt hat, buckskin breeches, long trousers, coarse white yarn stockings, and shoes with brass buckles.[11]   Colonel Bouquet described the traders in March 1761 as "the scum of the neighboring provinces who have no visible means to live except a license."[12]   A month later, Bouquet sternly reported to General Gage that he had the houses of traders destroyed in punishment for illegal dealings and sale of rum to the Indians.[13]

To prevent abuse of the Indians, Pennsylvania issued licenses, approximately fifteen each year, but many traded without a license. Those who were licensed are nowhere else noted as being concerned with the Indian trade, and they apparently obtained a license to deal with the tribes living adjacent to settlements who came down from the hills from time to time to obtain liquor, ammunition, and other supplies.

After 1760, when Croghan, as Indian deputy, and General Monckton, commander at Fort Pitt, permitted trading in the tribal towns, business expanded rapidly to the west. Cargoes were taken to Detroit, Sandusky, the Lower Shawnee towns, the Delaware villages, and elsewhere by Robert Callendar, Michael Teaffe, Alexander Lowrey, John Hart, and Hugh Crawford.[14]   The Pennsylvania traders were primarily concerned with the territory immediately west of Fort Pitt in 1760, but soon spread out. Although there were thirty-seven colonial traders in western Pennsylvania in 1760, only one went to Detroit and none to Mackinac. In 1761, there were thirty traders in Pennsylvania; sixteen from either New York or Pennsylvania had reached Detroit, and one had gone to Mackinac.[15]

In addition to the traders, a large number of men were employed to handle the boats and drive the horses. Their names represented the many ethnic groups then in Pennsylvania. The saddlers, horse drivers, and bateau men were hired by the season from among the frontier farmers. These occupations were not lifelong, but were undertaken for a short period to obtain cash. In contrast, wagon masters and carpenters were professionals whose names appear year after year in the records.

A fourth group, local purchasers who bought furs and deerskins in Philadelphia, included smaller buyers, presumably tradesmen who needed leather and fur for the manufacture of breeches, gloves, hats, saddles, and other products. The larger buyers were often speculators who shipped the peltry to London for resale. A shipment brought from Illinois via New Orleans was sold in Philadelphia for more than £3,000 sterling ($600,000). Some of the buyers were probably using the peltry to balance accounts in England.

In summary, the Pennsylvanians in frontier-related business were of four types: merchant wholesalers in the East; petty traders on the frontier; wagoners, bateau men, and others who worked for both groups; and those who purchased furs and deerskin for processing or resale in London.

The route to Fort Pitt from Philadelphia went over roads traveled by wagon and horseback. There were two roads from Philadelphia to the Fort Pitt area after reaching Carlisle. One was via Bedford, called Forbes Road for the commander who built it, and the other was via Fort Cumberland in Virginia, called Braddock's Road for its builder. Both of these roads were approximately two hundred miles in length and at times were open to wagon traffic the entire distance. However, during this period, much of the merchandise was transferred from wagons to pack horses at Carlisle, the central depot from which merchandise went north to the trading post at Fort Augusta, north up the Susquehanna River near present day Sunbury, and west to the Fort Pitt area. The heaviest traveled route was west to Fort Pitt, a journey of about twenty days over the two hundred miles of road.[16]

Of the many routes that extended westward from Fort Pitt, the most significant was the Ohio River, flowing down to the rich Illinois market. To the north, the Allegheny and other rivers formed a water route via Venango and LeBoeuf to Presque Isle on Lake Erie. The nine-day trip from Fort Pitt to Presque Isle covered more than three hundred miles. Cargoes went by bateau from Fort Pitt to Fort LeBoeuf, then by pack horses to Presque Isle, and by water to Detroit.[17]

An alternate route to Detroit struck overland using pack horses following the Ohio River northwest until the river curved southward. The road struck straight west to Beavertown and then generally northwest to Sandusky where the trip was continued by canoe. Still another route used later in the period was down the Ohio to the Scioto River, up the Scioto to the Shawnee town, overland to the Maumee River, down the Maumee River to Lake Erie, and by canoe to Detroit. Using one of these routes, one could go from Fort Pitt to Detroit in only six days without a cargo.[18]

On the most significant route from Fort Pitt, the Ohio River leading toward Illinois, the traveller merely loaded his flatboat with goods and materials and with a skilled crew floated the eleven hundred miles to the mouth of the Ohio River on the Mississippi. Only during the spring was the Ohio navigable throughout its length for a heavily loaded boat, because the changes of level came with great rapidity. On May 19, 1766, the river rose several feet so rapidly that bateaux moved along with only moderate rowing at six to seven miles per hour.[19]

Shipments of merchandise averaged in value from £200 to more than £800 Pennsylvania, a little less than the value of a canoe load of goods in Canada. For example in 1760, Indian goods worth £831 Pennsylvania ($95,500) were shipped to Benjamin Wallace, the commission agent at Fort Hunter, in the wagons of Andrew Cox and James Irwin. Another shipment on April 30, 1760, worth £564 Pennsylvania went in care of Francis West, the commission agent at Carlisle, who in turn forwarded the goods to George Allen in Fort Pitt in Matias Hoffer's wagon. The merchandise included French match coats, cloth, silver work, and seventy-two beaver traps.

The commission set up stores in Fort Hunter, Fort Augusta, and Fort Pitt. The volume was notable as indicated by the invoice book for Fort Pitt showing £844 Pennsylvania (about $100,000) received for skins in November and December 1760.[20] Between December 1758 and April 1760, the Pennsylvania commission sent articles worth £7,797 Pennsylvania ($900,000) to Pittsburgh. The inventory of Commission goods was valued at £4,845 Pennsylvania ($660,000) at Fort Pitt on June 23, 1760. The inventory was the residue of a shipment worth £7,797 sent by April 1760, indicating that £3,000 in sales had been made in less than three months. The sales, mostly to Indians, ranged from one shilling to £5 ($6 to $575).[21]

The Pennsylvania Indian Commission continued to ship large quantities of goods to Fort Pitt. By the end of 1760, £28,122 Pennsylvania ($3,235,000) in goods had been sent to the trading posts of the commission, nearly equal to the trade from Montreal. In the last six months nearly £6,000 in value was sent to Fort Pitt in seven loads. One shipment worth £487 Pennsylvania was sent in the wagons of John Cox and James Irwin to Carlisle in the care of Francis West, and were forwarded by him to John Langdale, the agent in Pittsburgh.[22] Other loads included purchases of £773 from Edward Pennington, £314 from George Allen, £407 from Pennington and Child, and £1,000 from Robert and Amos Strettel.

Private merchants were not as quick to take advantage of the increasing business opportunities as was the Pennsylvania Indian Commission. John and Peter Chevalier, Philadelphia merchants, supplied the army contractors (Plumstead & Franks, the firm that furnished provisions for the troops) through Joshua Howell, their agent at Fort Pitt, before he was replaced on March 21, 1760. Baynton & Wharton made major purchases in 1760 from those involved in frontier commerce, including Ephraim Blaine, a Fort Pitt merchant, for £171; John and Peter Chevalier for £353; Callender and Spear, the Carlisle partnership, for £297; Francis Wade for £97; John Hart for £88; and James Becham of Lancaster for £97.[23]

The Philadelphia Jews were very active in 1760, dealing primarily with one another. David Franks (who had the army provisions contract in partnership with William Plumstead) had accounts with Joseph Simon, Levy Andrew Levy, and Levy & Company in April 1760.[24] Bernard Gratz at Philadelphia wrote to Franks in London regarding the sale of £86 in wampum to the Indian

Commission, and also dealt with Joseph Simon of Lancaster and Levy Andrew Levy in April 1760. Michael Gratz had transactions with Franks of about £300 Pennsylvania ($34,500).[25]

The Jewish merchants had other ties also. On May 16, 1760, a partnership to deal with the Indians that lasted nine years was formed at Lancaster by William Trent, Joseph Simon, David Franks, and Levy Andrew Levy. Trent was already indebted to Simon and Franks for £4,082 Pennsylvania ($470,000) and gave them a mortgage on his land.[26]

The Philadelphia merchants were expanding their scope of business rapidly in the second half of 1760. For example, Daniel Clark, a Philadelphia merchant, wrote to William Neal in London acknowledging an order including merchandise intended for the Indians, and placed another very long order for the next spring. Clark also ordered a small quantity of goods from Holliday, Dunbar & Company. In November 1760, Clark ordered a long list of fabrics from Daniel Mildred (who also supplied dry goods to the Chevaliers and the Indian Commission). In December, Clark sent a shipment of rum and sugar to William Baker in London to balance his account. John and Peter Chevalier were dealing with Baynton & Wharton and William West in this period.[27] Much of this commercial activity was in anticipation of a vast increase in trade with the Indians in 1761.

At Fort Pitt, resumption of trade with the Indians in the early part of 1761 met with considerable controversy and disagreement among the army, the Indian Department, and the traders. In March 1761, Colonel Bouquet refused to permit the traders to sell other than at established posts to prevent conflict. In June 1761, Campbell, the commandant in Detroit, sent fifty men from Detroit to rescue some Pennsylvania traders being threatened at Sandusky after ignoring Bouquet's rules not to trade off the posts.[28] Rather than confining trade to the posts, Croghan thought that the sooner the traders went out to the Indians the better. Without traders in the tribal towns, the Indians were forced to come to Fort Pitt and caused trouble after getting too much rum.[29]

The traders who remained in Fort Pitt suffered because many traders had been permitted by Bouquet and Croghan to go to the Indian towns and others went without passes, intercepting the Indians before they arrived in Fort Pitt. In November 1761, Kenny noted that many traders went to the Indian towns. Two horse drivers with eight horses loaded with Indian goods were detained at Venango on the route from Fort Pitt to Presque Isle because they had no pass.[30] The underlying cause for the conflict at Fort Pitt was overlapping authority and intense competition. There were agents of the Pennsylvania Indian Commission and traders licensed by Pennsylvania, Bouquet and George Croghan, Johnson's deputy.[31]

The reports of Kenny reflect the problems of the trader at Fort Pitt. In August 1761, he reported that while trading with an Indian, another trader, John Ormsby, came in with an Indian who accused Kenny of using light steel yards (balances that showed light weight, thus cheating the customer). When Kenny's and Ormsby's steel yards were compared, there was a difference of one pound per hundred weight. Kenny expected that Ormsby had two "keys" or weights for his steel yard, one accurate and the other designed to discredit other traders.[32]

On another occasion, a Seneca chief came in to trade seven buckskins, while many Indians were crowding the store stealing. The warrior was not pleased with the trade, so Kenny gave him a loaf of bread. Another Indian hesitated in choosing a brass wire in exchange for a very small skin to divert Kenny's attention while the other Indians stole. The Indians tried to get behind the counter, but Kenny turned them back. One of the Indians took a keg that was behind the door, so Kenny turned them all out giving one a handful of salt for which he begged. Some buckskins were traded for powder.[33] These anecdotes reveal the conduct of trade and the behavior of both seller and customer.

The various factions accused the others of violating regulations, especially selling liquor to Indians. Rum was already a problem in 1760 when Croghan reported that there was too much rum around and that the Indians were drunk and killing the soldiers.[34] Although Croghan had encouraged General Monckton to prohibit the sale of rum in the fall of 1760, by March 1761, Colonel Bouquet informed Monckton that it was impossible to prevent the movement of rum to Fort Pitt. In a fight resulting from drunkenness, three Indians had been killed.[35] The matter was complicated by northern Indians stopping at Fort Pitt for weapons and provisions on their way to fight the Cherokees in the south. The presents given to these war parties by Croghan included rum and created a good market for the merchants at Fort Pitt. Captain Lewis Oury, commander at Fort Bedford, which was half way from Carlisle to Fort Pitt, informed Colonel Bouquet of the seizure of a shipment of one hundred kegs of liquor (about two thousand gallons), drunken laborers being shot, and traders being seized for illegal trading. On June 16, 1761, he reported seizing more liquor and having trouble removing the Indians from Bedford.[36]

To supply the huge quantities of rum being sold to the Indians, some Philadelphia merchants began to distill rum locally rather than importing it from New England and elsewhere. William McKee ordered six hogsheads of molasses, earthenware, and a thirty-two gallon still, obviously intending to set up the still for the manufacture of rum to compete with the stills of Philadelphia and the importing business.[37] The Chevaliers, in December 1761, in partnership with Baynton & Wharton, operated a still house and invested nearly £1,000 to buy Negro slaves, bricks, nails, and molasses. On December 21, 1761, they sold five sixty-three gallon hogsheads of rum to John Mitchell for £78 Pennsylvania and within the next few weeks sold twelve hogsheads to Townsend White for more than £200 Pennsylvania.[38]

The major complaint of the merchants in Fort Pitt was that although the traders were prohibited from bringing rum, the commission was bringing in large quantities.[39] The activities of the commission at Fort Pitt by the end of 1761 had reached expenditures of £18,592 Pennsylvania ($2.14 million). Cash credits by the end of 1761 were only £7,600, so the business was not yet a paying proposition. However, there was a large stock of goods on hand at the store in Fort Pitt.[40] More goods were being obtained in 1761 by the Commission in Philadelphia from Nathaniel Holland, Josiah Davenport, William West, and J. Morris. Payments for the sale of furs continued to be received from Thomas Lawrence, the public auctioneer in Philadelphia.[41]

Other Philadelphia merchants were becoming more involved in western trade. Baynton & Wharton, on March 17, 1761, delivered to William West for John Welch, an Indian trader, twenty quarter-casks of gun powder, a keg of bar lead, and a bale of match coating that were sent west by William White's wagon. They sold James Fox nineteen pieces of Indian blanket material for £190 Pennsylvania.[42] Daniel Clark sent to John Clark of Lancaster an assortment of goods on six months credit on March 15, 1761, and in July 1761, he received an invoice from William Neal of London for £2,316 sterling ($463,000). Clark complained that this invoice was far beyond the real value of the goods shipped and hoped that Neal had shipped no more because the goods would not sell at that price. In November 1761, Clark received an invoice for £811 from Neal and Pigou and a few days later sent them an order for Indian goods, cloth, knives, powder, lead, match coats, and strouds.[43] Clark made payments with shipments of tobacco and with sterling drafts.

In February, John and Peter Chevalier provided cloth and hardware to William McAllister, a sutler at Fort Pitt who absconded without paying his debts in April; and John Harris, a trader at Paxton.[44] On August 17, 1761, John and Peter Chevalier sent a shipment to London that included one-third of a chest of beaver valued at £175 Pennsylvania consigned to Mildred and Roberts. In December 1761, another shipment of furs consigned to Daniel Mildred netted £189 Pennsylvania.[45] Michael Gratz's ledger indicated a sharp increase in business in 1761 to more than £500 Pennsylvania in receipts with Frank's account at more than £220 Pennsylvania.[46]

Even the French traders in the Ohio Valley, who were cut off from their sources of goods from the St. Lawrence in 1761, tried to get goods from Fort Pitt rather than Illinois. In February, Colonel Bouquet reported that the British commander of the garrison on the Miami River had sent a Frenchman for clothes and other supplies for the Indians. Bouquet persuaded Trent, a merchant in Pittsburgh, to give the Frenchman credit for these goods in March 1761. A member of the Baby family of Detroit was in Fort Pitt trying to break the rule confining trade to the fort. Baby attempted to smuggle a shipment of goods for the Indians with the assistance of two men from Fort Pitt, but Bouquet seized and held the goods awaiting the decision of General Monckton.[47]

The Pennsylvania traders did very well in the summer of 1761. In July 1761, Patrick Allison, who purchased his goods from Baynton & Wharton, was in Lancaster waiting for his skins to arrive, having just returned from Fort Pitt. He already had seven horse loads of summer skins at John Harris' and would send the additional skins by the first wagon. His partner, Matthew McRae, was still in Fort Pitt intending to send thirty horse loads of skins to Philadelphia in three weeks.[48] In August 1761, Edmund Moran had returned from a trading venture at Fort Pitt and joined his partner George Ross in Lancaster. The two planned to return to Fort Pitt to check on their furs.[49] In September 1761, Daniel Clark complained that Moran had not paid a farthing on his account, although he had heard from Ross. All of these reports indicated a very high level of profitable trade in 1761. The Philadelphia market was glutted with fur because many furs had arrived from Albany in addition to those from Fort Pitt. The movement of furs down the Hudson to New York and then to Philadelphia to enter the local market in competition with fur from Fort Pitt had a depressing effect on the price of furs from the west.[50]

Having experienced a banner year in 1761, the Philadelphia merchants ordered large quantities of English goods for delivery in the summer of 1762. However, business in 1762 did not equal the previous year because of the overall tightening demanded by the British government including cuts in expenditures in the Indian Department (both salaries and gifts for the Indians) and a reduction in the military expenses in the colonies. These cuts had a direct influence on the Philadelphia merchants.

Although business with the British government declined in Pennsylvania, the trade with the Indians expanded greatly during 1762. Shipments by the Indian Commission to Pittsburgh in April 1762 had a value of more than £414 Pennsylvania of which £200 was in silver work made by Joseph Hollingshead and J. Richardson.[51] In June 1762, another shipment valued at more than £576 Pennsylvania was sent, and in September 1762, a further shipment of more than £263 which included eighteen rifles, valued at £4.10.0 each, was to be picked up in Lancaster from William Henry, the famous maker of early Pennsylvania rifles.[52] Goods came in large quantities from England. For example, in three invoices, John Strettel and Mildred and Roberts sent nearly £600 sterling ($120,000) in cloth.[53]

The Jewish merchants based in Lancaster continued their trade in 1762. Joseph Simon had stores in both Detroit and Fort Pitt, the latter operated by Abraham Mitchell.[54] With William Henry, Simon was importing goods directly from England. In June 1762, Joseph Simon sent ten bundles of fur on Shank's wagon to Bernard Gratz in Philadelphia to be sold. In August 1762, Simon wrote to Bernard Gratz that he intended to send fourteen chests of fur down and wished for an account of the furs that Bernard Gratz had sent to Baynton & Wharton for sale.[55]

On August 17, 1762, Simon and Mitchell sent fifty bundles of skins, worth about £4,000 Pennsylvania ($460,000) via wagons driven by Mathias Slough, Shank and Hans Swetzer. Another £2,000 shipment went to Mr. Bush, and other shipments went directly to Baynton & Wharton for sale. The complex arrangements that Simon had made for his fur trade were indicated by the list of partnerships that he formed. In Lancaster, he formed a partnership with William Henry; at Heidelberg he formed a partnership with Nathan. His partner in Fort Pitt was Abraham Mitchell. Another partnership was with Alexander Lowry in Detroit, and a fifth partnership was with Moses Franks and William Trent.[56] The trade in each locality was conducted by an agent who was in partnership with Simon.

Baynton & Wharton extended its influence during 1762. By December 1762, Robert Callendar, their associate in the western trade, sent two thousand pounds of dressed deer leather, nine hundred raccoons, and 346 pounds of fall skins to Baynton & Wharton. Callendar planned to send six or seven wagon loads more as soon as he could obtain wagons.[57] Baynton & Wharton were also in a new venture at the newly established post in Venango, on the Allegheny River north of Fort Pitt, with Andrew Wilkins as their agent. In October 1762, Wilkins reported that he was the only trader in Venango and would therefore have good access to skins. He hoped to make a full remittance of his credit by the next summer, as Croghan had promised him that no other trader would be permitted in Venango until the next summer.[58]

Daniel Clark, a merchant in Philadelphia supplying the army and Indian Department, referred to dealings with Callender and Croghan, and a debt owed by Martin McDonald in Pittsburgh in January 1762.[59] In letters to his three English correspondents, Neal & Pigou, Mildred & Roberts, and Holliday Dunbar & Co. in January 1762, Clark insisted on early shipment of Indian goods. In referring to an invoice for more than £700 sterling from Holiday, Dunbar & Co., Clark complained that the boat was late because of bad weather, and therefore the goods would not sell until the fall of 1762.[60]

Before the Indian uprising during the summer, Indian trade had been profitable in 1763. In early 1763, large shipments of skins and furs to the Indian Commission came down from Fort Augusta and Fort Pitt. In June 1763, twenty-one bundles with more three thousand pounds of peltry arrived. The peltry included both deerskin and furs. In August, twelve more bundles with fourteen hundred pounds of skins came in two wagons. By August 1763, seventy bundles with more than four tons of fur worth more than £2,000 Pennsylvania had arrived from Fort Augusta.[61] In addition, the Commission received cash for skins sold in Fort Pitt and for supplies provided to Plumstead and Franks, the army provisions contractor in Fort Pitt.[62] Although the commissioners did not make an unusually high profit, they were the major traders on the Pennsylvania frontier during this period. By April 1763, the Indian Commission had handled £37,323 Pennsylvania ($4.3 million) in business. The net loss for their three-and-a-half years involvement was only £185.[63]

Others were also doing well in the first half of 1763. Joseph Simon sent six hundred pounds of furs and skins, including 249 beaver to Bernard Gratz from Lancaster on May 30, 1763.[64] The partnership of Theodorus Swaine Drage of Bedford and John Hughes of Philadelphia supplied large quantities of rum to Croghan, and in the first four months of 1763, they had made payments of £3,754 Pennsylvania ($430,000) to suppliers and employees.[65]

Robert Callendar and his partner, Joseph Spear, were among the major traders in western Pennsylvania, supplying the army and buying fur. On January 12, 1763, John Nelson, the paymaster for British forces, gave them a bill for £2,002 Pennsylvania. Callendar also drew a bill to be paid by Nelson for goods from Baynton & Wharton for £2,758 Pennsylvania ($317,000).[66] In January 1763, Callendar and Spear sent twelve chests of peltry valued at £1,446 Pennsylvania to Baynton & Wharton, who in turn sent the fur to John Noble of Bristol, one of their agents in England. The net return received six months later was £1,071 sterling.[67]

Baynton & Wharton were also major players on the frontier in early 1763. They dealt with Philip Boyle, Abraham Mitchell, John Walch, Patrick Allison, Captain John Prentice, and William Trent, either receiving furs or shipping goods west to them.[68] The Quaker partners were also major losers when the Indians rebelled.

The profitable business on the frontier in 1763 came to an abrupt halt in May 1763, with the eruption of Pontiac's Rebellion. In that month, a large party of Mingoes and Delawares from the Ohio area came to Fort Pitt and sold £300 worth of peltry for powder and ammunition. They then went down the Ohio River and began robbing traders at Bushy Run.[69] Thomas Colhoun, who had been dealing along with fourteen other traders at the Tuscaroras, came in a few days later and reported that six men had been killed at the Salt Licks.[70] Probably one hundred men from Pennsylvania were killed during Pontiac's Rebellion, including horse drivers and other employees of the traders. Among those killed, were two Jewish traders who had been dealing with Franks & Company and Colonel John Clapham, who was killed on his way to Detroit.[71] In July 1763, Colonel Bouquet refused to permit any goods to pass Fort Pitt, and in October, Pennsylvania prohibited the sale of guns and powder to the Indians.[72]

The merchants were quick to demand compensation for their heavy losses to the Indians. On December 7, 1763, a large group of the losers met in the Indian Queen Tavern in Philadelphia and formed the "suffering traders," the Indiana Company. Others, including Croghan and William Franklin, secretly owned stock, even though they had lost nothing. The total losses claimed were £80,862 Pennsylvania (more than $9 million). Others who lost but did not join the suffering traders included Abraham Mitchell, Jeremiah Warder, Buchanan & Hughes, Daniel Clark, and William West, indicating that the £80,000 did not represent the total loss by the merchants.[73] Croghan and Moses Franks, a merchant in London, were given the task of presenting the memorial in London. The hope of the suffering traders was compensation by a grant of land to be obtained from the Indians in the peace settlement.

The financial effect of the Indian uprising was severe, as the debts of those robbed or killed would not be paid to merchants, including Baynton & Wharton. The latter firm expected to lose all of its Indian debts except Callendar's who had £4,000 Pennsylvania worth of goods in Detroit. If other merchants in

Philadelphia demanded immediate payment from Baynton & Wharton, they would have been in financial difficulty. They tried to salvage as much as possible and hoped that when everything was balanced the partners would have money left to continue business.[74]

To provide additional cash, Baynton & Wharton included in the partnership George Morgan, a wealthy young man employed as an apprentice. By September 1763, Samuel Wharton had vague plans for the tremendous expansion of the firm's western trade through a contract to supply the army posts west of Fort Pitt after the rebellion was ended. Wharton believed that the New York traders were in disfavor with Lord Amherst, while Wharton was very close to him. At the same time Wharton was negotiating with several firms in New York City to establish contacts with London and the West Indies to provide merchandise and rum for resale to the army.[75]

Joseph Spear, Callendar's partner and a major customer of Baynton & Wharton, proposed to send cargoes down the Ohio River to Illinois, and then down the Mississippi River to New Orleans, but Baynton & Wharton were reluctant because of the danger involved. Baynton & Wharton's final decision to enter the Illinois trade was made before early summer of 1763, when a large order for merchandise was sent to England for delivery by October 1763. The plan probably had been made before the Indian uprising, because in October 1762, Baynton & Wharton had a large cargo of merchandise from England. Baynton & Wharton divided the cargo with Callendar, who would take half of the goods to the trading posts on the Great Lakes. This first large shipment was apparently on the way west when the Indian uprising began in May 1763. The next question in the summer of 1763 was what to do with Baynton & Morgan's second large cargo, which was expected from England in October 1763 and had been ordered "when we first planned" to trade in Illinois. Spear and Callendar were involved in this second cargo, and Spear wished to proceed with the trade on the Mississippi. Baynton & Wharton suggested that Spear might do as he pleased with his part, but proposed an alternative. The merchandise would be sent to Illinois, but, because it was so late in the year, rather than sending it down the Ohio River, it could be sent by sea to Mobile and then up the Mississippi River by bateau.[76]

By December 26, 1763, Baynton, Wharton & Morgan wrote to John Noble, their correspondent in Bristol, asking for prices of deerskins at that port because the firm hoped to deal mostly in deerskins if peace was signed with the Indians.[77] In late 1763, Baynton, Wharton & Morgan were placing large orders with Richard Neave and David Barkley & Sons for goods to be delivered in spring 1764.[78] Croghan, who was to be in England seeking compensation for the suffering traders, would accept delivery of some of the goods. David Barkley & Sons and Neave were also asked to assist Croghan in his application for compensation for losses.[79]

Baynton, Wharton & Morgan's plan to expand trade with the west had been developed in consultation with Croghan who provided ties with Johnson.

Croghan had deposited a cargo of Indian goods with Baynton, Wharton & Morgan with the promise that Johnson would purchase the cargo. On April 6, 1763, having received a promise of a £5,000 sterling ($1 million!) advance from Gage, Johnson sent the order.[80] On April 30, 1763, with flourished penmanship, the firm wrote its first entry for Johnson on its accounts for a total of £2,618 Pennsylvania ($300,000).[81] The goods had been shipped on April 25, 1763, by way of New York, and payment finally came on September 15.[82]

The orders placed for goods in England were immense. On December 5, 1763, Baynton, Wharton & Morgan credited Richard Neave with £15,209 Pennsylvania ($1.7 million) for goods shipped to America. On December 5, 1763, alone, they received eighteen bales of woolens on board the *Britannia* valued at £2,338 Pennsylvania.[83] Their letter to Neave on December 26, 1763, stated the reason for the large order was that their present inventory had been sold. Baynton, Wharton & Morgan sales for the period November 7, 1763, to May 24, 1764, totaled £18,261 Pennsylvania, including their extensive commerce with the West Indies, the fishing ports, southern Europe, and England. The trade with the West was less than twenty percent of their total business, about £70,000 Pennsylvania ($8 million) for 1763.[84] Adding Baynton & Wharton's business to the £5,000 Pennsylvania of the Indian commissioners and the large trade of the associates of Bernard and Michael Gratz, the frontier trade in Pennsylvania had developed extensively by 1763.

Even though the Indian trade was halted in May 1763 by Pontiac's Rebellion, commerce with the West was not at a standstill in 1764. Because of the military activity, there was a vigorous market selling provisions and sundries to the army. Bargaining with the Indians required a large supply of presents both on the Pennsylvania frontier and through new connections with Johnson providing presents for the Great Lakes area. The hub of western commercial activity was in the firm of Baynton, Wharton & Morgan, who turned over large amounts of cash and goods in 1764. Early in the year, they were in very healthy financial condition often paying accounts in full with cash. Their remittances to London in the form of bread and flour were valued up to £15,000. They were also sending cargoes to the West Indies, Halifax, Boston, Madeira, Lisbon, and Leghorn. Early in 1764, they were purchasing sterling bills of exchange with Pennsylvania currency to pay Neave and others, rather than sending specie to London.[85] In general, the monthly turnover of cash and goods of the firm averaged about £5,000 during 1764.[86]

The increased tempo of business that Baynton, Wharton & Morgan had planned began with large orders to their two major London suppliers, David Barclay & Sons and Neave, at the end of 1763. In May 1764, Baynton, Wharton & Morgan received goods valued at £4,395 Pennsylvania from Barclay, and on the same ship, a cargo of goods valued at £5,789 Pennsylvania from Neave.[87] Even though the Indian rebellion was continuing in 1764, Baynton, Wharton & Morgan was supplying merchandise for the treaties. The largest parcel was the £2,800 sold to Johnson, but the firm hoped to send out all of the goods on hand, plus goods that had been ordered for the trade in Quebec. They ordered John Collins and William Govet, their agents in Quebec, to send all of the goods by the first ship to Philadelphia or to New York, to be forwarded to Philadelphia. Prospective sales were so good that Collins was instructed to ship regardless of the freight cost. The expected delay in payment of three or four months was better than waiting all winter with the hope of selling to the Canadians in the spring of 1765.[88]

Baynton, Wharton & Morgan was also concerned with supplying the troops. Joseph Spear at Carlisle tried to sell all of his goods to the army when the plan was announced to send troops down the Ohio to Illinois.[89] At Fort Pitt he sold some goods and received a bill of exchange from the 42nd Regiment for £200 Pennsylvania that he forwarded to Baynton, Wharton & Morgan to credit his account.[90]

John Hughes, who had been trading with the Indians since 1756, was supplying the army in Pennsylvania in 1764, with Joseph Spear acting as his agent. In July 1764, Spear reported that all of the goods and liquor belonging to Spear & Hughes was being sent forward but that prospects were poor, as too many people were permitted to trade with the army.[91] However, Spear did well and in August 1764, he reported that sixty horse loads of goods had been loaded as part of Colonel Bouquet's expedition.[92] Hughes was having difficulty with Neave over the matter of payment, although the problem in this case was the delay of the British government in paying bills.[93]

Spear was very active in many business affairs in 1764. He not only acted as Baynton, Wharton & Morgan's major contact at Carlisle and had entered partnership with Callendar for a large shipment of goods, but on May 11, 1764, he made a purchase of £745 Pennsylvania on behalf of the partnership of John Hughes, Theodorus Swaine Drage, and Spear. At the same time, he purchased £278 Pennsylvania on his own behalf from Baynton, Wharton & Morgan.[94] He also acted on behalf of Edmund Moran who left his goods with Spear's clerk at Fort Pitt when Moran went off with Bouquet's expedition.[95]

At Carlisle, Callendar was supplying the army contractors, Plumsted & Franks, receiving in return drafts from the army paymaster, John Nelson. On August 18, 1764, Callendar turned over to Baynton & Wharton in payment of his debts a draft of £2,000 sterling, a major boost to the firm's financial position at that time.[96] The army business was replacing the Indian trade. Robert Leake, the army quartermaster in New York, had nearly £1,000 sterling in outstanding bills to Callendar in August 1764.[97] On October 1, 1764, Callender's account with Baynton, Wharton & Morgan was credited with £908 Pennsylvania for cash received from John Nelson, the army paymaster.[98]

However, a crisis developed in Baynton, Wharton & Morgan's affairs when Neave in London demanded payment in June 1764. The partners pleaded that they could not pay because the fur trade in Canada had been closed for twelve months stopping the supply of furs, and the wheat trade also was at an end because of the poor quality of the harvest. The partners claimed that they had taken great effort to create a major trade in Canada and had lost because of unforeseen conditions.

Attempts to discharge their debts to Neave included applications to Johnson for early payment of his large debt and to Robert Leake for payment of £1,000.[99] On July 25, 1764, the firm demanded that Collins, their agent in Canada, make a remittance to England that summer.[100] In their concern to repay Neave, the firm borrowed 4,266 Spanish dollars from Richard McWilliams of Newcastle, Pennsylvania, valued at £1,600 Pennsylvania ($184,000) and sent the money on board the ship *Dragon* for London.[101] On August 9, 1764, the firm expressed indignation that Neave had lost confidence in the ability of Baynton, Wharton & Morgan to pay and claimed to be blameless in the matter. They sent a list of remittances made to Neave since June 1, 1764, which totaled more than £30,000 Pennsylvania ($3,450,000), including £2,700 in dollars and a little more than £1,500 in bills of exchange. Baynton, Wharton & Morgan listed cargoes worth more than £12,000 Pennsylvania that were to be sent including furs from Montreal that Callendar had saved from Detroit. The firm also expected skins and furs to be sent from Mobile to Neave equal to the £2,000 worth of Indian goods sent to Mobile in November 1763 and May 1764.[102]

However, Baynton, Wharton & Morgan still had financial problems, and were having great difficulty in paying debts. John Baynton thought the root of the problem was the ambitious scheme in Illinois, which he had opposed.[103] Samuel Wharton agreed that affairs did not look promising and hesitated to buy more fur in Detroit from Henry Van Schaack, as there was no money to pay for it.[104] To add to the difficulties of the firm, Croghan arrived in Philadelphia and established a household, which he equipped at the expense of the firm. In October 1764, Croghan spent nearly £500 Pennsylvania for household goods and liquor in less than six weeks.[105]

Meanwhile, the plans for the expedition to Illinois went forward. Spear was to accompany Colonel Bouquet's troops to the Mississippi, and the firm was building up its stock of goods. Spear and Callendar had formed a partnership and expected to receive a share of the Illinois business along with Baynton, Wharton & Morgan. However, Spear was somewhat concerned about the large supply of goods on hand. To him, the situation seemed so bad that he would rather have his share of the cargo to sell immediately, rather than holding it for future trade.[106]

The army and the Indian Department were the keys to the financial salvation of Baynton, Wharton & Morgan. A major change in the trade occurred when the contract of Plumsted & Franks of Philadelphia to supply the army expired on June 7, 1764.[107] In July 1764, the men of the 60th and 77th Regiments at Fort Pitt mutinied because of the bad flour provided by the contractors.[108] General Gage had little confidence in the company, and believed that they would use every chicanery to get their demands paid. Franks, with new partners, John Inglis of Philadelphia and his son-in-law, David Barclay, received the new contract.[109]   Franks was a Jewish merchant in Philadelphia with ties to Croghan, Johnson, the Gratz family, and Baynton, Wharton & Morgan. Inglis had been buying and selling in the West Indies and shipping slaves.

By the end of 1764, the Pennsylvania merchants had almost abandoned trade with the Indians on the frontier and had turned their attention to supplying the army and the Indian Department and to prospects of a new market in Illinois. In an attempt to salvage something from the disaster of the rebellion in 1763, many had joined the suffering traders to seek compensation in land for their losses. All of these alternate sources of revenue were dependent on a favorable British government. When, instead, the British imposed taxes to pay for the very force that was limiting their activity and to bribe the Indians who had robbed them, the merchants were outraged. British suppliers who were unable to collect their debts were in turn concerned at the turn of events and joined the protest against the new taxes.

NOTES

1. Marc Egnal, *A Mighty Empire, the Origins of the American Revolution* (Ithaca: Cornell University Press, 1988), 78-80.

2. Ibid., 81.

3. Ibid., 84-86.

4. W. N. Franklin, "Pennsylvania-Virginia Rivalry for the Indian Trade of the Ohio Valley," *Mississippi Valley Historical Review*, 20 (1934), 477.

5. *Pennsylvania Archives*, 1st ser., 12 vols. (Philadelphia: Joseph Severns & Co., 1851-1856), 3:734-35.

6. London Invoices, February 5 and 11, 1760, Pennsylvania Indian Commissioners, Gratz Collection, Pennsylvania Historical Society.

7. Charles H. McIlwain, *Wraxall's Abridgment of New York Indian Records, 1678-1751* (Cambridge, MA: Harvard University Press, 1950), xvi; *Pennsylvania Archives*, 2d ser., 19 vols. (Harrisburg: Joseph Severns & Co., 1874-1893), 2:619-27.

8. Mercer to Bouquet, March 21, 1759, *Canadian Archives Report*, 1889 (Ottawa: Canadian Archives, 1890), 130 (hereafter cited as *CA*).

9. Robert Anderson, John Philip Dehas, George Price, John Baird, Fred Hambuck, Joseph Richardson, James Bird, James McCaister, Joseph Scott, William Buchanan, William McDowell, John Simpson, Robert Callendar, Alexander McKee, Thomas Smallman, John Clark, William Patterson, Edward Ward, Hugh Crawford, John Potts, Andrew Wilkie, Joshia Davenport, and John Prentice. Walter S. Dunn, Jr., "Western Commerce, 1760-1774" (Ph. D. Dissertation, University of Wisconsin, 1971), Chart E.

10. Francis Parkman, *A History of the Conspiracy of Pontiac and the Indian War after the Conquest of Canada* (New York: MacMillan Co., 1929), 98.

11. *Pennsylvania, Minutes of the Provincial Council of Pennsylvania from the Organization of the Propriety Government . . . To the Termination of the Revolution, 1683-1790*, 16 vols. (Harrisburg, PA: Theophilus Fenn, 1838-1852), 9:490.

12. Bouquet to Monckton, March 20, 1761, *Massachusetts Historical Collections* (Boston: Massachusetts Historical Society, 1871), 4th ser., 9:397.

13. Bouquet to Gage, April 22, 1761, ibid., 405.

14. Nicholas B. Wainwright, *George Croghan Wilderness Diplomat* (Chapel Hill: University of North Carolina Press, 1959), 176.

15. Dunn, "Western Commerce," Chart E.

16. Edward P. Hamilton, *The French and Indian War* (Garden City, NY: Doubleday, 1962), 18–19.

17. Captain Lee's Journal, 1759, *CA*, 1889, 149–51; Bouquet to Major Stewart, November 3, 1760, ibid., 297–98.

18. Johnson to Gage, August 21, 1767, Edmund O'Callaghan, ed., *The Documentary History of the State of New York*, 4 vols. (Albany, NY: Weed, Parsons & Co., 1849–51), 2:501; Sir William Johnson, *The Papers of Sir William Johnson*, 14 vols. (Albany, NY: State University of New York Press, 1921–65), 2:866.

19. Richard E. Banta, *The Ohio* (New York: Rinehart & Co., 1949), 111.

20. Invoice Book of Skins, Pennsylvania Indian Commission, May 1760, Gratz Collection.

21. Wainwright, *George Croghan*, 162; Franklin, "Pennsylvania–Virginia Rivalry," 473–74.

22. Invoice, October 15, 1760, Pennsylvania Indian Commission, Gratz Collection.

23. Baynton & Wharton, Journal A, Baynton, Wharton & Morgan Collection, Microfilm F7, 43–70.

24. John and Peter Chevalier Daybook, April–May 1760, Pennsylvania Historical Society.

25. William V. Byars, *B[ernard] and M. Gratz* (Jefferson City, MO, The Hugh Stevens Printing Co., 1916), 47–48.

26. Baynton & Wharton, Journal A, BWM Microfilm, F7, 43–70.

27. Daniel Clark to Daniel Mildred, November 13, 1760, Clark Accounts, Historical Society of Pennsylvania.

28. Campbell to Amherst, June 17, 1761, *Johnson MSS*, 3:439.

29. Croghan to Horatio Gates, May 23, 1760, *MassHC*, 4th ser., 9:248, 252.

30. Entry, November 12, 1761, James Kenny, "Journal of James Kenny, 1761–1763," *The Pennsylvania Magazine of History and Biography*, 37:26.

31. Johnson to Richard Peters, March 4, 1761, *Johnson MSS*, 10:231.

32. Kenny, August 17, 1761, 18–19.

33. Kenny, December 8, 1761, 30.

34. Croghan to Gates, May 23, 1760, *MassHC*, 4th ser., 11:248.

35. Bouquet to Monckton, March 20, and 28, 1761, *MassHC*, 4th ser., 9:397, 402.

36. Lewis Oury to Bouquet, April 12, 1761 and June 16, 1761, *CA Report* (1889), 106–7.

37. William Mckee to Bernard Gratz, July 9, 1761, Byars, *B. and M. Gratz*, 54.

38. December 10, 1761, John and Peter Chevalier Daybook.

39. Croghan to Johnson, January 13, 1761, *Johnson MSS*, 3:303.

40. Invoice Book of Skins, Fort Pitt, 1761, Pennsylvania Indian Commission, Gratz Collection.

41. Invoice, April 9, 1761, Pennsylvania Indian Commission, Gratz Collection.

42. Baynton & Wharton Journal, A-F, May 29, 1761, BWM Microfilm, F7.

43. Daniel Clark to William Neat, July 14, 1761, and Clark to Neale & Pigou, November 8, 1761, Clark Accounts.

44. Baynton, Wharton & Morgan Memo Book, BWM Microfilm, F10, March 17, 1761; Daniel Clark to John Clark, Lancaster, March 15, 1761, Clark Accounts; February 3, 1761, John and Peter Chevalier Daybook.

45. August 17, 1761 and December 12, 1761, John and Peter Chevalier Daybook.

46. Byars, *B. and M. Gratz*, 49.

47. Bouquet to Monckton, February 24, 1761, *MassHC*, 4th ser., 9:391.

48. Patrick Allison to Baynton & Morgan, July 21, 1761, BWM Microfilm, F2.

49. Patrick Allison to Baynton & Morgan, August 20, 1761, ibid.

50. Daniel Clark to John Ormsby, October 24, 1761, Clark Accounts.

51. Invoice to Pittsburgh, April 12, 1762, Pennsylvania Indian Commission, Gratz Collection.

52. Pittsburgh Invoice, June 26, 1762, Pennsylvania Indian Commission, Gratz Collection.

53. John Strettel to the Pennsylvania Indian Commission, February 17, 1762 and May 28, 1762; Mildred & Roberts, Invoice, March 1, 1762, Pennsylvania Indian Commission, Gratz Collection.

54. Byars, *B. and M. Gratz*, 55.

55. Joseph Simon to Bernard Gratz, August 29, 1762, ibid., 57.

56. Simon & Mitchell to Bernard Gratz, August 17, 1762, ibid.

57. Robert Callender to Baynton & Wharton, December 1, 1762, BWM Microfilm, F2.

58. Andrew Wilkins to Baynton & Wharton, October 25, 1762, ibid., F2.

59. Daniel Clark to Donnellan, January 20, 1762, Clark Accounts.

60. Daniel Clark to Neale & Pigou, January 25, 1762; to Mildred & Roberts, January 25, 1762; and to Holliday, Dunbar & Co., January 21, 1762, Clark Accounts.

61. Invoice Book of Skins, May and June 1763, Pennsylvania Indian Commission, Gratz Collection.

62. Pittsburgh Store Invoice Book, Pennsylvania Indian Commission, Gratz Collection.

63. Invoice Book of Skins, April 1763, Pennsylvania Indian Commission, Gratz Collection.

64. Joseph Simon to Bernard Gratz, May 30, 1763, Byars, *B. and M. Gratz*, 62.

65. John Hughes Papers, Historical Society of Pennsylvania.

66. Baynton & Wharton Accounts, January 12, 1763, BWM Microfilm, F7.

67. John Noble to Baynton & Wharton, July 7, 1763, BWM Microfilm, F3.

68. Baynton, Wharton & Morgan Accounts, ibid.

69. Captain Ecuyer to Bouquet, May 29, 1763, *CA Report* (1889), 225.

70. Report of Thomas Colhoun, June 1, 1763, ibid, 226.

71. S. Wharton to J. Baynton, June 5, 1763, BWM Microfilm, F2.

72. Bouquet to Amherst, July 13, 1763, *CA Report* (1889), 25; *Pennsylvania Minutes of the Provincial Council*, October 22, 1763, 9:64.

73. A List of Losses of Indian Traders, February 1763, *Johnson MSS*, 11:613–14.

74. Samuel Wharton to J. Baynton, June 5, 1763, BWM Microfilm, F2.

75. Samuel Wharton to John Baynton, September 12, 1763, ibid.

76. Baynton & Wharton to Callender, October 16, 1763, ibid., F1:230–31.

77. Baynton, Wharton & Morgan to John Noble, December 26, 1763, ibid., F1.

78. Baynton, Wharton & Morgan to Richard Neave, December 26, 1763, ibid.

79. Baynton, Wharton & Morgan to David Barclay, December 15, 1763, ibid.

80. Baynton & Wharton to Johnson, April 4, 1764, *Johnson MSS*, 4:384; Johnson to Baynton & Wharton, April 6, 1764, ibid., 4:385.

81. Baynton, Wharton & Morgan, Journal A, April 30, 1764, BWM Microfilm, F8.

82. Baynton & Wharton to Johnson, April 1764, *Johnson MSS*, 4:407; September 15, 1764, Journal A, BWM Microfilm, F7.

83. Baynton, Wharton & Morgan to Richard Neave, December 26, 1763, BWM Microfilm, F5; Journal A, December 5, 1763, ibid., F7.

84. Baynton, Wharton & Morgan Memo Book, June 25-September 29, 1763, ibid., F10.

85. Baynton, Wharton & Morgan Journal A, 1764, ibid., F8.

86. Baynton, Wharton & Morgan Memo Book, ibid., F10, 532–69.

87. May 31, 1764, Journal A, ibid., F8.

88. Baynton, Wharton & Morgan to John Collins, July 25, 1764, ibid., F3.

89. Joseph Spear to Baynton, Wharton & Morgan, July 13, 1764, ibid., F5.

90. Memo Book, December 24, 1764, ibid., F10.

91. Joseph Spear to John Hughes, July 27, 1764, Hughes Papers.

92. Joseph Spear to John Hughes, August 10, 1764, ibid.

93. Richard Neave, Jr. to John Hughes, September 14, 1764, ibid.

94. May 11, 1764, Journal A, BWM Microfilm, F8.

95. Edmund Moran to Evan Shelby, October 21, 1764, Edmund Moran Papers, State Historical Society of Wisconsin.

96. Baynton, Wharton & Morgan, Journal A, August 18, 1763, BWM Microfilm, F8.

97. Robert Leake to Callendar, August 4, 1764, ibid., F6.

98. October 1, 1764, Journal A, ibid., F7.

99. Samuel Wharton to Baynton, August 27, 1764, ibid., F5.

100. Baynton, Wharton & Morgan to John Collins, July 25, 1764, ibid., F3.

101. June 30, 1764, Journal A, ibid, F8.

102. Baynton, Wharton & Morgan to Richard Neave, August 9, 1764, ibid., F5.

103. Baynton to Wharton, August 24, 1764, ibid., F2.

104. Samuel Wharton to Baynton, August 27, 1764, ibid., F5; Henry Van Schaack to Baynton, Wharton & Morgan, October 2, 1764, ibid.

105. November 23, 1764, Journal A, ibid., F8; Baynton, Wharton & Morgan Memo Book, December 1, 1764, ibid., F10.

106. Joseph Spear to Baynton & Wharton, [September 1764], ibid., F3.

107. *Michigan Pioneer and Historical Collections* (Lansing, Wynkoop, Hallenbeck, Crawford Co., 1874-1929), 19:261.

108. Captain Grant to Bouquet, July 24, 1764, *CA Report* (1889), 261.

109. Ibid., 69, 310.

6

Detroit

Because of its accessibility, Detroit was the major center of commerce on the upper Great Lakes, and it was also the headquarters of the British army garrisons in that area. The fort, located on the Detroit River, was accessible from Fort Pitt by the rivers feeding into Lake Erie, for example, the Scioto River from the Ohio River north to the Maumee River and then to Lake Erie; through Lakes Ontario and Erie from Montreal and Albany; and by the Ottawa River and Lake Huron from Montreal. Because of these good routes, more business was transacted in Detroit than in any other area in the five years following 1760. Here, the Pennsylvania and New York traders entered into head-to-head competition with French for the Indian trade. Pontiac's Rebellion in 1763 forced out the colonial traders, leaving the French in the possesion of the fur trade in cooperation with the Scottish traders in Montreal and Quebec. Because there was no viable alternative, the British government accepted the situation in 1764, with the French again in control of the fur trade.

After the capitulation of Montreal in 1760, Major Robert Rogers was selected to occupy Detroit on September 9, 1760. In October, Rogers arrived at Fort Pitt and, joined by Croghan, led a party up the Allegheny River, then over a series of portages to Presque Isle on Lake Erie. The troops left Presque Isle on November 4, 1760, using all the boats available on Lake Erie to carry Rogers' two hundred Rangers, and arrived in Detroit on November 29, 1760.[1]

In 1760, Detroit had three hundred houses and about twenty-five hundred inhabitants. There were seventy or eighty houses in the fort laid out in regular streets. Outside the fort, there were farms stretching about ten miles on both sides of the river. The river at Detroit was nine hundred yards wide and very deep.[2] Although the primary industry was the fur trade, agriculture was adequate to feed the populace and helped provide food for the men trading in Mackinac and the other upper posts.[3]

Very little fur had been exported from Detroit since the British occupied Niagara in 1759, and Bellestre, the French officer commanding at Detroit, offered to sell to Rogers furs worth more than £100,000 sterling ($20 million) at a low price.[4] Captain Brewer of the Rangers informed Amherst that there was an incredible quantity of fur at Detroit in 1760 because the French had been unable to ship it out after the British blocked the St. Lawrence route.[5] Traders flocked to Detroit to take advantage of the opportunity, and a cargo of merchandise valued at £3,423 New York ($430,000) was sent from Niagara to Detroit in October 1760 by a partnership including Major Robert Rogers, Edward Cole, Nicholas Stevens, John Vansire, and Cezar Cormick.[6]

Rogers and Croghan held a conference with the Indians in Detroit December 3 through 5, 1760, promising rum, presents, and an open trade with the English. They also promised that the new commander, Captain Donald Campbell, would ensure that the tribes were given just treatment by the traders.[7] On December 11, 1760, Campbell urged Colonel Bouquet to send traders from Fort Pitt during the winter because the Indians needed goods and lacked horses for a trip to Fort Pitt.[8] Bouquet urged traders at Fort Pitt to go, but they were not authorized to take liquor, and were required to sell at prices fixed by Croghan and Campbell.[9]

While the traders were setting up shop in Detroit, Amherst was planning to send the 80th Regiment with three hundred men to Detroit in 1761, under Major Henry Gladwin, who would then send small garrisons to Mackinac, St. Joseph, Green Bay, Miami, and Ouiatanon. One hundred men of the 80th were to be left at Fort William Augustus on Lake Erie. Gladwin was also instructed to explore the Great Lakes, and then to return to Fort William Augustus, leaving as much of the 80th Regiment with Captain Campbell as needed to garrison the various posts. In addition, one hundred New York troops were to go from Oswego to Fort William Augustus to help with repairs. This widespread scattering of troops indicated that Amherst had no fear of an Indian uprising.[10]

In April 1761, Amherst ordered Johnson to supply the Indians in Detroit with presents, as they were in great need, and the gifts were to continue until trade was opened and the Indians would be able to buy supplies.[11] Johnson was aware that the Indians in Detroit needed clothing, ammunition, and other goods, and he agreed that traders were the best method to solve the problem. A sufficient number of passes were given to Albany traders to trade in Detroit to make goods plentiful and prices cheaper.[12] Captain Campbell disliked the Dutch traders, some of whom came from Niagara with cargoes only of rum. The needed supplies had come with the traders from Fort Pitt and with James Sterling, a former army commissary.[13] Campbell was forced to purchase cattle to feed his troops from Fort Pitt. He was already tired of Detroit by early July 1761, and hoped to be relieved. "I begin to know the people too well, I do not think they improve on a long acquaintance."[14]

In July 1761, Sterling commented that he had received his share of business, even though he had arrived late in the season. Sterling was joined in a partnership by John Duncan, a Scot formerly an officer in the 44th Regiment who became the agent at Niagara. The partners brought carpenters to Fort Niagara to build a sailing ship to use on Lake Ontario. Their ship would reduce transportation costs from Oswego to Niagara and would give the partners a decided advantage in cost, speed, reliability, and safety when moving goods to Niagara and Detroit.[15]

Sterling made a large purchase of furs from Campbell in Detroit, presumably from the French government stock confiscated by the British army, intending to send fifty packs of fur back to Fort Niagara.[16] He complained about the quality of the fur held by the French in Detroit because the furs were rotted and infested with worms. The French, however, insisted on selling decayed fur along with new quality fur. On the other hand, the Indians' new fur was in excellent condition and selling direct to the Indians brought a higher profit. Sales were brisk, and by the end of July 1761, Sterling had sold half his cargo for cash and furs worth £3,000 New York ($378,000), more than any other two merchants in Detroit. Campbell favored Sterling, who ordered some good wine for the "gentlemen of the army." When Campbell sent troops to Mackinac, Sterling was permitted to send along two canoe loads of merchandise.[17]

In 1761, the merchants in Detroit were able to sell their merchandise at double the prices paid in New York and Pennsylvania. Sterling sold a stroud made of two yards of material for three or four beaver; a blanket or matchcoat for two beaver; and a large shirt for two beaver. Sterling sold rum at 18/10p to 30/17p per gallon ($30 to $45 per quart) according to the amount purchased and the promised date of payment. Army officers were good customers and paid with bills of exchange.[18] By September 1761, business in Detroit was going well and Sterling was complaining about the quality of merchandise sent by his suppliers. Sterling reported that silver and chintz were the best items and wampum and ribbons the poorest.[19] He complained that the shirts were badly made of poor quality linen.[20] In October, Sterling ordered Madeira wine, shrub (a beverage with some alcoholic content), loaf sugar, fine salt, and gunpowder from James Syme, a London supplier who later formed a partnership with Christopher Kilby, who had been a provisions contractor for the British army in America.[21]

Other traders came from Fort Pitt to share in the newly opened trade, including Trent and Alexander Lowry. In February 1761, Monckton allowed Pennsylvania traders to travel overland to Detroit if they conformed to the rules of trade provided by Croghan.[22] The rules were to sell at agreed prices, cultivate good understanding with the Indians, trade justly, grant credit, show their invoices to Campbell as soon as they arrived in Detroit, and follow Campbell's instructions on where to trade and what could be sold to the Indians.[23] When Trent and Lowry arrived in Detroit in May 1761, Campbell asked to see their invoices and the prices of the goods and assigned them a location where they were permitted to trade.[24]

Other Pennsylvania traders included T. D. Hambuck from Lancaster, a former officer in the Pennsylvania militia and a friend of Bouquet. In January 1761, Hambuck planned a trading venture to Detroit in partnership with Isaac Vandervelden, a young storekeeper in Lancaster who put up £500 in goods for his half share. The plan was to obtain six horse loads of goods for Detroit and trade for twelve horse loads of furs to be returned to Fort Pitt. Arrival in Detroit early in the spring was essential in order to sell their goods and double their money before other traders arrived and cut the prices. Vandervelden returned to Fort Pitt in July 1761, with one thousand pounds of fur and skins.[25]

Some of the traders from Pennsylvania did not reach Detroit, stopping at Sandusky even though doing so was against Bouquet's rule. Campbell sent fifty men to bring the renegades into Detroit, and complained that the traders from Fort Pitt did not know how to trade with the Indians, and thus they brought goods for the French inhabitants, rather than for the Indians.[26] In December 1761, the Indians begged Campbell for supplies, but he had nothing for them as the French had left no supplies for the British.[27]

The biggest problem in Detroit, however, was the prohibition of rum under the rules of Colonel Bouquet. When the French held Detroit, there was little danger for the British to sell rum at Fort Niagara to the Indians who usually took it away with them, but in 1761, the English held Detroit, and rum created serious problems because the Indians remained in the area and became uncontrollable when drunk.[28] By May 1761, many traders (including Callender, Hambuck, and John Baird, a former Pennsylvania militia officer) were ignoring the rule, and brought rum from Fort Pitt. Campbell tried to prevent rum sales to the Indians in Detroit, but the Indians could obtain rum from the Albany traders at Fort Niagara and bring it back to Detroit. The ready flow of rum made the Indians troublesome and difficult to manage.[29]

Regardless of the rules, large quantities of rum came via Niagara to Detroit, although transportation was always risky. In August 1761, Sterling brought in forty-one barrels of rum in four bateau manned by twelve men. The barrels were damaged by the soldiers when carried around the falls at Niagara and a great deal was lost. Sterling believed that rum was the worst thing to sell to the Indians because the people in Detroit suffered when the Indians were drunk. He hoped to sell the rum to the soldiers and the French, but he also sold "a keg now and then quietly with immense profits" to the Indians.[30]

In September 1761, Sterling reported that another forty barrels of rum were on the way to Detroit, but that he still had some on hand, because Campbell prohibited open sale of rum to the Indians. Sterling's goal was to have a man skilled in making wine in Detroit because the wine would sell at a greater profit than the rum. The sale of rum must have run into deep difficulties because in October 1761, Sterling requested that no more rum be sent to him for sale.[31]

Communication between Detroit and Fort Pitt was very tenuous during the winter months, using Indians who traveled by horse overland. On January 31, 1762, Sterling sent a letter with an Indian carrier to Croghan regarding the rental of a house. The Indian lost the letter, however, and returned to Detroit. On February 12, Sterling sent a duplicate letter.[32]

Sterling acted as the banker for the garrison in 1762. He purchased army vouchers used to buy supplies from other traders at a twenty-five percent discount, because there was no army deputy quartermaster general in Detroit to reimburse the merchants with cash or bills of exchange. The local merchants (especially the French) would not wait for the vouchers to be paid, so Sterling provided the merchants with bills of exchange drawn on his New York City partners in return for the merchants' vouchers. The local merchants could use these bills to pay their debts in Montreal and elsewhere.[33] Sterling sent to his partners in New York for payment the vouchers that he had purchased and bills of exchange from the paymaster of the 80th Regiment, Mr. Hall, and two other officers, Captain Balfour and Lieutenant Williams. In January 1762, Sterling sent to James Syme in London £150 New York ($19,000).[34] Sterling apportioned £60 New York of the bill to pay Gerrard Banker for a small keg of merchandise that Sterling had sold for him in return for acting as Sterling's agent in New York City. Sterling sent Syme another bill of exchange for £90 Pennsylvania ($10,350) drawn by Captain Thomas Barnsley, the paymaster of the 1st Battalion of the 60th Regiment (the Rangers). The cash provided by Sterling was used to pay the troops.[35]

In April 1762, a warrant (an authorization to spend) for £3,000 New York ($378,000) arrived from Fort Pitt to pay for military expenses in Detroit until September 14, 1762. Spear, an associate of Baynton & Wharton, purchased the warrant from Campbell for £3,601 Pennsylvania ($414,000) in bills of exchange drawn on Baynton & Wharton with which Campbell paid the army's debts to the other merchants. Sterling's share was £900 New York, almost one-third. Spear sent the army warrant with a list of bills he had drawn to Baynton & Wharton.

In June 1762, Sterling was in the banking business in earnest. He sent his partners a bill of exchange for £1,477 Pennsylvania ($170,000) from Callender and Spear drawn on Baynton & Wharton, which Sterling had purchased with billets (French paper money) obtained from the French in return for his merchandise. In addition, Sterling sent three other bills including Lieutenant McDonald's bill on Captain Barnsley, the paymaster of the 60th Regiment for £200 Pennsylvania; another bill by Lieutenant McDonald on Lieutenant Hall, the paymaster of the 80th Regiment; and a bill for £85 from Sir Charles Davers on William McAdam of New York City. The paper money paid by the French to Sterling for merchandise was sold to Campbell to pay the troops.[36]

At the end of the season, the British officers wound up their accounts. Campbell was being replaced by Major Gladwin; Captain George Etherington was going to Mackinac; and Lieutenant Gamet was going to St. Mary's. Sterling planned to send a draft for £2,000 New York from Campbell for the French billets that Campbell would redeem when he closed his accounts. Spear, the Baynton & Wharton agent, would carry the draft to New York.[37]

James Sterling was the major merchant in Detroit during 1762. In January, he wrote to his partner, John Duncan, complaining that business was slow during the winter because the Indians were hunting, but that it would pick up in the spring. Some Indians had already returned to Detroit and reported that game was abundant. Rum was selling well to the soldiers and to the French, but Sterling still had a six months' supply. He was working hard to gain the respect of the French. Sterling preferred to purchase merchandise in England at lower prices, rather than from American merchants in New York and Philadelphia, but was concerned that the cargo of European goods ordered by John Livingston in New York would not be adequate for his needs. Duncan was instructed to send merchandise to Albany by ship, then by boats to Niagara using the Mohawk River route. Sterling would later hire French canoe men to go to Niagara and pick up the cargo. In the event of extreme need, Sterling could send a sleigh to Niagara, which he did in January, for a load of ammunition that was in demand in Detroit.

In April 1762, Lake Erie was free of ice, commerce was under way, and more colonial traders flocked to Detroit. Among them was John Ormsby, the western agent of the Philadelphia merchant, Daniel Clark. Richard Winston and Edward Cole went to St. Joseph.[38] Sterling sent five bateaux and three canoes with twenty-seven men under Blondeau (probably Maurice Blondeau, a French trader who was active in the fur trade throughout the period) to Niagara to bring to Detroit all of the merchandise owned by Sterling. Blondeau took with him sixty-two packs of fur to be sold and a small box for Mrs. Rutherford. Food was in short supply in Detroit, so Sterling asked that eight to ten barrels of meat, especially pork, be sent along with the merchandise.[39]

Also in April, Sterling inquired about the status of six boat loads of merchandise that were coming from Schenectady to Fort Niagara. Sterling suggested to Duncan that a sailing ship of ten to twenty tons capacity be built on Lake Erie, in addition to the ship on Lake Ontario, to save money on transportation. Only a few sailors were needed to man a ship carrying twenty tons, compared to at least four men for each bateaux carrying four tons or less. Because the ship did not have to go ashore each night as did the canoes, the danger from Indian attack was greatly reduced, and the voyage shortened.[40]

Sterling had serious problems with the delivery of a cargo in May 1762. The bateaux had arrived from Fort Niagara with the goods in poor condition because of inadequate management by Colbeck, Sterling's agent at Fort Niagara, who was drunk for fourteen days with the sergeants and a seraglio of Indian women at the fort. Blondeau believed that Colbeck had a private arrangement with another Frenchman, DeQuoiney, a Detroit merchant. Sterling asked Duncan, who was going to Niagara, to investigate Colbeck.[41]

The price of transportation across Lake Erie continued to be a major issue. In June 1762, Sterling had forty packs of fur, not sent with Rinkin as promised, because the wages of bateaux men had risen, and Sterling was not certain that there were goods in Niagara to carry on the return journey. Again, Sterling recommended that Syme have a sailing ship built at Niagara with a capacity of eighteen to twenty tons to cut the cost of transportation.[42]

By June 1762, the posts on the Great Lakes were oversupplied with goods for sale to the Indians. Green Bay, Mackinac, and St. Joseph all had more goods than they could sell even at prices cheaper than Detroit. In addition to the oversupply of goods, the price of beaver had fallen at Detroit, indicating an oversupply of fur as well. Sterling planned to send cargoes to the Miami River and to Ouiatanon, but had to wait until late June when Morrison, one of Sterling's clerks, arrived in Detroit from Fort Niagara to transport the cargo, as Sterling would not trust the French with his goods.[43]

The army officers and the French were good customers for the finer quality of liquor. In June 1762, Sterling sent two bateaux to Niagara for six barrels of brandy, six barrels of shrub (a beverage made of fruit juice, sugar, and rum or brandy), and four kegs of cordials (aromatic, syrupy alcoholic beverages). Campbell provided a special pass for this shipment that was intended for the army and the French.[44]

In July 1762, Sterling sent articles worth £42 Pennsylvania to Ensign John Holmes, the commander of the post on the Miami River. Sterling sent Holmes all the liquor in his stock, but rum was in short supply in Detroit because of the enforcement of Amherst's order prohibiting its sale. Therefore, Sterling sent brandy and asked payment in fur.[45] Sterling complained of the competition from traders at the smaller posts who were preempting his business. Because of the prohibition of selling rum to the tribes, Sterling believed that fewer Indians would come to Detroit.[46] However, a short time later, five canoes of natives arrived from Mackinac and Sterling received a share of the business.[47]

In September, Sterling sent a Frenchman, Amable Foucher, with two bateaux of merchandise to trade at St. Mary's.[48] Sterling had originally asked his clerk, Morrison, who refused. Sterling discharged him. Morrison's refusal was indicative of the great danger facing a British trader who lived with the Indians over a winter.[49] The French were somewhat safer as they had better relations with the tribes, but they could not always be trusted. French *voyageurs* who ran away after running up a large debt were a continuing problem. In June 1762, Sterling wrote to Lieutenant William Lesly to collect 84 French livres ($840) from Lavoin Chevalier who had run away from Detroit. Sterling told Lesly that he was sending one or two bateaux to Mackinac and Green Bay and would send Lesly anything that he needed.[50]

Sterling complained to Duncan about his share of the profits. In order to maintain status in Detroit, he had to "support an appearance" that was expensive. In addition, the other merchants in Detroit received half of the profits, whereas Rutherford, the other partner, objected to giving Sterling more than one-third. Apparently, Duncan, Rutherford, and Sterling had agreed on one-third each, but Sterling believed that because he was taking the risks and had extra expenses, he deserved more than the other two.[51]

Trade with the Indians continued at a brisk pace. The quality of the merchandise was extremely important in Detroit. William McAdam, a New York City merchant and later New York commissioner of Indian affairs, had provided Sterling with merchandise that was unsalable, for example silver pieces that were too thin and too light weight. Therefore, Sterling made no remittance to McAdam in June.[52] In June 1762, Sterling ordered from Syme twenty-four one-gallon kettles, checked linen, corned gunpowder (gunpowder with a preservative added for use by the Indians, rather than the usual glazed gunpowder), four hundred to five hundred French blankets, ten pieces of stroud, and nearly six hundred scalping knives.[53] Sterling described French blankets as having a blue stripe not more than one-and-one-quarter inches wide with capital letters in a row arranged near one of the stripes. Sterling's agents were cautioned never to send blankets with black stripes or English blankets with red stripes because they never sold.[54] Nine days, later Sterling ordered an additional three thousand pounds of gunpowder for the Indians.[55]

In July 1762, Sterling sent ninety-one packs of furs to Colbeck at Fort Niagara in four canoes with about twenty-three packs in each canoe along with three Frenchmen to paddle. Later, another canoe was sent with fur belonging to VanderVelden and Hambuck. The furs were sent to Oswego on a schooner from Fort Niagara in July.[56]

By July, the trading season had ended. Sterling planned to send a clerk to Saginaw Bay where the Indians wintered and to other winter hunting grounds to increase his trade despite the prohibition of this practice by the army.[57] In August, Sterling sent another large shipment of fur (sixty-three packs including beaver, raccoon, bearskins, and deerskins), on the schooner *Huron* to Presque Isle. From there, the fur would go by bateaux to Niagara.[58] However, the schooner ran into bad weather, turned back, and the furs were sent again in bateaux.[59]

Sterling was extremely prejudiced against the Albany Dutch traders, "the damned set" of Claus, Hans, and Derrick from Albany and Schenectady. The Albany traders had arrived on July 12, 1762, and were already in Sterling's bad graces by August 4. However, he was not antagonistic toward the Jews. Sterling purchased French billets and certificates for provisions worth £430 New York ($54,180) from Chapman Abraham, a Jewish trader, before Abraham left Detroit for Montreal on July 20. Chapman took a discount of £40 for the convenience of ridding himself of all of his paper money in exchange for a bill of exchange for £390 drawn on James Syme that would be negotiable in Montreal. Sterling also had good relations with John Stedman, purchasing 4,512 livres ($45,120) in billets from him for £300 New York ($37,800) when Stedman left Detroit on July 26.[60]

Spear had a good year in Detroit despite his complaint in spring 1762 that trade was dull and overstocked with goods. Although the Indians found no presents of rum and powder awaiting them in Detroit in the spring, they did find traders with powder to sell, a few gifts, and a gunsmith.[61] The prohibition of rum had a noticeable effect in Detroit by June, and although the Indians grumbled about the lack of rum, at first threatening the English, they resigned themselves to hunting and to the care of their corn and were less trouble than the previous year.[62]

Despite French resistance in early 1763, the British and colonial traders in Detroit had a prosperous trade before the uprising. Among the traders in Detroit when the outbreak occurred were James Howard, John Chinn, Edward Chinn, James Stanley Goddard, Henry Bostwick, Forest Oakes, Gershen Levy, Holmes & Mensen, James Sterling, and Sampson Fleming. Croghan had sent a cargo worth £1,230 Pennsylvania ($141,450) to Detroit with a trader who was later killed. Callender had a cargo worth £400 Pennsylvania.[63] The principal French merchant in Detroit was Jacques Baby and his family.[64]

The major issue in 1763 was how to control the Indians. The conspiracy began at a council between the Indians and the French in May or June 1762 to plan an attack on the British in 1763. Campbell's belief in the improved conduct of the Indians in 1762 in fact was not true. Attending the conference were some of the principal French inhabitants of Detroit (Navarre, Augustin Sicotte, Currie, Baptiste Campeau, Francois and Baptist Meloshe, Sancho P. Obain, Domelte, Pero Barth, and Louisan Denter). The French would not fight with the Indians because of the risk to their families and property, but they told Pontiac that they would supply ammunition and young Frenchmen disguised as Indians would fight with them.[65]

Neither Gladwin nor Amherst understood the gravity of the situation in May 1763, and believed that the Indians could not hurt the British if they remained on guard. However, if the Indians did revolt, the British would show no mercy. Amherst approved the hanging of the Indian women who were convicted of murdering John Clapham on his way to Detroit in July 1762, which caused relations to deteriorate further.[66]

The Indians planned to surprise the British garrison by coming into the fort with firearms hidden beneath their blankets, but the plot failed because Major Gladwin had been warned and was ready when the Indians came. The siege that followed was not restrictive; some sorties were made; and boats arrived from Niagara with reinforcements and provisions. Gladwin had about one hundred soldiers and twenty British traders to defend the fort.[67]

On the other hand, Gladwin had a serious problem with the French in Detroit. In a letter to Amherst he stated, "that one half of the settlement merit a gibbet and the other half ought to be decimated."[68] On May 12, 1763, four days after the siege began, Pontiac sent five Frenchmen, Minni Chesne, Jacques Godfroy, Charles Beaubien, Chauvin, and Labadie, Jr. to arouse the Indians in Illinois to fight the English and to support Pontiac and the Indians in their uprising. On their way, at the mouth of the Miami River, they met John Welch with two canoes of fur. Aided by the Indians with them, the Frenchmen captured Welch and divided his goods. Welch was later murdered by the Ottawa, who also seized the stolen fur from the French. Four other prisoners were taken by Chesne and Godfroy to Illinois. Later, Chesne, Godfroy, and the Indians attacked the garrisons at Miami and Ouiatanon.

Although the merchandise in Detroit was saved, traders coming into the post were caught unawares and captured or murdered as they approached the town. On May 13, 1763, a Jewish merchant, Benjamin Chapman, on his way from Niagara with five boat loads of trading goods, was taken prisoner just outside of Detroit. On May 20, 1763, Major Thomas Smallman, a trader from Pennsylvania and a cousin of Croghan, Gershon Levy, Levy Andrew Levy, and two British employees were also taken prisoner outside of Detroit.[69]

Help was soon on the way to Detroit. On June 30, 1763, a ship arrived in Detroit with reinforcements of fifty men under Captain Dalzell with one hundred and twenty barrels of provisions and ammunition. The soldiers at the fort were in good health. Only one had been killed and twelve wounded during the sixty-four day siege that ended July 12, 1763, whereas twenty Indians had been killed and thirty wounded.[70] In July, Dalzell made a sortie that resulted in many soldiers being killed and wounded without any positive result. Otherwise, the siege in Detroit was not going badly for the British. However, Gladwin was completely disgusted with the situation in Detroit. In a bitter letter to Johnson he stated that he had gone to Detroit against his will, as he foresaw what would happen. Results were expected of him that could not be performed. He was forced into a bad situation and then abandoned. He blamed the French scoundrels living in Detroit.[71]

The French attempted to blacken the reputation of the Six Nations in New York who remained faithful to the British, by insinuating that the Iroquois had informed Pontiac of the expected arrival of some vessels from Niagara, but in reality the Frenchmen had warned the Indians.[72] The reinforcements came from Niagara, and although the Indians had planned to attack the soldiers in thier boats on Lake Erie, they missed them, and the troops reached Detroit in October.

Among the reinforcements was Major Robert Rogers who on October 7, 1763, sent a letter to Johnson ordering a large supply of Indian goods including 540 shirts, 8 gross of knives, and 108 pounds of vermillion. Cezar Cormick carried the order to Johnson with a bill of exchange drawn on Croghan to pay for the Indian goods ordered.[73] An officer of the British army on active service amazingly used the credit of an Indian Department officer and funds available to Sir William Johnson to provide supplies including 1,150 knives to the Indians who were still at war with the British!

On October 12, 1763, the Indians abandoned the siege of Detroit to leave for their winter hunting grounds. Another convoy of troops left Niagara on October 19, 1763, with six hundred men and provisions for Detroit. They were driven ashore by a storm, losing seventy of the men and spoiling all of the provisions and ammunition, so the convoy returned to Niagara. Because of the lack of provisions in Detroit, Gladwin was forced to have 240 soldiers return to Niagara in December 1763, leaving only 212 men in Detroit for the winter.[74]

By November 1763, Detroit was in business as usual. Edward Cole, a partner of Major Rogers and a friend of Croghan, wrote to Henry Van Schaak in Schenectady outlining plans for the following year. Cole had sent Nicholas (John Nicholas, a Pennsylvania trader?) to Niagara for goods earlier, but because the Indians blocked the way, Nicholas returned with nothing. Cole placed an order for goods that were to be sent to Detroit early in the spring of 1764, urging Van Schaak not to miss the first sailing ship from Niagara to Detroit.

The only other way to obtain the goods was to send Frenchmen from Detroit in bateaux with the army convoy to fetch them. If the goods could be shipped to Niagara, Cole promised to make remittances the following summer. He already had enough money to pay his debts to Jelles Fonda and Volkert Douw, two Albany merchants; and Daniel Campbell, a British merchant in the Schenectady area. Cole himself could not leave Detroit because spring was the best time to collect debts from the traders returning from the winter hunting grounds.

Cole reported that the Indians were peaceful and that in the spring a great push must be made to bring in supplies of powder and rum to be sold when the trade was reopened, but he warned Van Schaak to be cautious and obtain instructions from John Sterling or John Stedman at Niagara.[75] This informative letter sketched the operation of the trade in Detroit in 1763. An Englishman, Edward Cole, was the agent in Detroit, and a Dutchman, Henry Van Schaak, provided supplies from Albany. They obtained their goods on credit from important Albany merchants such as Jelles Fonda and Volkert Douw. Cole was not reluctant to ignore the rules against selling rum and gunpowder to the Indians and was advised on methods to smuggle the rum and gunpowder past Fort Niagara by Sterling and Stedman, important British merchants at Niagara.

The tempo of the trade was clearly indicated—goods must arrive early in the spring in order to be sold at high prices. An agent of any partnership must be in Detroit in the spring to collect debts from the Indians and French who brought in furs taken during the preceding winter. Regardless of the fact that only a truce existed, the merchants were eager to sell powder to the Indians. Remittances in the form of furs were made during the summer. Merchandise arrived by canoes manned by Frenchmen, who were sent to Niagara from Detroit and returned with the goods. The safer sailing ships were preferred, but a merchant could not be certain that his cargo would be loaded because military traffic took priority on the ships. French canoes were more reliable.

Most of the activity in Detroit in 1764 centered around Bradstreet's expedition which is described later. Sir William Johnson commented in 1764 that Bradstreet had allowed the French from Detroit to trade among the western Indians, but would not allow the English traders to bring goods from Detroit. Among those favored by Bradstreet were Jean Baptiste Chapaton, Marsack (Nicolas Marchessau?), Louis Campeau, and Cheuchet (Miny Chesne?), who were in fact some of the principal ringleaders in the attack against the British.[76]

Gladwin complained that the Indians were obtaining supplies from the French in Illinois to continue their attacks on Detroit.[77]

Detroit remained a center of the fur trade from 1760 to 1764. Few of the French inhabitants left after the French surrender. They resisted British rule and retained their strong influence over the Indians.   The established colonial merchants controlled the wholesale business in Detroit in 1764 because they had access to merchandise in the east, but they had to use the French as middlemen to trade with the Indians.   Among the most important merchants in Detroit were William Edgar (with ties to John Duncan and Robert Callender), the partnership of Livingston, Duncan, Rutherford, and Phyn (represented by James Sterling and John Porteous). Robert Callender was an associate of Baynton & Wharton of Pennsylvania and represented their interests in Detroit through William Edgar.[78] Pontiac's Rebellion had forced the colonial traders to restrict their activity to the larger garrisoned posts, whereas the French merchants sent their agents into the woods and purchased most of the furs from the Indians.

Detroit was the bulwark of British military control, especially as the use of sailing ships on the lakes increased, providing cheap reliable transportation from Niagara. In 1764, Colonel Bradstreet saw Detroit as the most important post because it was the best suited to raise provisions for the troops and provided a base for two army battalions. The large garrison in Detroit served as a force that could be used for immediate retaliation.[79] Under the protection of the garrison in Detroit, British and colonial traders had flourished, but the changes in British imperial policy that followed the uprising would drive out most of the colonials, while the discharged Scottish officers in Montreal formed alliances with the French to dominate the trade.

NOTES

1. Walters to Bouquet, November 8, 1760, *Canadian Archives Report* (1889), 165; Sewell E. Slick, *William Trent and the West* (Harrisburg: Archives Publishing Co. of Pennsylvania, 1947), 92.

2. Campbell to Amherst, 1761 in Clarence M. Burton, *The City of Detroit, Michigan, 1701-1922,* 2 vols. (Detroit: The J. S. Clarke Publishing Co., 1922), 1:118.

3. Calvin Goodrich, *The First Michigan Frontier* (Ann Arbor: University of Michigan Press, 1940), 56-57.

4. Paul Burpee to Captain Abraham Dow, September 22, 1760, Robert Rogers Papers (1766-1769), photostats in the State Historical Society of Wisconsin.

5. Amherst to Johnson, February 1, 1761, Sir William Johnson, *The Papers of Sir William Johnson*, 14 vols. (Albany, NY: The State University of New York Press, 1921-65), 3:315-16.

6. Paul Burpee to Captain Abraham Douw, September 22, 1760, Rogers Papers; R. Shuckburgh to Johnson, December 29, 1760, ibid., 3:293; Amherst to Johnson, February 1, 1763, ibid., 3:315-16; Account of Merchandise, March 11, 1763, Rogers Papers; Certificate by Edward Cole, Askin Papers, Burton Historical Collection, Vol. B4.

7. Proceedings of an Indian Conference at Detroit, December 3-5, 1760, *Johnson MSS*, 10:199; Tadeau to Gladwin, December 24, 1763, *Canadian Archives, Transcripts of Indian Papers*, 9:26.

8. Donald Campbell to Bouquet, December 11, 1760, *Michigan Pioneer and Historical Collections*, 40 vols. (Lansing, MI: Wynkoop, Hallenbeck, Crawford Co., 1874-1929), 19:47.

9. Nicholas B. Wainwright, *George Croghan, Wilderness Diplomat* (Chapel Hill: University of North Carolina Press, 1959), 176.

10. Amherst to Johnson, May 30, 1761 and June 11, 1761, *Johnson MSS*, 10:274, 285; Orders to Henry Gladwin, 80th Regiment, June 22, 1761, ibid., 10:293.

11. Amherst to Johnson, April 8, 1761, ibid., 10:255.

12. Johnson to Amherst, April 23, 1761, ibid., 10:257.

13. Campbell to Amherst, June 17, 1761, ibid., 3:439; Campbell to Johnson, July 8, 1761, ibid., 3:450; Campbell to Bouquet, June 1, 1761, *MPHC*, 19:71.

14. Campbell to Bouquet, July 3, 1761, ibid., 19:154 and July 22, 1761, *CA Report* (1889), 186.

15. Sterling to John Duncan, July 8, 1761, Sterling Letter Book, Clements Library.

16. Sterling to James Syme, September 1761, ibid.

17. Sterling to John Duncan, July 8, 1761 and July 24, 1761, ibid.

18. Sterling to Walter Rutherford, October 27, 1761, ibid.

19. Sterling to William McAdam, September 1, 1761, ibid.

20. Sterling to James Syme, September 1761, ibid.

21. Sterling to James Syme, October 14, 1761, ibid.

22. Monckton to Bouquet, February 12, 1761, *CA Report* (1889), 54.

23. Croghan to Trent and Lowery, February 5, 1761, *MPHC*, 19:58.

24. Slick, *William Trent*, 95.

25. T. D. Hambuck to Bouquet, January 1, 1761, *MPHC*, 19:50–51.

26. Campbell to Bouquet, June 8, 1761, *CA Report* (1889), 181; Campbell to Amherst, June 17, 1761, *Johnson MSS*, 3:439.

27. Campbell to Bouquet, December 1761, Howard H. Peckham, *Pontiac and the Indian Uprising* (Princeton, NJ: Princeton University Press, 1947), 66.

28. Campbell to Monckton, June 1, 1761, *Massachusetts Historical Collections*, 4th ser. (Boston: Massachusetts Historical Society, 1871), 9:416; Campbell to Bouquet, May 21, 1761, *MPHC*, 19:68.

29. Campbell to Johnson, July 8, 1761, *Johnson MSS*, 3:450.

30. Sterling to John Duncan (?), August 25, 1761, Sterling Letter Book.

31. Sterling to James Symes, September 17, 1761 and Sterling to Colbeck, October 27, 1761, ibid.

32. Sterling to Croghan, February 12, 1762, ibid.

33. Sterling to James Syme, January 10, 1762, ibid.

34. Sterling to James Syme, January 11, 1762, ibid.

35. Sterling to Syme, April 14, 1762, ibid.

36. Sterling to James Syme, June 8, 1762, ibid.

37. Sterling to Duncan, September 5, 1762 and October 2, 1762, ibid.

38. Joseph Spear to Baynton & Wharton, April 24, 1762, Baynton, Wharton & Morgan, Microfilm, F3.

39. Sterling to Colbeck, April 14, 1762, Sterling Letter Book.

40. Sterling to John Duncan, April 14, 1762, ibid.

41. Sterling to Captain George Etherington, May 31, 1762, ibid.

42. Sterling to James Syme, June 8, 1762, ibid.

43. Sterling to Syme, June 17, 1762 and Sterling to James Syme, June 8, 1762, ibid.

44. Sterling to Syme, June 1762, ibid.

45. Sterling to Ensign Robert Holmes, July 6, 1762, ibid.

46. Sterling to Syme, June 17, 1762, ibid.

47. Sterling to Syme, June 17, 1762, ibid.

48. Sterling to Duncan, September 5, 1762, ibid.

49. Sterling to John Sterling, August 28, 1762, ibid.

50. Sterling to Lieutenant William Lesly, June 3, 1762, ibid.

51. Sterling to Syme, June 8, 1762, ibid.

52. Sterling to William McAdam, June 7, 1762, ibid.

53. Sterling to Syme, June 8, 1762, ibid.

54. Sterling to James Syme, July 15, 1762, ibid.

55. Sterling to Syme, June 17, 1762, ibid.

56. Sterling to Robert Colbeck, July 8, 1762 and Sterling to James Syme, July 12, 1762, ibid.; Sterling to James Syme, July 20, 1762, ibid.

57. Sterling to Walter Rutherford, July 15, 1762, ibid.

58. Sterling to John Sterling, August 19, 1762, ibid.

59. Sterling to John Sterling, August 28, 1762, ibid.

60. Sterling to Duncan, August 4, 1762 and Sterling to Syme, August 6, 1762, ibid.

61. Peckham, *Pontiac and the Indian Uprising*, 92.

62. Donald Campbell to Johnson, June 9, 1762, *Johnson MSS*, 3:758.

63. Croghan to Amherst, September 26, 1763, ibid., 10:823.

64. F. Baby to Mons. Lobinie, September 13, 1763, Colonial War Section, Simon Gratz Auto Collection, Historical Society of Pennsylvania.

65. Charles Moore, "The Gladwin Manuscripts," *MPHC*, 27:640; Declaration of Tadeau to Gladwin, December 24, 1763, *Johnson MSS*, 10:985.

66. Amherst to Gladwin, May 29, 1763, ibid., 4:98.

67. James McDonald to Croghan, July 12, 1763, ibid., 10:739.

68. Goodrich, *First Michigan Frontier*, 61.

69. Declaration made to Cezar Cormick, June 11, 1763, *Johnson MSS*, 10:692–94; James McDonald to Croghan, July 12, 1763, ibid., 741.

70. James McDonald to Croghan, July 12, 1763, ibid, 10:744.

71. Gladwin to Johnson, October 7, 1763, ibid., 10:873.

72. Gladwin to Johnson, October 7, 1763, ibid., 10:873.

73. Robert Rogers to Johnson, October 7, 1763, ibid., 10:872.

74. Colden to Lords of Trade, December 19, 1763, Edmund B. O'Callaghan, *The Documentary History of the State of New York,* 4 vols. (Albany, NY: Weed, Parsons & Co., 1849-1851), 7:589–90; Robert Rogers to Johnson, October 7, 1763, *Johnson MSS*, 10:872.

75. Edward Cole to Henry Van Schaack, November 19, 1763, ibid., 4:246.

76. Johnson's Remarks on Bradstreet, November 24, 1764, ibid., 4:599.

77. Gladwin to Johnson, May 11, 1764, ibid., 11:191–92.

78. Virginia D. Harrington, *The New York Merchant on the Eve of the Revolution* (New York: Columbia University Press, 1935), 236.

79. Franklin B. Hough, *Diary of the Siege of Detroit in the War with Pontiac...* (Albany, NY: J. Munsell, 1860), 149.

7

Illinois

From 1760 to 1765, the French in Illinois were in a quandary. Subordinate to New Orleans as part of Louisiana rather than Canada, they were not included in the Capitulation of Montreal and therefore were actively at war with the British until 1763. Trade with Illinois was relatively inactive because until the end of the Seven Years' War, French vessels could not reach New Orleans with merchandise from France. However, communications with Montreal were open and French winterers from Illinois continued to trade with the Indians in the Great Lakes area, at times obtaining goods from French sources in Canada. After 1763, the French government was bound to turn over Illinois to the British, but the British were unable to move troops into the area even though merchandise was peacefully sent up the Mississippi River by the French in New Orleans. Therefore, French traders from Illinois continued to influence the Indians without British regulation until 1765.

On September 24, 1763, news of the Treaty of Paris, signed on March 4, 1763, finally reached Fort Chartres in Illinois. Villiers, the French commander, was ordered to turn over the colony to the British, but the people were free to go to new settlements on the west side of the Mississippi that would be under Spanish rule under the terms of the treaty.[1] By autumn 1763, Florida had been occupied by British troops from Cuba, but no immediate steps were taken to occupy the Illinois territory.

Theoretically, the Illinois trade passed into the hands of the British, and only a small amount of trade up the western branches of the Mississippi remained in Spanish hands. As detachments of the French army moved west to escape capture in 1760, many French *voyageurs* fled with them, some in organized militia companies. Therefore, large areas of the West remained under French control when the British occupied the posts on the Great Lakes in 1761. Only after the Treaty of 1763 were the most western French posts ceded to Britain.

The three-year interim from 1760 to 1763 gave the French ample time to reorient the Indians toward trading in Illinois.

Continuing French activity was the leak in the monopoly that undermined any British attempt to regulate commerce. After 1763, the French *voyageurs* from Illinois resumed operations, receiving merchandise transported up the Mississippi River and shipping furs down to New Orleans for transport to either France, England, the West Florida ports, or to other nations. The *voyageurs* obtained goods in Illinois and traded in the Indian villages, whereas the British army prohibited the colonial traders from leaving the posts. The *voyageurs* traded in great numbers throughout the area of present Illinois, Indiana, Ohio, Michigan, Wisconsin, Minnesota, and west of the Mississippi. The French effectively turned the trade from its natural course to Quebec and competed with colonial traders to within a few miles of Detroit and Fort Pitt.[2]

French knowledge of the Indian language and customs and long connections also gave the French a distinct advantage over the colonial traders. Continued French presence in Illinois helped the French stir up the Indians. General Gage believed that to retain control of the fur trade, the French were inciting the Indians and would use any lie to extend control for as long as possible.[3] The French lied to the Indians in 1762, telling them that a French army was coming up the Mississippi to restore French rule.[4]

Illinois provided a haven for renegades, *voyageurs* who had obtained goods on credit from the British, traded for furs with the Indians, and then paddled their canoes to Illinois to sell the furs to French merchants and keeping the profits, rather than returning them to those who had provided the credit. Occasionally, Frenchmen hired to trade with the Indians by colonial merchants murdered their employers, took the goods, and went to Illinois.

French posts were located at strategic points along the rivers flowing from the Great Lakes area to the Mississippi River. Vincennes on the Wabash River, built in 1727, was typical of the villages established by the French. The territory along the Wabash River provided an excellent hunting ground for the Indians, and Vincennes enabled the French to block traffic between Lake Michigan and the Mississippi. Although the British sent a garrison to Vincennes in 1761 to protect the colonial traders, the French garrison remained. The French traders maintained their friendly contact with the Indians in the neighborhood and continued to trade at the post.[5] In 1763, Aubrey described Vincennes as a fort surrounded by a picket (a wall formed by logs with the larger end driven partly into the ground). The garrison consisted of twenty married French soldiers and some French inhabitants.[6] After the British garrison of Vincennes was captured in 1763, during Pontiac's Rebellion, the British army was unable to regain control, although Baynton, Wharton & Morgan tried to establish a store in the village after 1764.

Fort Chartres, built of stone by the French, was the most important post on the Mississippi with a garrison of six companies of three hundred soldiers and twenty cannon. In 1763, there were still nearly two hundred men in the garrison and one hundred inhabitants. The village surrounding the fort had about forty families in 1765.[7]

St. Louis was established by Max Laclede & Company in 1764 under an exclusive grant in 1762 for trade with the Indians. The company built a large storehouse and forty homes for families. When the British occupied Illinois, the garrison from Fort Chartres moved to St. Louis along with many inhabitants. A petition signed by the people of St. Louis and the militia roster showed that most of the population of the town were French from Canada and Illinois. Less than five percent had come from New Orleans.[8]

Harry Gordon reported that Laclede at St. Louis had monopolized the trade of the Missouri River, the north Mississippi, and the Illinois, as well as trade with the Indians near Green Bay, Lake Michigan, and St. Joseph. The St. Louis governor, Kerlerec, estimated the value of the Missouri trade at 8,000 French livres ($80,000) in European goods, a relatively small volume.[9]

British occupation of Illinois was necessary because the French traders were capitalizing on Indian hatred, sustaining the hostilities between the Indians and the British in order to retain the fur trade in French hands. The British occupation of Illinois would suppress that source of trouble according to Dr. Richard Shuckburg, Johnson's agent in Detroit. He believed that the Indians were eager to resume trade with the British and end the war.[10] Colonel Bradstreet, who led the expedition to relieve Detroit, recognized that as long as the French and Spanish sent traders up the Wabash and the Scioto Rivers from the west, the Detroit and Fort Pitt merchants could not compete.[11] An Albany trader in Detroit in 1767, complained that even after the British occupation, the French traders from Illinois brought goods to Vincennes, Vermillion, Ouiatanon, and as far north as Miami.[12]

There was some effort on the part of the Spanish officers after 1763 to control the incursion of the French into British territory, and they officially halted communication across the Mississippi. The British attempted to keep the Illinois French out of British territory by prohibiting traders from obtaining credit for a cargo of goods east of the Mississippi River if the furs were to be returned to St. Louis to repay the debt.[13]

Despite all of these efforts, great numbers of French continued to trade with the Indians east of the Mississippi and presented serious competition to the British traders. Not only did they compete in the Ohio Valley and along the Wabash River, they also made great inroads in the upper Mississippi. A trader would have to carry his canoe over more than ninety portages between Montreal and the Lake of the Woods at the west end of Lake Superior, whereas one could paddle all the way from New Orleans to the Lakes of the Woods on the Mississippi without taking the boat out of the water. In 1765, there were between four hundred and five hundred French traders in the upper Mississippi area.[14]

Under the French, the commerce of the Mississippi River flowed down to New Orleans from Illinois. Flour, bacon, corn, ham, corned pork, corned beef, beeswax, cotton, tallow, leather, tobacco, lead, copper, buffalo hides, wool, venison, poultry, bear's grease, oil, skins, and hides were all shipped to New Orleans. Indigo, rice, and tobacco went to Europe and lumber went to the West Indies.[15] The trip down river from Illinois to New Orleans was easy, as few as twelve days. However, the trip upstream was extremely difficult; rowing against the current was a seventy to ninety day trip. Sails, rope hauling, and rowing were all used to move the boats upstream more than seven hundred miles, not including the many bends in the river. The French estimated the trip at four hundred leagues, or twelve hundred miles (the league varied but was usually about three miles). The voyage was a three-month trip, and the men were weary by the time they reached Illinois. The heat ruined the food during the trip, so the only way that Illinois could be maintained was by increasing the number of farms to make it self-sufficient.[16]

Even after the British achieved control of the trade, much of the farm produce continued to go down the river to New Orleans, although there was some reluctance to send fur for fear it would rot in the warm climate and because of the greater prevalence of vermin. However, the transport was easier and the price of furs in New Orleans was more than in Canada. The colonial merchants who established themselves in Illinois were willing to ship their fur south rather than send it up the more difficult route via the Ohio River and overland to Philadelphia.[17]

A British officer described New Orleans in 1766 as a small town with few houses, but the people were healthy and prosperous. The main business was the fur trade from Illinois.[18] Although the Treaty of Paris had given the British navigational rights on the Mississippi, the British could not use the port of New Orleans, the only navigable opening of the river entering the Gulf of Mexico. The threat of British smuggling merchandise into Louisiana from West Florida led the Spanish to prohibit British merchant ships from trading in New Orleans.[19] Instead, the British ships loaded with Indian goods went to Mobile and Pensacola.[20] Most of the cargoes were for the large contraband trade with New Orleans that developed after 1763 from West Florida.[21] The trade was illegal because the furs and deerskin from New Orleans were enumerated articles (controlled merchandise) that had been unlawfully taken from British territory in Illinois and the hunting grounds west of Lake Michigan by unlicensed French traders. An attempt was made in 1764 to divert the fur trade from New Orleans by deepening the Iberville River to provide a bypass around New Orleans, an engineering feat that failed, as did General Frederick Haldimand's effort later in 1767. The Spanish also failed to check the illegal trade with the British.[22]

The alternate route to Illinois was down the Ohio river. Goods from Pennsylvania were sold to French traders or to the Indians. The fur received from the Indians in exchange for the merchandise was sent down the Mississippi River to New Orleans, where it would be exchanged for credits with traders in Pensacola and Mobile who sent them to New York City, Philadelphia, and Europe.[23] The bills of exchange, obtained in return for furs, were used in

New York City and Philadelphia to purchase merchandise that was then shipped down the Ohio River, and the pattern was repeated. Some furs were sold to Spanish and French merchants in St. Louis, who in turn sold them to New Orleans merchants, who sent the furs to Europe. In 1767, Baynton & Wharton estimated that at least £100,000 sterling ($20 million) worth of fur passed out of New Orleans each year to France. Geography dictated the most economical path for the commerce that included several illegal transactions.[24]

However, the Mississippi was impassable if the Indians were not friendly. The French retained control of the Indians with presents in 1764 because the French inhabitants were dependent on Indian good will for safety. The French were better than the British at dealing with the Indians, and with the help of a few Spanish troops and supplies to fit out the Indians, the French could delay the British occupation of Illinois either by the Ohio River or the Mississippi.[25] In January 17, 1764, Aubrey reported to Spain that the Indians were reconciled to the end of the war and the Treaty of Paris, but that the British could reach Illinois via the Ohio River only if the Indians did not resist. In addition, the British were trying to send the 22nd Regiment up the Mississippi, but Aubrey believed that the attempt would fail.[26]

The 22nd Regiment had 351 men, having been reinforced by drafting all the men from the Third Battalion of the 60th Royal American Regiment not entitled to discharge when the battalion was disbanded at Pensacola in Florida. Many of the men who were discharged from the Royal American regiment were persuaded to reenlist in the 22nd Regiment. The expedition began with an attempt to find a passage at Iberville, but the waterway was clogged with trees. The regiment then went to New Orleans on February 12, 1764, to prepare for the trip up the Mississippi, and while there, thirty of the troops deserted. Finally, on February 27, 1764, the regiment set out with 320 soldiers, 30 women, and 17 children in ten bateaux (flat bottomed boats that could be rowed) and two pirogues (dugout canoes made from large tree trunks). By March 15, 1764, fifty more men had deserted and seven had died. On March 19 and 20, the Indians attacked the expedition two hundred miles north of New Orleans, so the regiment returned to New Orleans on March 26, 1764.[27]

Although the British were unable to move troops up the Mississippi, the French had no difficulty moving merchandise up the river. Severe winter weather delayed the opening of navigation on the Mississippi and trade with Illinois in the spring of 1764. However, on April 18, 1764, the ship *Le Missouri* arrived with a cargo of merchandise for New Orleans from Bordeaux, France, via Santo Domingo. On April 19, the following day, four bateaux and one pirogue armed and loaded by private merchants set off up the Mississippi.[28] A second convoy on May 11, included seventy-seven persons in three bateaux under the command of Berard with supplies for the French garrison in Illinois.[29] While Indian opposition prevented the British regiment from ascending the Mississippi, the French governor sent two convoys without incident.

In June 1764, Croghan suggested to the Board of Trade that a British colony be established in Illinois on the Mississippi to prevent the Indians from dealing with the French.[30] General Gage had this objective in mind when he ordered the 22nd Regiment to make a second effort to go up the Mississippi. Major Farmer at Mobile was ordered to clear the Iberville channel, to establish a post at Natchez, and to make treaties with the Indians allowing the British to pass. Gage who had replaced the deserters and provided supplies for the 22nd Regiment, considered the establishment of a post on the upper Mississippi essential to control French influence in Illinois.[31]

Even before the failure of the first expedition of the 22nd Regiment, Sir William Johnson expressed his belief to General Gage that despite the claim of French impartiality, the governor of Louisiana and other French officials were stirring up the Indians and supplying them with arms and provisions.[32] General Gage and Colonel Bouquet were convinced in May and June 1764 that the French in Illinois had supplied the ammunition that the Indians had used in the rebellion in 1763. Gage believed that the French had actually stirred up the trouble in order to keep the fur trade in their own hands, but the French merchants in Illinois were then short of ammunition and had little to give to the Indians.[33]

The French continued to spread false anti-British rumors among the Indians in 1764. A report from Green Bay relayed information from the tribes there that a Frenchman, LeVorn, from Illinois said that the English would kill the Indians if they went to Montreal for supplies. Instead of going to Montreal, LeVorn said that he would bring goods to the Wisconsin area from Illinois.[34]

At Oswego, Sir William Johnson received reports that the Indians at Detroit had received large amounts of ammunition from the French in Illinois to keep out the British.[35] The governor of New York believed that ammunition for the Indians was being moved up the Ohio River from Fort Chartres. With all communications cut between the Indians and the British, the French in Illinois were reaping the benefits of the fur trade. Many of the Indians had traveled to Illinois during the winter of 1763–64 with large quantities of furs.[36] Colden expected the French to use every excuse to evade or delay the evacuation of their troops from Illinois.[37]

General Gage was concerned about the formation of an alliance between the Indians and the Illinois French. If the tribes on the British frontier withdrew to Illinois and allied themselves to the western Indians, the alliance would be too powerful for the British forces. A campaign in Illinois would cost a great deal and the colonists would not willingly support a war that far west. On the other hand, Gage did not believe that the French were giving the merchandise to the Indians, rather that the Indians were purchasing the goods with furs.[38]

Contrary to British fears, the French officials and army were leaving Illinois. On July 2, 1764, a convoy of twenty-one bateaux and seven pirogues arrived in New Orleans with six officers, sixty-three soldiers, and others.[39] In Illinois in June, 1764, Louis St. Ange, a French official, told the Miami, Wea, Kickapoo,

Mascoutens, and Piankashaw tribes (all from the area south and west of Lake Michigan) that they would no longer receive gifts from the French and recommended that the tribes make peace with the British. Furthermore, if the tribes surrendered to the British, they would be given as much help as they had received from the French traders. The Indians refused to surrender, but St. Ange gave them some powder anyway. From the Indians, St. Ange learned that they planned to lay siege to Detroit again in the summer of 1764 along with the Shawnee, the Mohicans, and the Ottawa.[40]

In August 1764, St. Ange continued his attempts to pacify the Indians. Under pressure from Governor Dabbadie to reduce expenses, St. Ange claimed that avoiding some expenditure was impossible because the Indians pleaded misery and must be given something. St. Ange told the Indians that they need not continue fighting the English in order to be loyal to the French and that the French wanted peace. The Indians refused to stop fighting, saying that they were protecting the French by continuing the war and that they would be mistreated by the English.[41]

On August 16, 1764, Eugene Dabbadie, the French commanding officer at New Orleans, wrote to General Gage expressing his regret regarding the difficulty caused by the Indians. Dabbadie had ordered the post commanders to try to calm the Indians, but the Indians remained bitter. Dabbadie disavowed the belief that the French officials opposed British occupation of Illinois; the French would benefit if the British controlled Illinois because of the considerable cost of maintaining the forts there.[42] On August 24, 1764, Dabbadie sent a third convoy to Illinois under M. Dernis with seven bateaux and one pirogue and another pirogue for Arkansas with 132 people.[43] Explaining his policy to the Spanish government, Dabbadie claimed that the Indians must be given a small quantity of powder and bullets because they relied on their guns for hunting, and through hunting they obtained their food and the furs that contributed to the Louisiana trade.[44]

In September 1764, a dispatch arrived informing the French officials that as of April 21, 1764, Louisiana had been ceded to Spain, but no Spanish troops had arrived to occupy New Orleans.[45] In Illinois, the Indians attacked a French hunter, so St. Ange prohibited the *voyageurs* from traveling north until relations improved.[46]

The reports of the French sending large quantities of merchandise up the Mississippi were forwarded to Sir William Johnson by the Indians. Many of the Indians had traveled to Illinois and had received presents from the French. Johnson proposed that the British increase their level of giving to compete with the French.[47] Captain William Howard at Mackinac received a report in November 1764, that the French had sent an officer to St. Joseph on the east shore of Lake Michigan to urge the Potawatomi to continue the war, while at the same time St. Ange claimed that he had refused to supply the Shawnee because they continued the war with the English. St. Ange claimed to be embarrassed by the Shawnee demands that created expenses contrary to

Dabbadie's orders, but he had to give them a little ammunition to avoid antagonizing them and to maintain French influence.[48]

The Indian agent, McKee, at Fort Pitt reported that the French had sent five large canoes of merchandise to the Shawnee. Smallman, another agent, reported that the French had sent supplies to the Shawnee twice previously during 1764.[49] Colonel Bouquet also informed Johnson that Killbuck, the Delaware chief, would tell Johnson privately of intrigue by the French officials who supplied the Indians with powder. From this information Johnson was to judge whether the powder was supplied with the connivance of the French commanding officer.[50]

St. Ange continued to play a double role, claiming that the Indians would not agree to make peace with the English, thereby preventing the British from taking Illinois and relieving the French of their responsibilities there. As a result, St. Ange requested funds to supply presents to the Indians. St. Ange belittled the peace made by Colonel Bradstreet in 1764, for the Indians intended to betray the British when the time was right according to a letter from Pontiac. Pontiac was circulating a belt six feet long and four inches wide to all the nations to request aid in the uprising against the British. The belt was made of beads in a pattern that served to remind the carrier of all of the details that he was to convey orally to each tribe. Each group of beads represented a part of the message, and a six-foot belt would have represented a long discourse.[51]

The British, on the other hand, were making plans to occupy Illinois from the north, having failed from the south. Governor Colden of New York believed that the route overland from Philadelphia to Fort Pitt and then down the Ohio, or the other route via Lake Erie, the Maumee River, and the Wabash River (navigable only during the spring high water) were both preferable to the Mississippi.[52] Early in November 1765, General Gage ordered Colonel Bouquet to send an officer down the Ohio River to Illinois accompanied by Shawnee and Delaware escorts to inform all the tribes that peace had been made with the French. Bouquet drew supplies from Franks and Barclay, the army contractors, as the supplies previously provided by Callendar probably had been exhausted.[53]

Bouquet informed Johnson in late November 1764, that the only way to eliminate French influence was a display of force; therefore Bouquet proposed a military expedition down the Ohio River to the Mississippi.[54] Colonel Bouquet questioned the wisdom of sending a single officer as a messenger down the Ohio River because he would be treated badly by the Indians aroused by the French. The Indians mistrusted the English officers and did not feel that the English had any power over the tribes. Bouquet believed that the French must be driven by force out of Illinois. Travel up the Mississippi was impossible because the Indians could fire continually on the boats as they rowed slowly upstream against the current at only ten miles per day. On the other hand, boats going down the Ohio River with the current moved at fifty miles per day and could outdistance the Indians on land. The planned military expedition down the

Ohio had to be kept secret to prevent the French from assembling the Indians to stop the convoy. Once in Illinois, the British could dictate peace terms to the Indians, who would then be cut off from their supply of ammunition.[55] Among the peace terms that Colonel Bouquet recommended to Johnson for the Shawnee and Delaware were allowing free navigation of the Ohio River, no traders in the Indian villages, and not allowing the French to trade with the Indians. The last term could be enforced only after Illinois was occupied.[56]

General Gage, in December 1764, ordered Bouquet to proceed with the Ohio River expedition and hoped that Pontiac could be won over to the British side. Gage believed the trouble came from the French traders, not the French officials in Illinois.[57] Johnson agreed with Bouquet that the problem with the Shawnees was caused by French supplies and that the occupation of Illinois would end the problem.[58] On December 18, 1764, he wrote Gage that peace could not be attained as long as the French supplied the Indians, but that the first goal was to obtain the consent of the Indians for the British to occupy Illinois.

Johnson proposed to send Croghan to attend a peace conference at Fort Pitt and then take two or three companies of troops and some Indians via Sandusky and Lake Erie to the Miami River to meet with Pontiac. Later, Croghan would travel overland to Illinois with a large load of gifts on pack horses and promise the Indians in Illinois that the British would reopen the trade in the spring of 1765. However, if no plans were carried out until spring, the French might stir up the Indians again.[59] Also on December 18, 1764, Johnson ordered Croghan to come to Johnson Hall in upper New York to confer with him on the proposed expedition and to meet with the Shawnee and Delaware who were also coming to Johnson Hall. At that time, Johnson hoped to obtain the assistance of the Indians in occupying Illinois. Illinois had to be occupied and Croghan was to enlist Shawnee and Delaware chiefs to accompany him and the troops down the Ohio.[60]

General Gage agreed with Johnson that the way to Illinois was blocked by the Indians and the solutions were either by treaty or by force. Forceful passage down the Ohio River was not possible because neither Pennsylvania nor Virginia would provide troops. The French were obstructing a peaceful solution, capitalizing on the fears of the Shawnee and Delaware that the British were insincere. In late December, the Delaware told Colonel Bouquet that the French commandant at Fort Chartres had promised aid to the Indians within a short time, and that meanwhile the French traders would supply ammunition and clothing. The French traders had carried this message to the Delaware and Shawnee at Muskingum.[61]

In a letter to the Board of Trade, Johnson stated that taking Illinois was important for two reasons, first, to prevent the French from stirring up the Indians, and second to regain a significant portion of the fur trade going to the French in New Orleans. Johnson hoped that Croghan could take Illinois by traveling overland during the winter if he obtained the support of the Shawnees and the Twightwees tribe.[62]

General Gage finally decided in favor of sending Croghan down the Ohio River with a French-speaking British officer, Lieutenant Alexander Frazier of the 78th Regiment, who was ordered to leave Fort Pitt in early January 1765 with letters for the French commander in Illinois.[63] Gage was still waiting for news of the treaty with the Delaware and Shawnee, as Croghan needed their support to persuade some Indian chiefs to travel with him down the Ohio. The timing was critical because the 34th Regiment would try to come up the Mississippi from New Orleans in February 1765, and Indian resistance had to be eliminated if the regiment were to succeed.[64]

While the army and Johnson were making plans to occupy Illinois in 1765, Baynton, Wharton & Morgan, one of the largest mercantile partnerships in Philadelphia, had been making plans to go to Illinois since 1763. When the partners learned of the army proposal to go up the Mississippi in February 1764, they joined with Daniel Clark and Jeremiah Warder in a venture sending goods worth £1,500 Pennsylvania ($172,500) to Mobile for shipment to Illinois.[65] On May 31, 1763, a huge shipment of goods valued at £13,915 Pennsylvania ($1.6 million) was sent from Philadelphia to Callendar and Spear at Carlisle, Pennsylvania, intended for Illinois. The partners in the venture were Callendar & Spear (forty-five percent), Samuel Eldridge (ten percent), and Baynton, Wharton & Morgan (forty-five percent).[66] However, this large stock of goods was stalled when the route was blocked by the Indians and was probably sold to the Indian Department in 1764. In November 1764, Croghan became a partner of Baynton, Wharton & Morgan, Robert Field, and Robert Callender in a venture to take £20,000 Pennsylvania ($2.3 million) in merchandise to Illinois. Croghan promised to buy part of the shipment at Fort Pitt at inflated prices for the British Indian Department as presents for the Indians. He was to have twenty-five percent of the profits from the total enterprise, a clear conflict of interest. The other three partners were each to receive twenty-five percent as well. Croghan obtained a pass from Colonel Bouquet to take the goods to Illinois, pretending that the entire stock would be purchased by the Indian Department, because the only goods permitted to pass through Fort Pitt were those intended as gifts of the British government to the Indians.[67]

Baynton, Wharton & Morgan began preparations for the venture, including additional employees. John Jennings was hired for twelve months' service on behalf of the partnership at Fort Pitt beginning December 3, 1764.[68] Obtaining the large number of shirts provided an example of the complexity of preparing for such a large venture. Each ruffled shirt required more than two yards of cloth, ninety percent linen or garlix and ten percent muslim. First the partners obtained an Indian shirt from Callendar & Spear and had patterns made by Samuel Mason's widow. Pieces of Irish and princess linen, garlix, and muslim, each about thirty yards, were purchased. The materials, including thread, were given to Jane Campbell, Nancy Martin, Hannah Coffin, Margery Fare, Sarah Humphreys, Mrs. Coburne, Dorothy, and Mary Morris. These women were engaged to make more than twenty-five hundred Indian shirts from December

8 to December 12, 1764. The finished shirts were delivered by the end of January.[69] The cost of the shirts ranged from 6p to 8¼p (about $3 to $4). By January 8, 1765, the company's books listed £220 to be paid for shirts at a maximum rate of twenty-six shirts per £, indicating that fifty-seven hundred shirts had been made.[70] Considering that there were fewer then ten thousand Indian adult males in the northwest, the partners expected to monopolize the trade.

Other merchandise was prepared for the expedition. On December 7, 1764, five wagon loads (each with one to one and a half tons) were sent to Callendar by the three business partners and "etc.," omitting Croghan's name from the transaction. One of the wagons contained five bales of cloth including one bale of blue stroud worth £60 sterling, a bale of twelve scarlet strouds valued at £95 sterling, and a bale of twelve aurora strouds valued at £75 sterling. The value of the five wagon loads must have been more than £2,000 sterling ($400,000). On December 12, 1764, five more wagons were sent to Callendar from all four partners, including Croghan's name on this order, and on December 14, 1764, three more wagons were sent. The three shipments might well have had a value of more than £10,000 Pennsylvania ($1,150,000).[71] On December 24, 1764, Baynton, Wharton & Morgan received a shipment on the brigantine *Grace* from their primary supplier in London, Neave, for merchandise valued at £2,809 sterling ($562,000). The firm was well prepared to enter the western trade.[72]

Samuel Wharton wrote to Benjamin Franklin on December 19, 1764, concerning the proposed trip by Croghan down the Ohio River, indicating that Croghan was waiting for orders to hold a treaty with the Indians. Wharton emphasized that peace was impossible until Indian contact with the French in Illinois was terminated. Wharton also mentioned that the Pennsylvania Provincial battalions were being disbanded and that the 1st Battalion had been paid off in Lancaster on December 20, 1764. Given the unsettled relations with the Indians, the disbandment clearly indicated that the Pennsylvania leadership was transferring frontier defense to the British army.[73]

The Pennsylvania merchants dealing in Illinois had a gross of about £80,000 sterling ($16 million) according to Croghan in the late 1760s. The Pennsylvania firms competed with each other, with Virginians, and with the French. Trader Edward Cole, who had moved to Niagara in 1760 and to Detroit with Rogers' expedition in 1761, resurfaced at Fort Chartres in 1767, having transferred his activity in an attempt to restore his fortune. He was not successful, but another Detroit trader, Winston, who had hidden with Hambuck at St. Joseph in 1763 during the Pontiac Rebellion, did well in Illinois and soon paid his debts.[74]

The colonial traders had a difficult time competing in Illinois. The goods brought up the Mississippi River were thirty percent cheaper than those brought down the Ohio River from Fort Pitt. Furs sold at a price twenty-five percent higher in New Orleans than in Fort Pitt. Even if traders sold the Pennsylvania goods from Fort Pitt in Illinois, the furs were sent down the Mississippi to take advantage of the higher prices in New Orleans. The Pennsylvania merchants finally began to ship furs to New Orleans intending to send them to England, but once in New Orleans the furs could be sold and shipped anywhere. As a result, colonial attempts to dominate the trade in Illinois from Pennsylvania failed as furs and produce continued to be shipped down the Mississippi. By 1768 Baynton, Wharton & Morgan received less than five percent of the Illinois trade and the partnership went bankrupt. The few colonial traders left in Illinois then shipped their furs either to New Orleans or Natchez.[75]

In 1763, the fur trade in Illinois offered little profit, because the Spanish controlled New Orleans, hampering the import of goods and the export of furs. The apparent major benefit from commerce in Illinois was the sale of British goods imported by way of West Florida or Fort Pitt. Some furs were exported illegally from New Orleans, and General Haldimand sent an officer to New Orleans to investigate the smuggling. However, the officer found no evidence of furs coming from British territory, only farm produce which was perfectly legal. Various plans were devised to stop the illegal trade in furs. The most extensive was building a post at Point Iberville and deepening the river to provide access to the sea from the Mississippi on British soil. Construction of a canal was attempted twice and failed. Forts were considered too expensive and ineffective, and even bribes were tried in the form of presents to the Indians, but no plan succeeded in halting the illegal export of pelts from Illinois down the Mississippi.[76]

Competition with Illinois eventually developed from the Great Lakes when the British regained control with their French-Canadian associates. The lake route was used by schooners and sloops that reduced the cost of transportation. Cheap transportation of heavy goods over the lakes combined with the lower original price that the British had to pay for rum, flour, blankets, and other necessities lowered British prices below the costs of the French from Illinois in the winter hunting grounds. Upstream travel on the Mississippi was slow and difficult in comparison to the swift crossing of the lakes by the sail driven sloops and schooners. The northern route also eliminated the danger of deterioration to the furs posed by the warm climate of New Orleans.

As the British revived their commerce to the north, New Orleans remained a potent exporter of deerskins, with exports ranging from 120,000 to 250,000 skins per year in the early 1770s. A factor in the continuation of New Orleans as an export center may have been importing trade goods on the northern route and exporting via New Orleans taking advantage of the easier route entering and leaving Illinois.[77]

In conclusion, the Illinois French traders for five years continued to trade in Ohio, the upper lakes, and territory west of South Carolina taking the furs out via the Mississippi. The colonial traders could not compete until Illinois was occupied because of the British rules restricting trade with the Indians to the confines of designated posts. The *voyageurs* working for British merchants in Canada violated the rules with ease, but the Pennsylvania, New York, and Virginia traders were hamstrung. The occupation of Illinois in 1765 helped the colonial merchants as they moved into Illinois to supply both the army and Indians, but the Pennsylvania merchants could not compete. The competing British-French partnerships from Canada finally appropriated the trade from both the Illinois French and the Pennsylvanians.

NOTES

1. Villiers to inhabitants of Fort Chartres, September 27, 1763, Sir William Johnson, *The Papers of Sir William Johnson* (Albany: State University of New York, 1921-1965), 10:821.

2. Franklin B. Hough, *Diary of the Siege of Detroit in the War with Pontiac...* (Albany, NY: J. Munsell, 1860), 143; Wayne E. Stevens, *The Northwest Fur Trade, 1763-1800* (Urbana: University of Illinois, 1928), 25-26.

3. Gage to Shelburne, November 11, 1766, Marjorie Reid, "The Quebec Fur Traders and Western Policy, 1763-1774," *Canadian Historical Review,* 6:26.

4. *Illinois Historical Collections* (Springfield: Trustees of the Illinois State Historical Library, 1903-to date), 10:521 (hereafter cited as *IHC*); Johnson to Colden, December 24, 1763, Hough, *Diary of the Siege*, 216-17.

5. Paul C. Phillips, *The Fur Trade*, 2 vols. (Norman: University of Oklahoma Press, 1961), 591-92.

6. Aubrey's Account of Illinois, 1763, *IHC*, 10:3.

7. Clarence W. Alvord, *The Illinois Country 1673-1818* (Springfield: Illinois Centennial Commission, 1920), 192; *IHC*, 10:xxxi, Phillips, *Fur Trade*, 596.

8. Douglas Dunham, "The French Element in the American Fur Trade," Ph.D. Dis., University of Michigan, 1950, 97-98.

9. Ibid., 71-72.

10. Dr. Shuckburgh to Johnson, July 14, 1765, *IHC*, 10:521.

11. Hough, *Diary of the Siege*, 143.

12. Van Schaack to Hay, September 4, 1767, *IHC*, 16:3-4.

13. Phillips, *Fur Trade*, 598.

14. Theodore C. Pease and Marguerite J. Pease, *George Rogers Clark and Revolution in Illinois, 1763-1787* (Springfield: Illinois State Historical Society, 1929), 8.

15. Francois X. Martin, *History of Louisiana, From the Earliest Period*, 2 vols. (New Orleans: Lyman and Beardslee, 1827-29), 1:179.

16. Dabbadie to Minister, January 10, 1764, *IHC*, 10:209; Alvord, *Illinois Country*, 213.

17. Dunham, "French Element," 100-101.

18. Captain Harry Gordon's Journal, 1766, Charles A. Hanna, *The Wilderness Trail*, 2 vols. (New York: G. P. Putnam's, Sons, 1911), 2:55.

19. Phillips, *Fur Trade*, 596.

20. Clinton N. Howard, *The British Development of West Florida, 1763-1769* (Berkley and Los Angeles: University of California Press, 1947), 17.

21. Phillips, *Fur Trade*, 596; Howard, *British Development*, 17, 39; Linda Sellers, *Charleston Business on the Eve of the Revolution* (Chapel Hill: University of North Carolina Press, 1934), 169-70.

22. Pownall to the Board of Trade, February 19, 1765, Howard, *British Development*, 29–30, 41.

23. Ibid., 21; Dunham, "French Element," 81.

24. Virginia Harrington, *The New York Merchant on the Eve of the Revolution* (New York: Columbia University Press, 1935), 240.

25. Dabbadie to Minister, January 10, 1764, *IHC*, 10:209.

26. Aubrey to Minister, January 15, 1764, ibid., 214–15.

27. John Shy, *Toward Lexington, The Role of the British Army in the Coming of the American Revolution* (Princeton, NJ: Princeton University Press, 1965), 152–53; Report of Robertson, March 8, 1764, *IHC*, 10:216–17, 220; ibid., xli–xlii; Gage to Halifax, April 14, 1764, ibid., 225; Loftus Attempt Up the Mississippi, March 1764, ibid., 227.

28. Journal of Dabbadie, May 21, 1764, ibid., 186–87; April 19, 1764, ibid., 182–83.

29. Journal of Dabbadie, June 12, 1764, ibid., 188; Dabbadie to Minister, June 29, 1764, ibid., 270–77.

30. Croghan to the Board of Trade, June 8, 1764, Canadian Archives Microfilm II, State Historical Society of Wisconsin.

31. Gage to Halifax, May 21, 1764, *IHC*, 10:248–49.

32. Johnson to Gage, January 12, 1764, *Johnson MSS*, 4:295.

33. Bouquet to Gage, May 27, 1764, *Canadian Archives Report* (1889), 66; Gage to Bouquet, June 5, 1764, ibid., 67; Gage to Johnson, April 30, 1764, *Johnson MSS*, 11:167–68.

34. Trader's Reports, Gladwin MSS, 1764, Reuben G. Thwaites, "The British Regime in Wisconsin," *Wisconsin Historical Collections*, 18 (1908), 268.

35. Johnson to Gage, June 29, 1764, *Johnson MSS*, 11:245.

36. Johnson to Gage, January 12, 1764, ibid., 4:295.

37. Johnson to Gage, June 29, 1764, ibid., 11:245.

38. Colden to Halifax, July 9, 1764, *Colden Papers, New York Historical Society Collections*, 1876, 335; Gage to Halifax, July 13, 1764, *IHC*, 10:283–84.

39. Journal of Dabbadie, July 2, 1764, ibid., 189–90.

40. St. Ange to Dabbadie, July 15, 1764, ibid., 289–91.

41. St. Ange to Dabbadie, August 12, 1764, ibid., 292–94.

42. Dabbadie to Gage, August 16, 1764, ibid., 300–01.

43. Journal of Dabbadie, August 20, 1764, ibid., 196.

44. Dabbadie to the Minister, September 10, 1764, ibid., 312.

45. Dabbadie to the Minister, September 30, 1764, ibid., 314–15.

46. St. Ange to Dabbadie, September 30, 1764, ibid., 296.

47. Johnson to Gage, September 30, 1764, *Johnson MSS*, 11:364–65.

48. Journal of William Howard, November 3, 1764, ibid., 696.

49. Alex McKee to Johnson, November 17, 1764, ibid., 475.

50. Bouquet to Johnson, November 30, 1764, ibid., 4:607.

51. St. Ange to Dabbadie, November 9, 1764, *IHC*, 10:355–57.

52. Colden to Lords of Trade, October 12, 1764, Edmund B. O'Callaghan, ed., 4 vols., *The Documentary History of the State of New York* (Albany, NY: Weed, Parsons & Co., 1849-51), 7:668.

53. Gage to Bouquet, November 9, 1764, *IHC*, 10:353–54.

54. Bouquet to Johnson, November 30, 1764, *CA Report* (1889), 34.

55. Bouquet to Gage, November 30, 1764, *IHC*, 10:366–67.

56. Gage to Johnson, December 6, 1764, ibid., 369.

57. Gage to Bouquet, December 7, 1764, ibid., 371.

58. Johnson to Bouquet, December 17, 1764, *Johnson MSS*, 4:620.

59. Johnson to Gage, December 18, 1764, ibid., 625.

60. Johnson to Croghan, December 18, 1764, ibid., 11:509-10.

61. Gage to Bouquet, December 20, 1764, *CA Report* (1889), 74; Indian Intelligence, December 22, 1764, *Johnson MSS*, 4:627-28.

62. Johnson to the Lords of Trade, December 26, 1764, *IHC*, 10:394.

63. Gage to Bouquet, December 24, 1764, *CA Report* (1889), 74.

64. Gage to Johnson, December 31, 1764, *Johnson MSS*, 11:515-17.

65. Daniel Clark to Baynton, Wharton & Morgan, April 28, 1764, Baynton, Wharton & Morgan Microfilm, F3.

66. Journal A, February 28, 1764, ibid., F7.

67. Nicholas B. Wainwright, *George Croghan, Wilderness Diplomat* (Chapel Hill: University of North Carolina Press, 1959), 212, 214.

68. Baynton, Wharton & Morgan Memo Book, December 3, 1764, BWM Microfilm, F10.

69. Baynton, Wharton & Morgan Memo Book, December 8, 11, 12, 27, 1764, ibid., F10.

70. Baynton, Wharton & Morgan Memo Book, December 22, 1764, ibid., F10.

71. Baynton, Wharton & Morgan Memo Book, December 7-14, 1764, ibid., F10.

72. Journal A, December 24, 1764, ibid., F8.

73. Samuel Wharton to Benjamin Franklin, December 19, 1764, *IHC*, 10:376-77.

74. Dunham, "French Element," 91; W. N. Franklin, "Pennsylvania-Virginia Rivalry for the Indian Trade of the Ohio Valley," *Mississippi Valley Historical Review*, 20:477; Cole to Edgar, August 3, 1767, William Edgar Papers, 1750-1775, Burton Historical Collection, vol. 15.

75. Pease, *George Rogers Clark*, 20; Marjorie Reid, "The Quebec Fur Traders and Western Policy, 1763-1774," *Canadian Historical Review*, 6:21; Stevens, *Northwest Fur Trade*, 26.

76. Dunham, "French Element," 89; Clarence W. Alvord, *The Mississippi Valley in British Politics*, 2 vols. (Cleveland, OH: Arthur H. Clark, Co., 1917), 1:304; Pease, *George Rogers Clark*, 8-9, 11.

77. Harold A. Innis, "Interrelations Between the Fur Trade of Canada and the United States," *Mississippi Valley Historical Review*, 20: (December 1933), 325; Cecil Johnson, "Expansion in West Florida, 1770-1779," *Mississippi Valley Historical Review*, 20 (March 1934), 483; Dunham, "French Element," 97; Dabbadie to Minister, January 10, 1764, *IHC*, 10:209.

8

Imperial Policy, 1762–1763

The end of the fighting in North America in 1760 plunged the thirteen colonies into an economic depression as military spending declined sharply. This depression was echoed later in England where the termination of military purchases depressed the economy there as well and led to a tightening of credit. As English merchants demanded payment from the colonists in the early 1760s, the American merchants were hard pressed to meet demands.

Prior to Pontiac's Rebellion, the imperial policy toward frontier trade was one of *laissez faire*, leaving the Pennsylvania and Albany traders free to trade and abuse the Indians with minimal control. The rebellion demonstrated that some regulation was required and the signing of the Treaty of Paris in 1763 opened the path for permanent arrangements at the expense of the colonists. The proposed solutions would require funds that the British taxpayers were unwilling to provide. In the face of their own economic woes, the American merchants were unwilling to pay taxes to fund a system that would deprive them of profits on the frontier.

The Treaty of Paris would have a dramatic impact on the frontier. During the negotiations for the settlement of the Seven Years' War, economic factors played a dominant role. The British government had to choose which of its conquests to acquire permanently, Canada or Guadeloupe, as the British believed that the French would be unwilling to give up both. Additional sugar from Guadeloupe would eliminate American smuggling of sugar and molasses, and robbing France of her West Indies trade would reduce that country's ability to train sailors for the navy.[1] The proponents of Guadeloupe claimed that the fur trade was of less economic importance compared to Guadeloupe, as Canada exported only a few furs to England in 1761, while Guadeloupe, also under British control in 1761, exported £603,269 sterling ($120 million), two-thirds sugar and one-fifth cotton.[2]

Acquisition of Guadeloupe was opposed by the British West Indies planters, who were well represented in Parliament, because the addition of Guadeloupe sugar to the British market would reduce the price and hurt them personally. The trade with the existing British West Indies was already two to one against England and Guadeloupe would make it worse. Canada was a better potential market for British goods, whereas Guadeloupe had no comparable future as a market. Acquiring Canada would reduce the danger to the American colonies from the French.[3]

The economic difficulties of the British hat-making business during 1752 to 1762 may have resulted in considerable pressure to acquire the source of the furs. The hat merchants were desperate and petitioning parliament for many forms of aid: labor regulation, prohibitory tariffs, and prohibition of colonial manufacture, and this argument might well have won over some members of Parliament who would otherwise have voted for Guadeloupe.

While these arguments were being broadcast in a pamphlet war in England, the real war carried on into 1762. Spain entered the war, and England responded by taking Havana in September 1762. Faced with further defeats, France signed the Treaty of Paris on February 10, 1763, relinquishing Canada in return for Guadeloupe. The interests of the colonial rum manufacturers, who would have benefitted from legal access to molasses from Guadeloupe, were sacrificed for those of the sugar plantation owners of Great Britain who would have faced stiff competition from sugar from Guadeloupe.

The colonial interests were not well served by the treaty, although the removal of the French threat made the colonists less dependent on Britain. The French Canadians soon forced the colonial merchants out of the fur business, and the new colony of Florida made inroads into the Charleston deerskin trade that had already been challenged by Georgia. Access to new land west of the mountains was denied the colonists by the Proclamation of 1763. The treaty brought little reward to the colonists.

The end of the war brought a period of severe economic conditions in the American colonies that would make American merchants hyper sensitive to any reductions in expenditures by London that would worsen an existing dismal situation. In 1761, British military expenditures in America (£1,044,000) plus exports (£848,000) had provided the seaboard with credits to balance the enormous imports (£1,652,000). In 1762, the tempo of the war tapered off in North America to an even slower pace than in 1761. Although some of the British regiments had returned from the West Indies to New York City, they came back in a depleted state with many of the soldiers sick.[4] Some regiments were disbanded and the officers returned to England. Others were recruited to full strength with American recruits because there were few potential soldiers remaining in England after six years of war.[5] Income for the colonies from military sources was greatly reduced, and this loss of revenue was a factor in the drop in the level of imports from England to £1,377,000 sterling in 1762. The value of exports to England also dropped to £742,000 sterling, lower than the 1760 rate and another indication of the depressed commerce. The value of the exports does not include the hidden factor of the loss of the army bills of exchange that had been used to offset the deficit balance. In 1762, military expenses were cut to £525,000.

Despite the overall colonial adverse balance of trade, New York and Pennsylvania realized some advantages. The increased availability of fur and the bills of exchange created to pay for the Indian Department and the British army on the frontier in Pennsylvania and New York may have been a factor in the better performance in these two colonies. Despite the indications of economic depression with regard to international trade, higher prices in the colonies indicated a healthy demand for goods and services in the colonial economy. This demand may be partially explained by the very small amount of British goods available on the market, raising the prices. In addition, the military actions in 1761–62 in the Caribbean may have created a shortage of West Indies products (molasses and sugar), raising these prices. Army purchases in New York and Pennsylvania for the expedition to the West Indies against the Spanish possessions also increased prices. In April 1762, William Corry, a merchant in Albany, reported to Sir William Johnson that no provisions were for sale except beef, and that hay and fodder were in short supply.[6] The shortage was caused by the West Indies expedition because British agents had hired all of the ships at Philadelphia and purchased great quantities of provisions in May 1762 in Philadelphia.[7]

Despite the steady increase in exports from 1759 to 1765, the colonial debt to England created by the spending spree in 1759 and 1760 remained, and the means to pay debts in England were scarce. The shortage of cash and bills of exchange to pay obligations in England was indicated by the merchant records, as well as the statistics. In June 1762, Daniel Clark wrote to Holiday and Dunbar, his correspondents in Liverpool, that he was unable to make any payments on his balance of £1,135 sterling because he had been disappointed by his rural customers.[8] James & Drinker, in Philadelphia, wrote to Neal and Pigou in July 1762 that bills of exchange were so scarce they would have to remit in silver dollars.[9] John Sanders of Albany, for the first time in this period, remitted to England in Spanish dollars worth £110 New York along with a bill of exchange for £100.[10] In August 1762, John and Peter Chevalier sent £500 sterling in Dutch bills of exchange drawn on J. Henriques of Amsterdam, to their correspondents in London, Mildred & Roberts.[11] In Albany, William Corry wrote to Johnson in April 1762, that money was very short among the trading people.[12] Governor Colden requested from Lord Amherst in March, that, even though war with Spain would soon begin, William Walton, a New York shipowner, should be given clearance for a ship to carry provisions to the Spanish post in St. Augustine, Florida, because the quantity was small and Walton expected to collect 150,000 Spanish dollars ($6 million) when the ship arrived. Collecting this amount would be a great advantage to Britain.[13] These are but a few examples of letters regarding the shortage of means to remit to England in 1762.

The signing of the preliminaries of peace in November 1762 decelerated the war in North America, and more British regiments returned to North America from the West Indies by the end of 1763. Injury and death in battle combined with illness had thinned the ranks of all the regiments that had fought in the tropics. Some of the regiments that had seven hundred to one thousand men when they left Canada and the American colonies returned with only two hundred. By the end of 1764, there were twenty regiments in North America including seven in Canada, four in the Province of New York, two in Pennsylvania, five in Florida, and two in other areas of North America.[14] The major movement of troops from the West Indies was to Pennsylvania, New York, and Florida. Florida had been given to Britain as compensation for the return of Cuba to Spain. The expenditures to maintain the regiments from the West Indies boosted only slightly the colonial economy which was sagging after the war boom years. The return of the British regiments, however, with their need for rations and other supplies, provided some sterling bills of exchange.

An additional source of remittances came in the form of Spanish silver dollars. The conquest of Havana had resulted in a great demand for colonial provisions and other goods in Cuba, paid for in Spanish dollars. More than £3 million sterling (compared to total American exports in 1763 of £1,106,000) was distributed to the army in Cuba as prize money, given to soldiers and sailors as their share of captured Spanish assets. The prize money was paid in Spanish silver dollars, and, as a result, Spanish dollars were plentiful in Philadelphia and New York early in 1763 when the soldiers returned. At the end of 1763, many merchants were using these dollars rather than sterling bills to pay their debts in England. John and Peter Chevalier, in November 1763, sent a shipment of 2,800 Spanish dollars ($1,120,000). Baynton, Wharton & Morgan shipped 4,667 Spanish dollars in December 1763 to their correspondent Richard Neave. John Sanders in Schenectady sent 250 Spanish dollars to pay his obligations to Moses Franks in London.[15] In February 1763, Collins and Govet in Montreal purchased 1,207 dollars from Jenkins, Tyre & Co. and used the Spanish coins to pay Willing and Morris in April.[16] This influx of Spanish dollars in the pockets of soldiers returning to North America was not recorded in trade statistics, but may have been an essential part of the boom in 1763.

Although the Seven Years' War had brought laurels to Britain, the conflict left a debt of £132 million sterling ($26,400,000,000) to be borne by a population of 8 million with annual exports of only £15 million. The taxpayers in England, the landed gentry and the merchants, demanded relief from heavy taxation, much of which was used to administer the colonies. Rather than a reduction of colonial expense after the war, England was faced with an increase for the additional territories acquired by the war. Efforts were made to reduce expenses in all activities. Military expenses of the empire were reduced from £15,252,000 in 1762 to £6,849,000 in 1763, and further to £5,264,000 in 1764.

The colonies had shown during the war that they could not be depended on to provide troops and money for their own defense without considerable urging. When the decision was made to retain twenty regiments in America to defend Canada and protect the fur trade, an attempt was made to support British regulars in America by parliamentary taxation of the colonies because the colonies obviously would not support the army directly.

The pressure to reduce the cost of presents to the Indians began in January 1762. The cost of the Indian Department was reduced to £7,300 by 1763. Amherst challenged Croghan's accounts that totaled £4,400 Pennsylvania for the Indians at Fort Pitt, despite the sharp decrease in the allocation for presents. Amherst objected also to the large amount spent by Captain Donald Campbell in Detroit and by Lieutenant John Butler. Again, he reiterated to Colonel Bouquet, the commander of the western department, that presents were to be limited, and that no rum was to be carried by the traders, as it was destructive to the Indians, whose misbehavior in turn was costly to the crown.[17] Also on January 16, 1762, Amherst wrote to Johnson reaffirming the prohibition of rum in the trade. Amherst planned to order the post commanders to stop any liquor passing so that traders would carry more useful articles. Ammunition was finally to be made available by the traders for hunting, and therefore there was no need for presents of ammunition in the future as had been past practice.[18] Johnson defended the high cost of the Detroit conference in 1761 and of Croghan's and Butler's accounts on the grounds that many more Indians were involved than in the past. Purchasing goods in Fort Pitt and Miami from traders also added greatly to the cost of the Indian Department. Even if the traders were permitted to carry more goods, including ammunition, some money was needed for presents in order to keep peace.[19] Despite his protests, Johnson did convey strict orders to Croghan to economize sharply on expenses and to make certain that only Indian expenses were charged to the department.[20] However, the actual savings that Johnson was able to implement were slight if any.

Amherst, despite his objections, did pay the accounts submitted by Campbell, Croghan, and Butler, although he considered the amounts very high. Meanwhile, Croghan was attempting to maintain some semblance of order in controlling the Indians, and his two assistants were continually visiting the tribes. In March 1762, Croghan reported to Johnson that his expenses since November 1761 were trifling, as the winter had been very severe, and few Indians had visited Fort Pitt other than some Senecas on their way to fight the Cherokees. The Senecas became angry when refused ammunition, vermillion, knives, and other warlike supplies prohibited by Amherst's orders. Bouquet and Croghan believed that the merchandise should have been given to the Indians.[21] In April 1762, eighty warriors of the Six Nations stopped at Fort Pitt on their return from the Cherokee expedition. Their request for supplies was refused also by Colonel Bouquet under Amherst's policy. Again, they objected, so Croghan delivered the necessary provisions and supplies at his own expense. In May 1762, Croghan reported only £317 expenses for the past six months, exclusive of salaries of the Indian Department agents in Detroit and Fort Pitt.[22] This reduction was tremendous from a monthly rate of £400 in 1761. In reducing the amount of expenses, Croghan hoped to please Amherst, and although two murders had been committed by the Indians, most of the tribes in the Fort Pitt area had been peaceful toward the traders.[23] Amherst was apparently satisfied as he promptly returned a warrant to pay the accounts and ordered Mr. Nelson in Philadelphia to issue the money as soon as the warrant was endorsed by Croghan.[24]

In July 1762, Johnson asked for an advance of £2,000 sterling for the pay of the Indian Department and for other expenses with the promise that accounts would be prepared and sent later, but Amherst refused and provided only £1,500 sterling. Amherst was definitely tightening the supply of money, insisting that Croghan's expenses were too high. He had already ordered Colonel Bouquet to dismiss one of Croghan's two assistants.[25] In August, Johnson again wrote to the Lords of Trade appealing the thrift policy, complaining that the Indians were under French influence, and that suddenly rather than gradually reducing the presents was dangerous. Johnson stressed the need for free trade to maintain the Indian friendship.[26] However, Johnson did cut the Indian Department at Fort Pitt from nearly £1,700 Pennsylvania to under £1,150 Pennsylvania in August of 1762.[27] In the fall of 1763, Amherst insisted that the Indians trade skins for powder, and that the British should not give them any powder unless it was absolutely necessary.[28] Johnson requested four hundred to five hundred pounds of powder for the use of the Indian Department as presents, and Amherst agreed after delaying nearly three weeks.[29]

In response to the reports of plots against the British, Johnson ordered Croghan to conduct an investigation, and he in turn, on April 3, 1762, sent Thomas Hutchins on a tour of the Great Lakes to give presents to the Indians. Hutchins reported discontent everywhere because of the lack of presents and ammunition.[30]

The management of the trade at Fort Pitt continued to be troublesome in 1762. In March, Bouquet complained to Amherst that although rum was forbidden, traders went into the woods and sold rum to the Indians. The traders involved knew the country well enough to avoid the posts with the help of the Indians.[31] Lieutenant Blaine stationed in Ligonier reported that preventing the traders from selling rum or trading without passes was impossible unless the army demonstrated with a severe example.[32] In April 1762, John Hart, a trader in Fort Pitt, had his rum confiscated by the army on Croghan's complaint that he had sold liquor to the Indians.[33]

In June 1762, Johnson called a meeting in Easton, Pennsylvania with the Delaware Indians. The Quakers quickly disagreed with Johnson and the Pennsylvania officials regarding the land question. As a result of the conference, the Walking Purchase of 1737 was abrogated and the land returned to the Indians.[34]

In August 1762, the Lancaster conference was held with Governor Hamilton, members of the Pennsylvania Council, representatives of the Quakers, and five hundred Indians representing the Six Nations, Delaware, Twightwee, Shawnee, Kickapoo, and other tribes. The objective was to secure the release of English prisoners and to establish a trade route in the west branch of the Susquehanna to the lakes. The Indians refused to permit use of this route, and the conference ended unsuccessfully on August 29, 1762.[35]

In September 1762, the Kickapoo Indians came to Fort Pitt asking for supplies and requested that Hugh Crawford be sent as a trader. Crawford was permitted to proceed, but presents were limited to the delegates to the treaties, rather than to the entire tribe as the natives expected. The Kickapoo were enraged and left threatening trouble.[36] In October, another party of Indians stopped in Fort Pitt on their way to fight the Cherokees, demanding ammunition and clothing. Bouquet instructed Croghan not to give presents until orders had been received from Amherst. On this occasion, Croghan refused the Indians, but feared that they would steal the supplies.[37] In November 1762, the Indians were uneasy for two reasons: First, no boundary had been run in Pennsylvania between the White and the Indian country. Second there was a shortage of ammunition. Croghan suspected the Quakers of stirring up the Indians, and in December, Croghan passed a report to Bouquet of a plot being hatched by the tribes who feared that the refusal of the British to provide ammunition was a sign that the English intended to attack them. The Delawares especially held their warriors near their towns to hunt and appeared sulky toward the traders living among them.[38] The Indians were disturbed about the new policies, for example, in December 1762, when a band of warriors from the Six Nations were refused presents in Fort Pitt, they protested the reduction of gifts since the end of the war and that traders were prevented from selling them ammunition and rum. Croghan responded that the war was over, and they must trap for pelts that could be used to buy supplies. Furthermore, the reason rum was not provided was because they misbehaved when drunk. Furthermore, because the Indians had not returned all of the prisoners, they had broken their promise as well.[39]

In the Fort Niagara area, the restriction on presents, especially gunpowder, was equally vexing to the Indians. In April 1762, the threats of Indian uprisings were current in western New York. Captain William Walters, the Indian agent in Niagara, reported that the Indians were uneasy about the lack of ammunition and the rumors that the English intended to kill them all. Amherst remained reluctant to give anything to the Indians, yet Walters saw no way to avoid presents. For the previous two years, he had furnished fish and ammunition to the Indians in order for them to survive. During the summer, those who came to trade had to be given small presents. He urged Johnson to relate his feelings to Amherst.[40] At a meeting in Johnson Hall in April 1762, Johnson met with four hundred Indians of the Six Nations. He asked them about the reports of plotting, and they replied that it had been stopped. They protested the bad treatment by the soldiers who threatened to shoot them and who would not feed them when they were starving. They reminded Johnson of the promises of cheaper goods and also requested that a trader be allowed to go to their villages because of the long distance to Niagara and Oswego.[41]

The Indians also realistically requested the prohibition of rum that was echoed in a petition from Niagara signed by twelve traders. The traders realized that too much rum would destroy the trade and therefore asked that the quantity of rum carried by a trader be limited to a reasonable amount compared to his other goods. The trader's attitude was based on the conviction that the tribes would not come to Niagara if they heard that there was no rum, and the traders would be bankrupted. The petition suggesting that a reasonable amount would be two gallons for Indians who came a long distance also suggested that the rum be given under the supervision of the post commander. The traders asked permission to sell only the stock that was already in Niagara, not to bring in additional supplies.[42] However, Captain Walters received a confirmation of Amherst's order to prohibit rum, and the passes from Johnson stated that no liquor was to be allowed. Therefore, in April 1762, Walters took all of the rum in Fort Niagara to the army storage area.

By the end of 1762, the Indians were planning to drive out the English by the spring of 1763. The Indians' main complaint in 1762 was the drastic reduction in presents. Further complicating the problem was the withdrawal of eleven regiments from the New York Province alone, and the general reduction of armed forces available to maintain order on the frontier. Also the French continued and, in fact, intensified the activity of arousing the Indians to resist British rule. Amherst was opposed to allocating money to buy Indian presents; he also thought bribery was not necessary because the Indians would be punished for misbehavior.[43] Amherst's policy was unwise for two reasons: First, the Indians did not consider the presents as bribes, but merely as an expected expression of good will. Second, there was a need to maintain Indian favor and to counter French influence.

Throughout 1762, the slow strangulation of the Indian Department efforts under Johnson by the economy measures of Amherst created dissatisfaction among the Indians. Of the consumer groups in the west—the army, the French traders and inhabitants, and the Indians—supplying the Indians had become more important since the end of hostilities. Through his policy of retrenchment, Amherst reduced significantly the Indian Department's ability to purchase from the merchants because the department was not allowed money to buy the necessary presents. This restricted policy also endangered the secondary market, that is, the direct exchange with the Indians of trade goods for furs. During his tour of the lakes, Thomas Hutchins noted in his journal on September 24, 1762, that the Indians complained because he did not bring presents, even though he went as an official messenger. The French had always given presents during both peace and war. During the hostilities, significant gifts had been offered three or four times a year, and there was always ammunition available at the post. The English had broken the custom so suddenly, and at the same time, the traders were allowed to bring only a limited quantity of ammunition. The few gifts from the post commanders were seen as mere trifles.[44]

The Indians, the army, and the Indian Department all had less to spend in 1762, and as the year ended, the Indians went to their winter hunting grounds filled with antagonism toward the British. The next year was filled with calamitous events that would profoundly alter the lives of everyone who lived and traded on the frontier.

In 1763, Amherst was directly responsible for Canada and the western lands, and British regiments were scattered throughout the area, which had no civil government. Without legislatures, there was no local machinery to levy taxes on Canada or the west, so the British government had to pay the complete cost of administration. A major economic upset occurred in Canada when the country was formally transferred to England by the Treaty of Paris in 1763. The French currency was no longer legal tender, and only part of the 41 million livres in French paper money ($410 million) in circulation in Canada in 1763 was redeemed. French merchants and wealthy farmers holding too much French currency were ruined, but given the time lag between the occupation and the peace treaty, few individuals would have been caught holding large amounts.[45]

The major event upsetting the colonial economy in 1763 was Pontiac's Rebellion. There were many causes for the uprising of the Indians in 1763. Among the divisive issues were Indian resentment regarding the small amount of powder and other merchandise given as presents, the high price of trade goods, the British prohibition of rum in contrast to their previous liberality during the war, the resentment of the Indians caused by thinly disguised British contempt for the natives, and the concern over settlements on Indian land. Indian bitterness was fanned by the unassimilated French and Pontiac who urged the Indians to strike out against the British.[46]

During April 1763, Amherst continued to receive reports regarding the unhappiness of the Indians. Croghan reported on April 30, 1763, that the Indians were disturbed by the surrender of their land to the British by the French in the Treaty of Paris.[47] A worried Major Gladwin in Detroit on April 20, 1763, reported that the traditional British allies—the Six Nations, the Shawnee, and the Delaware—were then ill disposed and tampering with the other Indians.[48] In a conference on April 21, 1763, the Onondagas, one of the Six Nations, complained to Johnson that they were short of ammunition to hunt in order to support themselves.[49]

The suspicious Johnson firmly believed that the French had stirred the Indians. In June 1763, he informed the skeptical Amherst of the French designs to agitate the Six Nations against the British. As early as April 1763, Johnson had written Croghan that he disagreed with the cost cutting at the expense of the Indians, but Johnson could not convince Amherst who was under pressure from London to reduce expenditures. In April, Johnson hoped that the Mississippi River would be the boundary with the French under the final terms of the Treaty of Paris. Illinois would then be a British territory with a resident Indian agent to conciliate the Indians, making it difficult for the French to arouse the Indians against the British.[50] As late as April 3, 1763, Amherst scornfully downgraded reports of Indian plots as "mere bugbears, and can never have any other effect than that of hurting ourselves by making us treat them as enemies and withdraw our friendship from them." Amherst could see no reason for supplying the Indians with provisions, as they would never provide for their families by hunting if they could be supplied by begging.[51]

The consensus among the British was that the French had created the atmosphere that encouraged the Indians to revolt by telling lies and spreading rumors with the objective of driving the British and colonials out of the Indian trade. F. Baby wrote to his relative in Detroit from LaRochelle in 1762, "I see with a heart full of bitterness the sacrifice of our youth passed in a barbarous country and our hard work brought to nothing by a stroke of fortune."[52] In Green Bay, Edmund Moran, a trader, wrote to his associate, Captain Evan Shelby, on May 14, 1763 (prior to the uprising), that the Indians seemed well inclined if it weren't for the "damd [sic] Canadians."[53] In April 1763, from the Ohio area, Alexander McKee, who had just returned from a tour of the Ohio meeting with the Indians, reported that the French instigated blocking of the passage down the Ohio by the Indians.[54] The French were using every means to harass British merchants according to John Welles, a merchant in Montreal.[55] The Albany trader, John Van Eps, reported that the French were agitating the Indians against the British.[56]

Once the rebellion was launched, Amherst believed that the French had been motivated primarily "to engross the trade to themselves," and that the French were surprised at the lengths to which the revolt had gone.[57] In September 1763, Amherst repeated this sentiment, believing that the clamor against the French was "great, owing to the jealousy of the traders." In a vengeful mood, Amherst ordered that if proof were found implicating the French, the guilty ones were to be sent to Montreal to be punished.[58]

The British administration placed the blame for the revolt squarely on the French and their desire to continue their profitable trade with the Indians. In December 1763, Johnson wrote Lieutenant Governor Colden of New York that the French had propagated the rebellion to strike at British trade and give the French some hope of reestablishing control by embroiling British affairs. The objective was to draw the fur trade to Illinois and down the Mississippi River.[59] Colden, in a letter to the Board of Trade during the same month, stated his belief that the Indian rebellion was closely tied to the availability of goods from Illinois. Early in the spring of 1763, the Indians had sent a large party down to New Orleans with beaver to purchase ammunition. The Indians claimed that a Frenchman, St. Luc Lecorne, had started to work on the Indians in 1761 and that the French Canadians had sent extra ammunition via the Ottawa River to avoid inspection at British posts.[60]

Colonel Bradstreet, who commanded the punitive expedition against the Indians in 1764, advised in a contemporary pamphlet that all the French and Canadians should be removed from the Wabash River valley, St. Joseph, Mackinac, and all of the other posts scattered among the Indians, and that the French should be concentrated in Detroit to prevent them from dealing with the Indians.[61]

There were reports from the Indians of the French in Illinois supplying the ammunition for the attacks.[62] Villiers, the French commander at Fort Chartres in Illinois, reported to Dabbadie, the French commandant in New Orleans, that the French traders had initiated the revolt, but that the rebellion had gone beyond what was expected. Villiers thought he could have stopped the conspiracy, but because he did not know about it, developments continued. When informed, he had sent belts (wampum belts serving as reminders to the person delivering an oral message) with Louis DeBeaujeu, Destauge, and Dequindre, but calming the Indians was difficult.[63]

Some of the French traders were convinced that once the Indians rose and drove back the British, a French army might be sent to assist the natives.[64] General Gage suggested that some of the French inhabitants in Montreal and Quebec be enrolled to fight the Indians to disprove the promises of French support for the uprising. On February 12, 1764, Gage ordered the recruitment of three hundred Canadians, but volunteers were not forthcoming, and the British had to resort to drafting men. The French Canadian soldiers were never used against the Indians.[65] The official denial of the story that the French would aid the Indians came from Villiers, the French commander in Fort Chartres. In October 1763, a French messenger arrived in Detroit with a definite statement that the French would not assist the Indians, as officially the French had made peace with England. This action by Villiers was of major importance in ending the rebellion because the Indians knew that the French would not help them.[66]

In Detroit, the French had supplied the Indians with food and ammunition before the revolt, and Major Gladwin, the British commandant, bitterly complained of French treachery, although the French also supplied the British with food. In St. Joseph, Louis Chevalier, the French leader, concealed two English traders, Richard Winston and Hambuck, while the garrison was being massacred. After Hambuck was taken prisoner, Chevalier appropriated Hambuck's goods and refused to pay for the stock in later years.[67] Although the French took financial advantage of the revolt, they gave the appearance of neutrality.

On June 29, 1763, the British army moved to deprive the Indians of ammunition. The complete prohibition of trade was initiated on August 3, 1763, by Gage in Montreal.[68] However, even Gage relented, and in September, when the Indians in Montreal pleaded for ammunition to begin hunting, Gage agreed to their request.[69] The Indians in the Toronto area also needed ammunition, claiming they had no part in the rebellion, and therefore begged that a trader be sent, as they were in distress for their necessities. Without the ammunition, they could not begin the winter hunt. Gage, on this occasion, refused to allow trade with the Indians, although Daniel Claus, the Indian agent, gave the three Indian deputies some merchandise.[70]

As reports of Indian victories were received, Amherst, who previously wrote bravely of punishing wrongdoers, had only a few military reserves to counter the attacks. The British regiments returning from Cuba were sickly and short of men.[71] On June 12, 1763, Amherst ordered the 42nd Regiment and the 77th Regiment, both recently returned from Cuba, to send their light infantry companies to Philadelphia to begin the reinforcement of western Pennsylvania. The remaining nine companies of the 77th Regiment had eighty men left, instead of the authorized nine hundred.[72] The light infantry company of the 17th Regiment went to Albany immediately, whereas the remainder of the regiment was to follow when ready. Amherst had probably ordered the three regimental commanders to transfer whatever healthy men were in their regiments to the light infantry companies and to dispatch those companies while Amherst searched for more men to fill the remainder of the companies in the regiments.

By June 25, 1763, Amherst had exhausted his reserves and then appealed to the governors of Pennsylvania, Rhode Island, Connecticut, and New Hampshire for garrison troops to relieve regular forces for active duty. The colonial government of New York refused to provide troops, as assembly approval was required and it was not in session. The Albany Dutch were willing to defend the frontier (twenty-five volunteered from Schenectady and twenty-five more from Canajoharie), but the volunteers had no ammunition and none was available.[73] Pennsylvania raised seven hundred men to protect the frontier settlements.[74]

In July 1763, Amherst received more military reinforcements from the West Indies. Five regiments arrived in New York, but the men were in poor condition and had to be placed on garrison duty. Men gathered from three regiments were sent to Detroit and were badly defeated by the Indians in an attempt to sally out of the fort and capture Indian supplies[75] The British received a further setback with the defeat of another force in Niagara on July 31, 1763.[76] Amherst was desperately trying to send as many men forward as possible to halt the Indians' attack.[77]

Amherst also asked Johnson to secure the assistance of the Mohawks.[78] In late June 1763, Johnson suggested bribing the Indians and urged that gifts be purchased for the Ottawas and the other western Indians to discourage them from joining the uprising. Amherst urged Johnson to preserve peace among the Indians in New York and approved of a meeting with the Six Nations.[79]

On July 18, 1763, Johnson assembled 340 Indians from the Six Nations except the Seneca. The Indians who attended were not in arms against the British; however, they did offer reasons for the rebellion, blaming the promises of the French, the high price of powder and trading goods, the ill treatment by the army, the garrison's refusal of provisions, and the existence of many small forts throughout their country maintained by the British. The Six Nations promised to remain peaceful, but they wanted the trade confined to the posts in Oswego and Niagara.[80]

On August 5, 1763, Bouquet won a battle against the rebellious Indians at Bushy Run near Fort Pitt. The English claimed a great victory even though only thirty were killed or wounded in the battle. The Indians maintained that there were very few warriors in the battle against the English.[81] The British continued to send more and more troops to the west, as the weakened regiments from the West Indies replaced the healthy regiments as garrisons in Montreal, Quebec, and elsewhere. Amherst even had plans for launching an attack from Fort Pitt toward Presque Isle with the objective of relieving Detroit, while Gage sent troops of the 80th Regiment from Fort William Augustus via Niagara to Detroit.[82]

During September and October 1763, Amherst and Johnson wrestled with conflicting ideas on resolving the problems of the frontier. In September 1763, the military situation had been stabilized, and the attention of the leaders turned to formulating policies to restore peace and trade to the west. In early September, Amherst relayed to Johnson that Lord Egremont in London had agreed with the bribery approach, and Johnson was authorized to expend £1,000 sterling as a present to the Indians. Amherst warned Johnson, however, that he was not to spend any additional money for bribes unless absolutely necessary to conciliate the tribes.[83] Johnson believed that because the £1,000 limit for presents had been established before the London government knew of the uprising, a much greater sum was necessary, and that Amherst would use his discretion to allow more money for gifts.[84]

On the matter of resuming trade, Amherst recommended that the tribes be permitted to buy goods only at the principal posts determined by Johnson with the exception of the Indians in the northwest who were to trade at Mackinac. Amherst refused the Indian demand to remove the small posts along the lines of communication. Johnson, on the other hand, believed that trade should be halted entirely, except in Montreal and Fort Stanwick. He suggested to Amherst that trade in Fort Pitt, Detroit, and Mackinac be closed until peace had been reestablished. However, the French supplied the unfriendly Indians from the Mississippi River, so closing the trade to them would have little effect.[85]

Johnson believed that only by treating the Indians as friends and allies and presenting gifts could the British occupy the western posts and carry on trade. If not well treated, the Indians would rob the traders. Hopefully, in a matter of a few years, the English traders would become strong enough to protect themselves, and then the cost of presents might be reduced.[86] On the other hand, Amherst was determined to punish the Indians before he would make peace. In order to retain some segment of Indian friendship for Johnson, Amherst ordered him not to be involved in this punishment, but to be ready to make a peace settlement at the appropriate time.[87]

The sharp division between the attitude of Amherst, the commander-in-chief, and the Indian Department was repeatedly expressed in late September and October 1763. Amherst believed that the Indians were troublesome because of the shoddy treatment by the colonial traders. However, the Indians must first be punished and subsequent negotiations would be on the basis that they would be forgiven and that trade would resume, but they would receive no presents. He was confident that Johnson would have the strictest regard for economy recommended by the Earl of Egremont, and that, in fact, because of the rebellion, the expense of the Indian Department should be lessened.[88] Contrary to this policy, Johnson sent a request for reimbursement of £700 New York for presents that Claus had given the Indians from the northwest who had escorted to safety the Mackinac garrison and traders. At the same time, Johnson asked for additional money for presents for the Six Nations.[89] Johnson's position was that ample gifts be made because the British should consider not only what the Indians had done, but what they could do in the future. The objective was to find "a method for rendering them as little consequence as possible." Johnson was aware that the Indians of the Six Nations had made it possible for Britain to win the French and Indian War in North America, but the tribes could still create havoc on the frontier. The only way to maintain peace, then, was to establish a strong Indian Department to prevent quarreling, which would be cheaper than conducting a war. Johnson believed that the British must make peace with the Indians east of the Mississippi because they could not be destroyed and driving them westward would only create a stronger enemy, if they allied themselves with the western Indians. Johnson maintained that the French were the cause of the trouble because they supplied the Indians from Illinois, and if the fur trade were stopped, the Illinois French would take over. The only policy open was to punish those who fought the British and give presents to those who were friends.[90]

Croghan was also at odds with Amherst during this period. He hoped to obtain leave to go to England to further his land schemes resulting from losses by merchants. Amherst refused while the Indians were still at war and, as a result, Croghan resigned. Croghan favored employing friendly Indians against the rebelling Indians, but Amherst refused because he did not believe they could be trusted.

The bad feeling between the Indian Department and the army was mutual. Robert Leake, a New York City merchant, told Croghan that the officers at Amherst's headquarters spoke very badly of the Indian Department and had no concern for the distress of the Indians.[91] Johnson supported Croghan's request for leave, believing that his personal affairs were urgent, and, because of the hostility of the Indians in the Ohio Valley, Croghan's dealing with them would be contrary to the British government's policy.[92]

Amherst was having other difficulties with the governors of the various colonies who refused to provide militia to assist the British army, and without the militia, the regular troops were required to garrison the posts. With the regulars tied to garrison duties, Amherst's hope for an offensive against the Indians in the spring would be at risk.[93]   The Earl of Halifax wrote the governors of Pennsylvania, New Hampshire, Massachusetts, Connecticut, Rhode Island, New Jersey, New York, North Carolina, and South Carolina, indicating the king's displeasure with their reluctance to provide provincial troops or militia and empowered Amherst to call on the governors for troops as needed. Yet on October 29, 1763, Amherst reported that Colden of New York claimed that he had no ammunition for the militia, nor could he obtain any until the assembly voted. The only promise that Colden would make was that he would put the militia on a respectable footing when the assembly met.[94] The difficulty in raising colonial troops confirmed the need for a regular army garrison in the west.

Colden was involved in controversy with the British government over a number of matters. He protested the complaint that New York had not provided militia when asked. The requisition for support from Amherst on October 30, 1763, asked for 1,400 men from New York and 600 from New Jersey, but none from New England, which Colden considered unfair. However, Colden had agreed to raise 300 men in addition to the 173 men already under New York pay at Oswego, Detroit, and Niagara. This number Colden felt was double the quota that New York should have been assigned had New England been requested to raise its fair share.[95]

Colden also protested the charge in British newspapers that the rebellion was caused by the Indians having been cheated of their lands.[96] Colden placed the entire blame for the rebellion on the French, who had been stirring up the Indians since the British conquest. The French had supplied the arms and ammunition, falsely telling the Indians that the French had not made peace, and that a French fleet and army was on the way.[97] Johnson pointed out to Colden that the French used presents, no matter what the cost, to hold the Indians to their alliance because presents were much cheaper than maintaining an army that could not control the Indians anyway.[98] Colden believed that the Indians made peace in the fall because the trade had been stopped and ammunition cut off. The Indians then realized that they could not do without the English goods. Colden believed that very little ammunition should be given to the Indians until a firm peace had been established and that the Indians should be punished for their deeds.[99] Johnson told Colden that he believed the Indians wanted peace because they expected better treatment, but the Indians would keep their promises only if the British fulfilled theirs. Peace would be maintained only if the Indians were treated well, because the French could always supply ammunition from Illinois.[100] Johnson did not believe that friendly Indians should be deprived of powder on the fearful supposition that they would give it to others. Not providing friendly Indians with powder would prove the French assertions that the British intended to kill all of the Indians.[101]

In conclusion, the Indian uprising in 1763 had a greater effect on the traders based in Pennsylvania than on any of the other groups of traders, because of all the posts taken, only Mackinac was not used by merchants from Pennsylvania. Croghan estimated that two thousand whites were killed by the Indians during the uprising, probably an exaggeration. About one hundred Pennsylvania traders were killed along with British traders in Mackinac, St. Joseph, and in the other posts. The deaths of other traders among the Indians were reported as the year passed. Most of the New York traders conducted business in Detroit, Niagara, and Oswego, none of which had been overrun. The Indian rebellion had comparatively little impact on the trade from Canada, as even at Mackinac only the colonial merchants were killed and robbed. Although most of the French traders left Montreal for the upper posts in April and May 1763, before the rebellion, the Indians directed their hatred toward the colonials and the British, and few if any Frenchmen were harmed.

The effect of the uprising in London was shattering. On August 13, 1763, Secretary of State Egremont wrote Amherst that the report of the Indian uprising had caused King George III great concern. The king agreed that the Indians deserved the severest punishment, yet he feared that the Indians would escape into the wilderness and finally force Amherst to bribe them with gifts to make peace, a method that had proved ineffectual in the past. Although the letter indicated that the king had firm confidence in Amherst's prudence and activity, soon thereafter the king relieved Amherst of his command and ordered him to return to England. Gage, second in command, replaced Amherst as commander, although he was not given the title of commander-in-chief in America.[102] After the crisis passed, Amherst followed instructions and returned to England, and Gage assumed command. With Amherst's departure, British policy changed. The rebellion had signaled the failure of Amherst's belief that the Indian objections to unregulated trade could be ignored.

NOTES

1. William L. Grant, "Canada Versus Guadeloupe," *American Historical Review*, 17 (July, 1912), 741.

2. Virginia D. Harrington, *The New York Merchant on the Eve of the Revolution* (New York: Columbia University Press, 1935), 310–11.

3. Jack M. Sosin, *Whitehall and the Wilderness, The Middle West in British Colonial Policy, 1760–1775* (Lincoln: University of Nebraska Press, 1961), 23.

4. John Shy, *Toward Lexington, The Role of the British Army in the Coming of the American Revolution* (Princeton, NJ: Princeton University Press, 1965), 108.

5. Egremont to Colonial Governors, December 12, 1761, Edmund B. O'Callaghan and Fernow Berthold, eds., *Documents Relating to the Colonial History of the State of New York*, 15 vols. (Albany, NY: Weed, Parsons & Co., 1853–87), 7:483.

6. Corry to Johnson, April 3, 1762, Sir William Johnson, *The Papers of Sir William Johnson*, 14 vols. (Albany: The State University of New York Press, 1921–65), 3:668.

7. Daniel Clark to [unknown recipient], May 4, 1762, Letter Book, Historical Society of Pennsylvania.

8. Daniel Clark to Holiday & Dunbar, June 4, 1762, ibid.

9. To Neale & Pigou, July 31, 1762, James & Drinker Letter Books, 1756-1762, Historical Society of Pennsylvania.

10. John Sanders Letter Book, New York Historical Society.

11. John and Peter Chevalier Daybook, August 13, 1762, Historical Society of Pennsylvania.

12. William Corry to Johnson, April 3, 1762, *Johnson MSS*, 3:668.

13. Colden to Amherst, March 31, 1762, *Colden Papers, New York Historical Society Collections* (1876), 184.

14. Chart D, Walter S. Dunn, Jr., "Western Commerce, 1760-1774," Ph.D. Dis. at the University of Wisconsin, 1971.

15. Baynton, Wharton & Morgan Memo Book, December 26, 1763, Baynton, Wharton & Morgan Microfilm, F10; John and Peter Chevalier Daybook, November 1763; John Sanders to Moses Franks, November 4, 1763, Sanders Letter Book.

16. John to Gage, August 25, 1763, *Johnson MSS*, 10:802-04.

17. Amherst to Bouquet, January 16, 1762, *Michigan Pioneer and Historical Collections*, 40 vols. (Lansing, MI: Wynkoop, Hallenbeck, Crawford Co., 1874-1929), 19:127-28 (hereafter cited as *MPHC*).

18. Amherst to Johnson, January 16, 1762, *Johnson MSS*, 10:353-54.

19. Johnson to Amherst, January 7, 1762, ibid., 3:598-601.

20. Johnson to Croghan, January 8, 1762, ibid., 604-05.

21. Croghan to Johnson, March 31, 1762, ibid., 662.

22. Croghan to Johnson, May 10, 1762, ibid., 732-33.

23. Croghan to Amherst, May 10, 1762, ibid., 10:452.

24. Amherst to Croghan, May 31, 1762, ibid., 459.

25. Amherst to Johnson, July 25, 1762, ibid., 475.

26. Johnson to Lords of Trade, August 20, 1762, ibid., 3:866-69.

27. Estimate of Western Department, August 28, 1762, ibid., 860-61.

28. Johnson to Amherst, August 28, 1762, ibid., 10:496; Amherst to Johnson, September 12, 1762, ibid., 508.

29. Johnson to Amherst, September 24, 1762, ibid., 3:884; Amherst to Johnson, October 17, 1762, ibid., 904-05.

30. Croghan to Johnson, May 10, 762, ibid., 733.

31. Bouquet to Amherst, March 7, 1762, *MPHC*, 19:131.

32. Lieutenant Blane to Bouquet, March 12, 1762, *Canadian Archives Report* (1889), 201.

33. James Kenny, April 6, 1762, "Journal of James Kenny, 1761-1763," *The Pennsylvania Magazine of History and Biography*, 37 (1913), 47.

34. Meeting at Easton with the Delawares, June 18, 1762, *Johnson MSS*, 3:760-91. The walking purchase received its name from the provision that all the land which a man could walk around in a given time would be included.

35. Croghan to Johnson, September 4, 1762, ibid., 873.

36. Sewell E. Slick, *William Trent and the West* (Harrisburg: Archives Publishing Company of Pennsylvania, 1947), 104.

37. Croghan to Johnson, October 8, 1762, *Johnson MSS*, 10:548-49.

38. Croghan to Johnson, November 10, 1762, ibid., 3:931; Croghan to Bouquet, December 10, 1762, ibid., 10:597.

39. Croghan to Johnson, December 10, 1762, ibid., 3:964-65.

40. William Walters to Johnson, April 5, 1762, ibid., 10:426-27.

41. Indian Proceedings, Johnson Hall, April 21-28, 1762, ibid., 3:690–717.

42. Collins Andrews, *et al.* to Johnson, April 27, 1762, ibid., 720.

43. Ibid., 345.

44. Thomas Hutchins Journal, September 24, 1762, ibid., 10:529.

45. Mason Wade, *The French Canadians, 1760–1945* (Toronto: Macmillan Co. of Canada, 1955), 48.

46. March 30, 1763, *Johnson MSS*, 4:97; Howard H. Peckham, *Pontiac and the Indian Uprising* (Princeton, NJ: Princeton University Press, 1947), 101.

47. Sosin, *Whitehall and the Wilderness*, 66.

48. Gladwin to Amherst, April 20, 1763, *Johnson MSS*, 4:95.

49. Journal of Indian Conference, April 21, 1763, ibid., 10:657.

50. Johnson to Amherst, June 6, 1763, ibid., 4:135; Johnson to Croghan, April 8, 1763, ibid., 10:651–52.

51. Amherst to Johnson, April 3, 1763, ibid., 649.

52. F. Baby to Duperon Baby, March 18, 1762, Baby Papers.

53. Edmund Moran to Captain Shelby, May 14, 1763, Moran Papers, State Historical Society of Wisconsin.

54. Captain Ecuyer to Bouquet, April 23, 1763, *CA Report* (1889), 224.

55. J. Welles to Johnson, November 1, 1763, *Johnson MSS*, 4:222–23.

56. Amherst to Johnson, August 14, 1763, ibid., 187.

57. Amherst to Johnson, August 14, 1763, ibid., 187.

58. Amherst to Johnson, September 30, 1763, *DCHNY*, 7:569.

59. Johnson to Colden, December 24, 1763, Franklin B. Hough, *Diary of the Siege of Detroit in the War with Pontiac...* (Albany, NY: J. Munsell, 1860), 216–17.

60. Colden to Board of Trade, December 19, 1763, *Colden Papers* (1876), 269.

61. Hough, *Diary of the Siege*, 148.

62. Intelligence from an Indian from Ouiatanon, July 11, 1763, *Johnson MSS*, 4:169.

63. DeVilliers to Dabbadie, December 1, 1763, *Illinois Historical Collections*, 10:49–50.

64. Nelson V. Russell, *The British Regime in Michigan and the Northwest, 1760–1796* (Northfield, MN: Carleton College, 1939), 41.

65. Alfred L. Burt, *The Old Province of Quebec* (Toronto: The Ryerson Press, 1933), 54–55.

66. Hough, *Diary of the Siege*, 148; Villiers to Inhabitants of Detroit, September 27, 1763, *Johnson MSS*, 10:222–23.

67. Hambuck to Edgar, March 23, 1767, Edgar Papers, 15, Burton Historical Collection.

68. Murray G. Lawson, *Fur, A Study in English Mercantilism, 1700–1775* (Toronto: University of Toronto Press, 1943), 55; Sosin, *Whitehall and the Wilderness*, 67.

69. Claus to Johnson, September 7, 1763, *Johnson MSS*, 4:200.

70. Claus to Johnson, October 1, 1763, ibid., 200; Hough, *Diary of the Siege*, 173–74.

71. Shy, *Toward Lexington*, 117.

72. Amherst to Bouquet, June 16, 1763, *CA Report* (1889), 229–30.

73. Johnson to Amherst, June 26, 1763, *Johnson MSS*, 10:717.

74. Amherst to Johnson, July 16, 1763, ibid., 4:173.

75. Sosin, *Whitehall and the Wilderness*, 68.

76. Alexander Duncan to Johnson, August 1763, *Johnson MSS*, 10:762–66.

77. Amherst to Johnson, July 7, 1763, ibid., 733.

78. Amherst to Johnson, June 26, 1763, ibid., 718–19; Sosin, *Whitehall and the Wilderness,* 67.

79. Amherst to Johnson, July 7, 1763, ibid., 10:733; Amherst to Johnson, July 28, 1763, ibid., 761.

80. Johnson to Amherst, July 24, 1763, ibid., 754–55.

81. DeCouange to Johnson, August 24, 1763, ibid, 790–91.

82. Gage to Johnson, August 12, 1763, ibid., 787–88; Amherst to Johnson, August 14, 1763, ibid, 4:187; Amherst to Johnson, September 9, 1763, *DCHNY,* 7:547.

83. Amherst to Johnson, September 10, 1763, *Johnson MSS,* 4:202.

84. Johnson to Amherst, September 14, 1763, *DCHNY,* 7:551.

85. Amherst to Johnson, September 10, 1763, *Johnson MSS,* 4:202.

86. Johnson to Lords of Trade, September 25, 1763, *IHC,* 10:33.

87. Thomas Moncrieffe to Johnson, September 13, 1763, *Johnson MSS,* 10:813.

88. Amherst to Johnson, September 30, 1763, *DCHNY,* 7:568.

89. Johnson to Amherst, September 30, 1763, *Johnson MSS,* 4:209–10.

90. Johnson to Amherst, October 13, 1763, ibid., 10:876–82.

91. Croghan to Johnson, September 28, 1763, ibid., 826.

92. Johnson to Amherst, October 13, 1763, ibid., 882.

93. Amherst to Johnson, October 16, 1763, ibid., 883.

94. Earl of Halifax to Amherst, October 18, 1763, *DCHNY,* 7:570; Amherst to Johnson, October 29, 1763, *Johnson MSS,* 10:912–13.

95. Colden to Halifax, December 8, 1763, *DCHNY,* 7:586–87; Gage to Johnson, November 30, 1763, *Johnson MSS,* 10:938.

96. Colden to Board of Trade, December 19, 1763, *Colden Papers* (1876), 270.

97. Colden to Halifax, December 22, 1763, ibid., 273.

98. Johnson to Cadwallader Colden, December 24, 1763, *Johnson MSS,* 4:275.

99. Cadwallader Colden to Johnson, December 28, 1763, ibid., 10:988.

100. Johnson to Colden, December 30, 1763, ibid., 4:282.

101. Johnson to Colden, December 30, 1763, ibid., 283.

102. Egremont to Amherst, August 13, 1763, *DCHNY,* 7:539–40.

9

New Imperial Policy, 1764

An imperial policy toward the Indians had been under discussion in London well before Pontiac's Rebellion. After the Capitulation of Montreal in 1760, there had been unfettered participation in trade with the Indians by discharged provincial and British soldiers who realized they could make enormous profits from the sale of liquor. In the early years, the rum peddlers secured a major part of the furs whereas the French, lacking a source of goods, received very few. No universal set of rules existed for the trade between 1760 and 1763 with British commanders (Amherst, Bouquet, and Gage), the Indian Department (Johnson and his deputies, including Croghan), and the colonial governors all issuing licenses and their own rules, but no one was able to enforce them.

Further aggravating the situation, the British government insisted on cutting costs. Amherst drastically reduced the presents given to the Indians and threatened punishment if they resisted. The rebellion, however, forced immediate action to replace the confused regulations that had been the norm until 1763. Amherst was made the scapegoat for the uprising and was ordered to turn over command to Gage. By encouraging the Indians to revolt, the French had ruined Amherst's career. Even though the rules were formalized in the proposed Plan of 1764, the policy was never introduced in Parliament, so funds were not appropriated to enforce the plan. The Proclamation of 1763, which prohibited land settlement, was a Royal edict, rather than a Parliamentary action.

At the same time that the conflicting philosophies were embroiling the frontier, the dispute boiled over to London. The British government was faced with two conflicting pressures: First, in order to prevent future rebellion, more money needed to be devoted to bribing the Indians and to supporting the garrisons on the frontier. Second, the English landowners in Parliament demanded economy to reduce taxes in England. An alternate to giving the

Indians the supplies they needed was to make the products available for purchase from traders. However, to force the Indians to trade their fur for needed goods, rather than rum, some form of regulation had to be developed.[1] Not only would regulation prevent the further loss of life, but a properly managed fur trade could be a source of profit to the empire.

In 1764, the colonial economy was in a recession. Daniel Roberdeau, a Philadelphia merchant, complained to his associates that times were very dull and that trade was slow. To Myler and Hall, his agents in London, he complained that goods could not be sold without nearly giving them away at very low prices. He commented that the Royal Navy warships were in the river hindering the smugglers. Less smuggling would favor honest men and therefore he expected his business to improve.[2]

Although a trickle of furs continued to come east from miscellaneous sources, there was an absolute prohibition of sending any goods west until peace was made with the Indians. Fur exports to England from both New York and Pennsylvania in 1765 dropped to 1760 levels.[3] The level of exports to Great Britain from the American colonies continued at a high level, £1,111,000 sterling in 1764, compared to £1,106,000 in 1763. This volume probably resulted from hurried shipments sent before November 1, 1764, to avoid payment of the stamp tax on clearance papers.[4] However, the combination of continued massive imports from England (£2,250,000 sterling) and the drop in military expenditures reduced the ability of the merchants to pay debts in England (see Table 1.1, p. 8).

The overall military establishment decreased in size from twenty regiments to eighteen. The greatest reduction was in New York where the 44th Regiment was withdrawn to Canada and the 55th and 80th Regiments were disbanded. Business with inhabitants in the west was reduced by the limitations imposed by the military on any shipments to Detroit and Fort Pitt and the great danger from the Indians. The result of this sharp imbalance was the lack of specie and bills of exchange to send to England in payment for goods received. This shortage was felt throughout the colonies in New York, Philadelphia, Boston, and Virginia. The New York newspaper, the *Mercury*, estimated the debt payable to England by the merchants at £4 million sterling ($800 million) in 1764.[5]

Baynton, Wharton & Morgan, through their connections in Havana, were still able to obtain Spanish dollars. For example, they sent to Neave on February 28, 1764, two shipments of Spanish dollars, one of 1,667 Spanish dollars and another of 3,000 on board the ship *Britannia*. These dollars had an estimated value of £1,800 Pennsylvania ($207,000).[6] Merchants in Albany, such as John Sanders, were sending silver dollars and Portuguese gold johannes in payment of their debts in England. The continued heavy shipments of specie abroad, however, resulted in shortages of money in the colonies. In January 1764, Henry Van Shaack wrote Johnson that a debt had not been paid because of the scarcity of money and the impossibility of obtaining cash in return for bills of exchange on New York City, indicating that money had been drained from not only the seaports but also from inner commercial centers such as Albany.[7]

The restoration of the fur trade as it had existed before 1760, was an important consideration in the writing of the Proclamation of 1763. The exclusion of the settlers prevented conflict with the Indians and protected the hunting grounds that were the source of the furs. Halting westward movement was intended as a temporary measure to allow time to carefully plan treaties and regulations. Colonial refusal to pay taxes to support the army and the Indian Department made the provisions of the Proclamation permanent, rather than temporary as planned. The Proclamation of 1763 prohibited settlement west of the mountains, but made few references to the regulation of the fur trade other than that trade with the Indians was to be open to everyone, provided that every person receive a license from Amherst, the commander—in—chief or a colonial governor and provide a bond to observe regulations to be made.

In early 1764, those in England concerned with the Indians in North America turned their thoughts to various plans for regulating the trade. The form of regulation and, of equal importance, the degree of enforcement, was hotly disputed. In August 1763, the Board of Trade invited the Indian superintendents for the northern and southern departments to propose regulations. In November 1763, Johnson replied that the Indian Department be given complete control of the Indians; that the trade be confined to posts; that there be a commissary at each post to control prices, supervise traders, and enforce regulations; and that each trader be licensed by the Indian Department.[8] If enforced, these rules would have given the colonial traders equal footing with the French, but there was little chance that the French winterers could be confined to the posts.

Johnson believed that trade should be permitted only at the principal posts such as Fort Stanwick, Ontario, and Niagara, where the traders would be protected from the Indians, rather than having the traders wander about the woods trading in the Indian towns. In the posts, the conduct of the traders would be under observation, and the Indians could be protected from cheating.[9] He believed that small posts were unwise because of the danger not only from the Indians, but also from the French traders, for as long as there were Frenchmen in the woods, they would promote quarrels between the British and the Indians.

Restricting trade to the major posts would reduce the cost of transportation and would lower the cost of the merchandise below the prices charged by the unsupervised traders in the Indian villages, who overcharged the Indians. Johnson believed that posts could be maintained where there was good communication by water using small vessels on the lakes. He believed that Detroit and even Mackinac could be maintained to draw furs from the western country. The concept of trade at the posts resulted from the experience in the Province of New York, where trade centered around Oswego, with the Iroquois acting as middlemen to carry the European goods to the tribes farther west.[10] The restriction to the posts was in direct contrast to the established French method of trading where the posts were mainly supply centers, and for the most part the individual traders lived with the Indians in their villages during the hunting season. Many of the French winterers who traded in the Indian towns were of mixed French and Indian parentage and technically were not in violation of the proposed post-only rule. The presence of the winterers eliminated the need of a trip to the posts for most Indians, and winterers delivered furs received from the Indians to their French employers.

The position of the British army was set forth in a book in 1763 by Colonel Bradstreet, commander of the northern expedition in 1764, whose conduct of Indian negotiations resulted in accusations of incompetency. Bradstreet believed that the trade should be confined to the trading posts. This policy would prevent the bateau men from being corrupted by life among the Indians because the natives would become the carriers of the fur to the posts. Prices could be established to prevent cheating by the traders and could be regulated by provincial commissaries from New York and Quebec. He saw Detroit as the main center of the trade, with Albany or Quebec serving as the intermediate depots. A strong fort in Detroit would gain the respect of the Indians. The fact that the French from the Mississippi would remain as competitors in the trade could not be ignored. The Indians would never be dependent solely on the English for their goods, so they must be treated with some care.

The role of the commander in Detroit, who would also be the commanding officer of the Great Lakes, would be to inspect the trade and punish abuses, and thereby gain the friendship of the Indians. The post commander would also be required to make gifts of rum, tobacco, and provisions, as had the French. Bradstreet also suggested that the Indians be assigned to various posts: the Six Nations to Oswego; the St. Joseph, Miami, Wabash, and Scioto tribes to Detroit and Fort Pitt; and the Indians west of Lake Superior to St. Mary's and Mackinac. He suggested that the amount of arms and ammunition be limited, and was especially concerned that the sale of rifles to Indians be prohibited because the rifles needed less powder and were more effective than the musket. He advised that goods in general be comparable to French goods sold at the same price. If all transport of goods on the lakes were in government vessels and the traders paid freight charges, the Indians could not rob the traders' boats on the way to Detroit and the other major posts. The government should control the portage at Niagara.

Bradstreet believed that restricting trade to the posts was fundamental, eliminating the winterers who led an evil life among the natives. The Indians could carry the furs to the posts, where prices would be regulated. The post commanders would punish abuses of the traders and distribute gifts. Many of these suggestions were included in the Plan of 1764.[11]

From December 1763 through July 1764, the Board of Trade discussed proposed regulations. In late 1763, Croghan, in part to support Johnson's program before the Board of Trade, resigned his post in the Indian Department and went to England, arriving February 11, 1764, with a variety of tasks. First, he was to represent the claims of the "suffering traders" to the government and attempt to gain compensation in the form of land grants. He also represented Johnson and his ideas regarding regulation. Amherst's harsh policy was in disfavor, and Croghan was in demand for his advice advocating more sensitive treatment. Army officers who had served under Amherst, for example Colonel Lee of the 44th Regiment, were leading an outcry against the former commander-in-chief, Amherst. His policies were thoroughly discredited as a result of Pontiac's Rebellion, but he continued to have a role in government councils in later years.

Croghan, the most sought after authority on the Indians in London, was called before the Board of Trade and Halifax, an influential man who was a friend of Johnson. Halifax believed that Johnson should have a fund for Indian relations independent of the army, but the political climate was concerned with economy, rather than additional expense.[12] Croghan believed that the real reason for the delays in enacting Indian regulation was the fear of introducing in Parliament any matter requiring additional expense, because any form of trade regulation had to include some means to obtain operational funds and raising money had to be approved by Parliament. Croghan believed that the minority party in Parliament would use the regulation issue to expose the false economy and other unsuccessful measures in Canada since 1759.[13]

Thomas Penn believed, perhaps naively, that the reason the Board of Trade did not discuss the matter of Indian regulation was because of the pressure of business while Parliament was in session, but he, along with Croghan, believed that as soon as Parliament adjourned, the Board of Trade would consider the matter of Indian regulation.[14] Trade regulation was delayed in the Board of Trade until the Houses of Parliament adjourned on April 20, 1764. After that, the Board of Trade could discuss the projected plans for Indian regulation without fear of criticism from Parliament.[15]

The impetus to remove the Indian Department from the control of the army and to create a separate source of funds to finance it was the result of Amherst's refusal to accept Johnson's advice in 1762 regarding liberal presents. Halifax believed that refusing to supply the Indians was an important cause for the Indian outbreak. Even though in 1763 Halifax had convinced Egremont, the secretary of state, that the policy of economy toward the Indians must be reversed, the only channel that Egremont could follow was to write Amherst advising him to follow Johnson's advice on the matter of presents. To prevent a repetition of that disaster, Halifax sought to transfer Indian affairs completely into Johnson's hands without army interference and directly subordinate to the Board of Trade.[16] Gage, commanding the army in North American, was advising Halifax concerning the plan for western affairs, urging that a series of military colonies be established in the west.[17] Bouquet, commander at Fort Pitt, also supported the policy of establishing a military frontier.[18]

In May 1764, Johnson once more urged the Board of Trade to establish regulations for trade and to provide funds for liberal presents. To support his position, he reported the success of the Indians friendly to the British in operations against the rebellious Indians. He strongly urged that only with regulated trade could either farming or the fur trade be carried on without constant war.[19]   In June 1764, the Board of Trade considered the matter of Indian regulation. As resource material, they had Johnson's report of November 18, 1763, a report from Croghan of June 8, 1764, correspondence from Gage and Stuart, the superintendent of the southern department, and testimony from Penn.[20]

Croghan's advice to the Board of Trade was that the Indians be guaranteed the permanent possession of their hunting grounds and that a trade should be established that would benefit both the Indians and British. Croghan saw no need for western posts that "neither support themselves nor protect the trade." He believed the secret to the success of the fur trade was presents, that the Indians considered presents a custom, and the British should regard the custom as good policy. Not to give presents was seen as a violation of the peace, and, although costly, was the cheapest and best method in the end to cultivate a friendship with the Indians. Croghan estimated that the war in 1763 cost more than £100,000 sterling ($20 million) and accomplished nothing, whereas annual gifts equal to the interest on £100,000 sterling would have ensured lasting peace. He believed "some favors annually bestowed on them will secure to us the valuable fur trade . . . with as many posts in that country as will be necessary for us to carry on the trade with them."[21]   On July 10, 1764, the Board of Trade issued its proposal, the Plan of 1764, based somewhat on Johnson's ideas.

The Plan of 1764, reflecting Johnson's ideas, was recommended to the British Cabinet. Of more than forty provisions, the most important were that the Indian Department have complete control of the Indians; all colonial regulations were to be repealed; licensed traders could deal only at posts or towns under the supervision of commissaries appointed by the two superintendents; prices were to be set by commissaries; no one was to acquire land except by negotiation with the Indians; Indian Department officers were to have the power of justices of the peace to settle disputes; and rifles and rum were prohibited. Credit to Indians was limited to 50/- ($500), an attempt to limit the use of Indians as winterers by the French to evade the post-only rule.[22]

To fund the expense of regulation, a variety of taxes were suggested, including an export duty levied at the ports proposed by James Grant, governor of East Florida. Stuart, the superintendent, of the Indian southern department suggested a ten percent duty on fur exports. Johnson disagreed with an export tax, suggesting either payment of a tax at the time of application for the trading license, or a five percent duty on all Indian goods, plus an additional five percent on liquor, arms, powder, and lead.[23]   Governor Murray of Canada objected to the entire idea of a tax on the fur trade, believing the only result would be smuggling or the diversion of the trade to other channels, for example down the Mississippi to New Orleans. Murray suggested that a well-regulated trade to prevent abuses was necessary, but did not offer any suggestions for financing this activity.[24]

The tax provision was the stumbling block that prevented the implementation of the plan. No tax could be levied without an act of Parliament, which was already embroiled in the problem of America and taxation. Throwing additional fuel on the fire for the sake of £20,000 for the Indian Department could not be considered. The Grenville-Bedford ministry in 1764 had promised Parliament to cut expenses and to alleviate the troubles with America. To present an additional tax for America was inconceivable. In 1765, the Board of Trade stated that "it would be advisable in the present state and situation of American affairs to postpone any representation thereupon." During the next four years, the Plan of 1764 was discussed but never brought before Parliament.

Although Parliament never considered the Plan of 1764, Gage authorized Johnson and Stuart to implement as many of the provisions as possible with money from the military budget. The first step of the implementation of the plan in the northern department was the distribution of gifts to the Indians by Croghan on a trip down the Ohio River to Illinois, and then down the Mississippi River to New Orleans. As a result, in October 1765, the British were finally able to occupy Illinois based on treaties made by Croghan. Trade was reopened in January 1765, under many of the provisions of the Plan of 1764, including the post-only rule, but the prohibition of rum was not attempted.

The restriction of trade to the posts caused a storm of protest from the Montreal and Quebec merchants. The required security bond was not obtainable because of the complex credit structure of the trade. The merchant provided goods on credit to the trader and in addition had to post a double bond on those goods. Should the trader have a petty falling out with an Indian officer, the merchant would lose three times the value of goods. Rather than security, merchants suggested confiscation of the goods and corporal punishment of the offender. Wintering, which was prohibited, resulted in having four times as many furs than if the trader simply waited for the Indians to come to the posts. If the British and colonial traders remained at the posts, the traders from Illinois would obtain all the furs and in addition stir up the Indians to cause more trouble. The credit structure did not work with the traders at the posts, for an Indian would have credit at one post and sell his furs at another.[25]

The major issue in Canada in 1764 was the disagreement among the French and British merchants and the military government under Murray concerning his arbitrary action to stop speculation in French paper money, war privileges, and the sale of liquor to the Indians. In February 1764, Haldimand reported that there was no paper money in Trois Rivieres, but that it was available in Montreal where merchants sold goods for paper money at a great discount. Haldimand had ordered the French not to sell paper money at a discount until a decision was made on its redemption.[26] Murray, on the other hand, accused the merchants of violating the suspension of trade and supplying the upper posts with goods to trade to the Indians by fraudulent practices.[27] Among the leaders of the opposition party were Thomas Walker, Zachary McCauley, and John Welles.[28] Walker, from Winchester, Pennsylvania, was later active in the Mackinac trade. Welles, a Montreal merchant from Albany and friend of Johnson, had opposed the policies of Amherst and believed that Amherst's poor military policy was basically at fault for the rebellion. Murray was also attempting to collect the duties on rum sent from New York to Canada, a measure that displeased both French and New York merchants, long accustomed to smuggling up Lake Champlain.[29] In March 1764, the Montreal gentry, merchants, and other inhabitants petitioned the Board of Trade to open the Indian trade to all who met the legal requirements and to eliminate all customs restrictions in Quebec and Montreal commerce.[30]

In reaction to Pontiac's Rebellion, Governor Ralph Burton had forbidden trade with the Indians in the upper lakes, but in April 1764, he authorized trade with the local Indians in Carillon on the Ottawa River and the Cedars on the St. Lawrence, while continuing the prohibition on the sale of arms, ammunition, and liquor to the Indians.[31] Although the Indians were anxious for peace, Burton refused to allow trade to resume.[32] No traders were permitted to pass the upper posts, and strict orders were given to the commanders to prohibit any trade.[33]

Canadian merchants were also making efforts to have compensation for their losses during the rebellion as part of any peace treaty. Gage agreed with the principle of compensation for losses; otherwise the Indians would be encouraged to run themselves into debt and then "cut our throats to clear off all scores."[34]

The major complaint by the French merchants against Murray was his favoritism toward the Scots. He appointed Captain Alexander Fraser, formerly of the 78th Regiment, as director of Indian affairs in Canada in direct competition with Daniel Claus, the Indian agent appointed by Johnson.[35] Welles and Ferrall Wade, Welles' associate, also complained of the Scottish influence on Canadian affairs.[36]

Welles estimated that the Canadian fur trade stood at £27,000 sterling ($5,400,000) annually in 1763, but could be increased to £85,000 sterling ($17,000,000) equal to nearly eight percent of all American exports to England in 1763, if business were properly conducted with open trade with the Indians.[37]

While the French and Scots were working out their differences in Canada, the problems of the New York and Pennsylvania merchants were eased in 1764 by the demand for supplies for the army garrisons in Canada and the upper lakes, and Indian presents. Most of the troops had returned from the West Indies by mid-1763 and were actively engaged in Pontiac's Rebellion. During 1764, two punitive expeditions were launched to demonstrate to the Indians that the British were masters of the western country and peace treaties were made with all the tribes.

The punitive expeditions required large expenditures for the British regular army and also the provincial troops—business that was beneficial to the merchants interested in western commerce. The great demand for presents, which were a necessary part of the peace treaties and congresses, also provided a large market.

In early 1764, Gage agreed with Johnson's liberal policy toward the Indians, but before any trade regulations were even specified, the war with the Indians had to be ended. Johnson had long favored the use of friendly Indians to fight the rebellious ones. By February 1764, he had sent two hundred Iroquois with White officers to fight the Delaware and the Shawnee in the Ohio Valley and was prepared to send more. Johnson thought this policy had a twofold value: It would result in alienation among the tribes that would continue after the war and make Indian management easier, and the Indians fought better than the regular troops, who took heavy losses fighting in the woods.[38] In March 1764, Johnson was able to report to Gage that he had sent out three hundred friendly Indians, who had been successful in their efforts against the rebellious Indians.[39]

The colonials continued their reluctance to provide men. Only Connecticut, New York, and New Jersey had offered troops by April 1, 1764. Pennsylvania procrastinated; they had voted to raise the men, but the governor and assembly disagreed about the supplies, and then adjourned until May 14, 1764.[40]

The economy drive in the British government in 1764 forced the Board of Trade to allow only £15,000 for surveying in the colonies and for the cost of the Indian establishment.[41] This sum included the cost of presents and the salaries of all employees of the Indian Departments both north and south. Therefore, Johnson had to draw on the military extraordinary expense account to supplement the sum allotted him.

The change in attitude of the army under Gage toward Johnson and the Indian Department and the liberal policy toward the Indians was dramatically demonstrated by the preparations for the peace negotiations in 1764. Johnson requested funds be made available to him to buy presents and, in order to economize, Johnson suggested that the goods be bought in New York, Philadelphia, or London, rather than from the traders in the Albany–Schenectady area. He believed that the most economical method would be for Gage to issue a warrant for £5,000 sterling (one million dollars) enabling Johnson to pay immediately and purchase goods at the lowest price to have on hand when the Indians arrived. He also requested two hundred good, light short guns for the Indians from army stocks.[42] Gage was favorable to the proposal and agreed that advance payment would enable procurement of goods at a lower price. Gage also promised to provide the guns from army arsenals, including 111 French guns and additional light guns of different sorts at Albany that would be delivered on request. The warrant for £5,000 sterling was duly issued on April 22, 1764, to Johnson.[43] This liberal policy differed sharply from Amherst's reluctance to issue warrants for even smaller amounts for presents. Johnson received the warrant for £5,000 sterling on May 3, 1764.[44]

Despite early hopes for peace, the Indians were reluctant to come to terms in April 1764. Johnson believed that their attitude was largely the result of French influence. The initial promises of peace were a result of the French failure to supply goods during the early part of 1764, as well as the Indians' need for English goods. With peace negotiations delayed indefinitely, more money was needed for presents to placate the Indians. Morally, the British could not kill off ("extirpate") all the Indians, nor did the merchants want to eliminate the Indians, because they were eager to resume trade with the tribes.[45] Therefore, the British continued to find a means to accommodate them.

However, Gage and Johnson were disappointed in the hope for a peaceful resolution of the Indian problem and made plans for two punitive expeditions, one under the command of Bradstreet via Niagara to Detroit, and the other under Bouquet to proceed from Fort Pitt down the Ohio River.[46] A conference with the Indians at Niagara was planned in conjunction with Bradstreet's arrival with the army. The terms proposed by Gage were (a) the Indians were to deliver the ringleaders of the war, as well as the murderers of the traders, to be executed for their crimes; (b) all captives, including White men, Negroes, and adopted French and British, were to be delivered; (c) all alliances between tribes, except the Six Nations, were to be renounced; (d) all claims to land east of the Ohio River from the head of the Ohio to the sea were to be renounced by the Western Indians, leaving the Six Nations with the only claim to land east of the mountains; (e) the traders were to be repaid for their losses; and (f) the Indians were to provide hostages if Johnson thought necessary.[47]

In June 1764, Johnson asked Gage for additional funds to carry out the planned negotiations and to supply Bouquet's army with Indian goods to take on their expedition. Johnson had already spent most of the previous warrant for £5,000 sterling in Philadelphia, nearly £3,000 Pennsylvania ($345,000) going to Baynton, Wharton & Morgan, a major transaction. Some of the merchandise had already arrived, having been ordered before Johnson received the warrant in April.[48]

During the summer of 1764, the Indians in Detroit were friendly, but were expecting presents from the British. Johnson demanded that the continuing abuses of the traders must be prevented in the future and restated the urgent need for frequent Indian congresses where presents could be offered.[49] Johnson outlined his policy for the Niagara meeting. Trade was to be closed temporarily to impress the Indians of their need, and all trade was to be prohibited at the small western posts that were not secure.[50] No further passes were to be given to the Indian towns, and trade was to be limited to the major posts: Detroit, Niagara, Oswego, and perhaps Mackinac and Fort Pitt.[51] Gage agreed with Johnson's plan to stop trade for a period to let the Indians feel their need and approved the recommended list of posts and limitation of trade to those posts. In late June 1764, Gage expected instructions on regulation of Indian trade from London that would include limitation to the posts.[52]

The first punitive expedition under Bradstreet had a slow start. When Bradstreet became ill in Oswego, the 17th Regiment and the New York troops were forced to wait from May until July 1764.[53] In July, Bradstreet arrived in Fort Niagara with twelve hundred soldiers and met more than seventeen hundred Indians. The Indians were suffering because trade had been cut off and they lacked food, powder, knives, axes, and other necessities. The Indians requested that they be allowed to trade furs for rum. Johnson initially refused on the grounds that until the Indians were made aware of their errors, there would be no trade, and the traders began to pack up. However, Johnson relented and gave the Indians a present of ammunition, clothing, and rum, and finally granted them trade in Niagara because of their promises to keep the peace and return prisoners.[54]

The Niagara meeting settled matters with the Huron, Ottawa, Chippewa, Sauk, Puan, Fox, and Menominee, all the major western tribes in the rebellion except about three hundred Indians on the Maumee River led by Pontiac and the Potawatomi.[55] On July 17, 1764, Johnson made a treaty with the Hurons under terms that included the cessation of the war, return of all captives, and full passage to the British in return for opening trade. Johnson wrote the Board of Trade that his terms were liberal because, unless they were promised trade, the Indians would resort to plundering. The traders were anxious to begin again to avoid being ruined, because they could not pay their bills in Europe.[56]

On August 2, 1764, the Senecas arrived and Colonel Bradstreet was forced to delay his departure for Detroit because he did not have enough men to leave a sufficient garrison at Fort Niagara, which was surrounded by nearly two thousand Indians. Sixteen hundred of these Indians were warriors. Bradstreet instead planned to leave on August 6, 1764, with an Indian escort.[57] The Senecas gave the British a large section of land at Niagara. The land was four miles wide on both sides of the Niagara River, giving the British control of the portage.[58]

Bradstreet reached Presque Isle and signed articles of peace with the Huron of Sandusky, Shawnee, Delaware, as well as other tribes from the Scioto plain. The Indians had begged for peace, and Bradstreet concurred on the terms that they agree to deliver their prisoners, give hostages, relinquish their claims to forts, allow the punishment of murderers, and make an alliance with the British against those breaking the peace. In return, Bouquet's punitive expedition from Fort Pitt would be stopped.[59] Prior to receiving news of Bradstreet's treaty at Presque Isle, Gage complained to Johnson that none of the tribes directly involved in the rebellion had asked for peace, and yet Bradstreet had not punished the guilty Indians.[60] The treaty that Bradstreet made at Presque Isle was seen later as being an Indian device to forestall an attack by Bouquet from Fort Pitt. The Indians at the treaty had no authority to make such promises and commitments on behalf of other tribes.

However, feeling that he had succeeded, Bradstreet went on to Detroit, arriving on August 26, 1764, and proceeded to make a treaty with the Indians in that area. The Indians agreed that Pontiac would be surrendered to the English and sent to the east coast. Bradstreet reported that the Detroit barracks were in bad condition and that he intended to build new ones. He had raised two companies of fifty men from among the inhabitants and planned to send them to Mackinac on August 29, 1764. He also sent word to the Illinois Indians that they must permit the English to come in or they would be attacked.[61]

On September 2, 1764, Gage received a copy of Bradstreet's treaty at Presque Isle and Johnson's report on the Niagara treaty. Regarding Johnson's opening the trade, Gage preferred to wait until he had more information. Regarding the Bradstreet treaty, Gage was angry that there was no mention of punishment for the murderers and that Bradstreet had no authority to make the treaty, only to refer the Indians to Johnson and to suspend fighting. Gage considered the treaty derogatory and refused its ratification. He ordered Bouquet and Bradstreet to resume the attack on the Indians.[62] Johnson arrived in Detroit in early September 1764, and held a congress with the Chippewa, Ottawa, Miami, Potawatomi, and Sauk tribes. The Ottawa and Chippewa had already made a treaty with Bradstreet stipulating that the Indians should keep the peace or be punished. The Indians also agreed to deliver their prisoners and, in return, a pardon was given Pontiac.[63]

On September 14, 1764, Bradstreet left Detroit and held a conference with the Wyandot in Sandusky on September 29, 1764. There he offered terms similar to the previously mentioned treaties. At the same time, he issued passes for Indian trade to the north and ordered that they be respected.[64] Bradstreet's expedition dissolved in early October 1764. The Indians of the Five Nations who had accompanied Bradstreet wanted to return home and refused to attack the Shawnee as Bradstreet requested. The Five Nations preferred to await the return of a party sent against the Delaware before beginning a war with the Shawnee.[65]

Gage and Johnson were opposed to Bradstreet's treaty at Presque Isle in August 1764, and Bradstreet began collecting evidence proving that Johnson had actually ordered the Indians accompanying Bradstreet to make peace with every tribe that released prisoners.[66] On October 15, 1764, Gage wrote Bradstreet berating him for signing the peace with the Shawnee and the Delaware. Bradstreet had been tricked by the Indians who had no intention of fulfilling the promises they had made in return for ending hostilities. In any event, Bradstreet had no authority to sign a treaty, and he should not have made the peace when the Indians came without the usual wampum belts that were the accepted form of preserving the proceedings of a conference. Gage's only hope was that Bradstreet had retained the hostages.[67] The northern campaign had failed because of Bradstreet's lack of ability and Gage referred to him as having immoderate vanity, self-opinion, puff, bluster, and being guilty of very suspicious behavior.[68] Johnson was also extremely critical of Bradstreet's conduct that had resulted in serious waste to the army and loss of face among the Indians. The Five Nations had been detained from their spring hunt because of their service with the army and were in need of ammunition. Johnson felt that all of this effort had achieved nothing because of Bradstreet.[69]

Although the punitive expedition in the Great Lakes area had failed miserably because of Bradstreet's ineptitude, a similar expedition in the Ohio Valley was marked with great success under the able leadership of Bouquet who prepared an army of fifteen hundred men in Fort Pitt for the a punitive expedition to Muskingum and the Scioto River. The Province of Pennsylvania had promised to raise troops for the expedition, but not replacements for the regular regiments; the Pennsylvanians preferred to serve with provincial regiments because of the higher pay. Bouquet suggested to Gage that because many deserters were in the country, a pardon might be offered to old soldiers who returned. Each of the old soldiers was worth three recruits in Bouquet's mind.[70]

Pennsylvania voted to raise one thousand men, but they were so late that planning was disrupted. Of the more than nine hundred men from Pennsylvania who were recruited for the campaign, two hundred had deserted before the army marched and more deserted later.[71] Bouquet was rather disgusted with the Pennsylvanians, writing in July 1764 that after all the talk, the frontiersmen preferred to be wagoners and drivers, rather than soldiers. Although many Virginians had volunteered to serve in the expedition, not a single Pennsylvanian volunteered. A great deal of money was being spent for the protection of Pennsylvania with no response on their part. Perhaps in the future, the frontiersmen would have to protect themselves. Bouquet was frustrated and hoped that would be the last time he would have to risk his reputation for their sake.[72]

On September 17, 1764, Bouquet started down the Ohio Valley with a battalion of the 60th Regiment, the 42nd Highlanders, and a detachment of the 77th Highlanders.[73] The army soon met with the Senecas living on the Ohio (the Delaware and the Shawnee), and held a conference in Muskingum in October 1764. Edward Moran thought that the Indians were "damnably scared" at seeing such a large army in their country.[74] Although the Delaware behaved well, the Shawnee were troublesome and finally cooperated only a few days before the treaty was signed on November 15, 1764. The terms included the return of captives, no further hostilities, and exclusion of traders from the Indian towns, including French traders. The British were to maintain garrisons at Fort Chartres on the Mississippi and Fort Massiac on the Tennessee River to cut off the French traders.[75]

Gage was pleased with Bouquet's dealing with the Shawnee in contrast with the ineptitude of Bradstreet.[76] By the end of November 1764, Bouquet's expedition was completed and the Royal American Regiment returned to the east coast, along with the two battalions of Pennsylvania troops. The garrison of Fort Pitt and the smaller Pennsylvania forts was reduced to the 42nd Regiment, with five companies at Fort Pitt, two companies each at Fort Ligonier and Fort Bedford, and a half company each at Fort Cumberland and Fort Loudon.[77]

Although a peace agreement had been signed and the Indians were to be treated as friends, there was no definite treaty, nor any method of trade regulation. Therefore, on November 29, 1764, Bouquet ordered the officers in Forts Bedford, Cumberland, Ligonier, Pitt, and all the other posts on the Ohio not to permit the passage of liquor, dry goods, or merchandise. If the traders tried to pass these items, their cargo was to be seized and held in the king's stores. Goods were to be sent to Fort Pitt for the use of the troops only with a pass from Gage.[78]

Whereas Bouquet's policy was to prevent or delay trade with the Indians, Johnson's intentions were far different. In November 1764, he instructed Croghan, who had returned from London, to proceed to western Pennsylvania to promote peace with the Indians. Croghan informed McKee, his agent in Fort Pitt, that a change had been made in managing Indian affairs that declared Indian agents independent of post commanders. Croghan reported that he was on his way to Fort Pitt to open the trade. McKee was to inform the Indians, who were to be ready to bring in furs when Croghan arrived, but until he arrived, they were not to trade. McKee was not to tell the army about these instructions, but could report that Croghan was on his way.[79] Bouquet was informed that Croghan was sending letters contrary to policy, and ordered Captain William Murray in Fort Loudon to open Croghan's letters and delay delivery.[80] When Gage reprimanded Bouquet for this action, Bouquet agreed that he would not interfere with Indian management. Nevertheless, Bouquet regretted that power had been delegated to a man such as Croghan who he considered "illiterate, impudent, and ill bred." He accused Croghan of subverting the purpose of the government and of a ridiculous display of his own importance. By destroying harmony among the branches of the armed service, Croghan hoped to hasten the opening of trade with the Indians.[81] There was a definite split between Bouquet's policy, which more or less represented the official army attitude, and the policy of Johnson. Opening Johnson's letters to Croghan created a considerable stir.[82] Nevertheless, Johnson's policy prevailed, and on December 7, 1764, Gage informed Governor Penn of Pennsylvania that New York's governor intended to publish a proclamation opening Indian trade on the condition that the traders take licenses from the governor and give bond and security to trade only at established posts. Therefore, Penn might do likewise, and Gage asked if there were any further regulations so that he might instruct the commanding officers at the posts to ensure that the traders complied with the terms of the government to which they belonged.[83] However, by the end of the year, trade still had not been opened in Pennsylvania. Three Delawares, who came to Fort Augusta in December 1764 to trade a canoe load of skins were refused and told not to come to the post until peace had been firmly established.[84]

In December 1764, Johnson hoped that shortly he would receive his final orders.[85] Gage, in the meantime, had reports from the post commanders in Detroit and Mackinac of their intent to make large purchases of presents for the

Indians. Gage asked for Johnson's opinion as to when the presents were necessary to maintain the Indians because the British could not meet all of their needs. Even though gifts were necessary, without guidelines the officers in the posts would recklessly provide clothing for entire nations. Gage was under constant pressure to cut expenses, and wrote Johnson, "We must curtail all our expenses as much as is possible which I must earnestly recommend to you for they grow very uneasy at home about it. I have very strong letters from the treasury on that subject."[86] As 1764 came to an end, the conflict between the liberal and the restrictive policy toward the Indians moved from America to London. Whereas in 1763 the conflict was between Johnson and Amherst in America, in 1765 the treatment of the Indians and the costs involved would become a major issue in Parliament.

In America, irreconcilable differences divided the economic and social groups, each believing that their needs should take priority in any policy. Several factions in America were opposed to taking land from the Indians. Two of these factions were the Indian Department under Johnson and the Quakers in Pennsylvania. The primary goal of the British government was to promote a policy that would reduce friction and possible conflict and to prevent any violence that would lead to major military expenses. Of all the groups, only the Indians with French support threatened violence, and under the pressure of humanitarian forces in England, the British government finally opted for a policy favorable to the French and Indians.

The post-only and no rum rules were finally enforced in New York and Pennsylvania, but only after the dangers of trading in the woods had been demonstrated by Pontiac's Rebellion. The French merchants circumvented the post-only rule by employing winterers of mixed parentage. The French had intermarried with the Indians and were more amenable than were the colonials to the welfare of the tribes.

As a result of the enforcement of the regulations, major merchants such as Baynton & Wharton abandoned the fur trade in Canada, Pennsylvania, and Detroit and turned to supplying the army. Many of the minor traders from Pennsylvania and New York were killed by the Indians during the uprising and few were daring enough to succeed them in direct trade in the Indian towns. Those who remained in the trade were forced to settle for whatever furs the Indians brought to the posts at Niagara, Oswego, Detroit, Fort Pitt, and other posts near the settled areas.

Pennsylvania and New York fur traders desired minimum regulation to enable them to profit from trade at the expense of the Indians; the land speculators wanted the west opened for claims, taking land from the Indians; the humanitarians, including the Quakers, promoted steps to protect the Indians against encroachment from both groups. The French traders in Canada and Illinois wanted a policy that would control the availability of rum and confine the colonial traders to the posts. The Indians realized that the French traders would best protect their interests.

NOTES

1. Croghan to Lords of Trade, June 8, 1764, Edmund B. O'Callaghan and Fernow Berthold, eds., *Documents Relative to the Colonial History of the State of New York*, 15 vols., (Albany, NY: Weed, Parsons & Co., 1853–87), 7:603 (hereafter cited as *DCHNY*).

2. Daniel Roberdeau to Hugh MacMurphy, July 7, 1764, Roberdeau Letter Book, Historical Society of Pennsylvania; Roberdeau to Myler & Hall, July 6, 1764, ibid.

3. U.S. Bureau of the Census, *Historical Statistics of the United States, Colonial Times to 1957* (Washington, DC: U.S. Government Printing Office, 1960), 762. In 1765, New York exported £5,565 in value and Pennsylvania £1,927. In 1760, New York exported £1,023 and Pennsylvania £1,879.

4. Merrill Jensen, *The Founding of a Nation* (New York: Oxford University Press, 1968), 129.

5. Virginia D. Harrington, *The New York Merchant on the Eve of the Revolution* (New York: Columbia University Press, 1935), 318.

6. Baynton, Wharton & Morgan Memo Book, February 28, 1764, Baynton, Wharton & Morgan Microfilm F10; Journal A, February 28, 1764, ibid., F7.

7. Henry Van Schaack to Johnson, January 28, 1764, Sir William Johnson, *The Papers of Sir William Johnson*, 14 vols. (Albany, NY: The State University of New York Press, 1921–65), 4:311.

8. Louise P. Kellogg, *The British Regime in Wisconsin and the Northwest* (Madison: State Historical Society of Wisconsin, 1935), 30.

9. Johnson to Colden, January 12, 1764, Franklin B. Hough, *Diary of the Siege of Detroit in the War with Pontiac...* (Albany, NY: J. Munsell, 1860), 228.

10. Johnson to William Eyre, January 29, 1764, *Johnson MSS*, 11:23.

11. Hough, *Diary of the Siege*, 146–53.

12. Croghan to Johnson, March 10, 1764, *Illinois State Historical Collections* (Springfield: Trustees of the Illinois State Historical Library, 1903-), 10:223 (hereafter cited as *IHC*).

13. Croghan to Johnson, April 14, 1764, *Johnson MSS*, 4:397.

14. Thomas Penn to Johnson, April 14, 1764, ibid., 11:125–27.

15. Croghan to Johnson, April 14, 1764, ibid., 4:397.

16. Thomas Penn to Johnson, April 14, 1764, ibid., 11:125–27.

17. Gage to Halifax, April 14, 1764, *DCHNY*, 7:620.

18. Jack M. Sosin, *Whitehall and the Wilderness, The Middle West in British Colonial Policy, 1760-1775* (Lincoln: University of Nebraska Press, 1961), 72.

19. Johnson to Lords of Trade, May 11, 1764, *DCHNY*, 7:624–26.

20. Sosin, *Whitehall and the Wilderness*, 75.

21. Croghan to Lords of Trade, June 8, 1764, *IHC*, 10:258.

22. Plan for Imperial Control, July 10, 1764, ibid., 10:273–79.

23. Johnson to Lords of Trade, October 8, 1764, ibid., 10:326; Clarence W. Alvord, *The Mississippi Valley in British Politics*, 2 vols. (Cleveland, OH: Arthur H. Clark Co., 1917), 1:224–25.

24. R. A. Humphreys, "Governor Murray's Views on the Plan of 1764 for the Management of Indian Affairs," *Canadian Historical Review*, 16 (1935), 166, 169.

25. Colonial Papers, Minnesota Historical Society.

26. Haldimand to Gage, February 27, 1764, *Canadian Archives Reports* (1885), 146 (hereafter cited as *CA Reports*).

27. Marjorie Reid, "The Quebec Fur Traders and Western Policy, 1763-1774," *Canadian Historical Review*, 6 (March, 1925), 22.

28. Burton to Lords of Trade, February 1, 1764, Gustave Lanctot, *Las Canadiens Francais et Leurs Voisins du Sud* (Montreal: Bernard Valiquettes, 1941), 96.

29. Murray to Lieutenant Colonel Irving, May 18, 1764, *CA Reports* (1912), 95.

30. Canadian Petition to the Board of Trade, John Welles to Johnson, March 30, 1764, *Johnson MSS*, 4:381.

31. Governor Ralph Burton to Johnson, April 17, 1764, ibid., 4:400.

32. Burton to Johnson, June 6, 1764, ibid., 4:441.

33. John Welles to Johnson, May 10, 1764, ibid., 4:418; Lieutenant John Donnellan to Johnson, August 11, 1764, ibid., 4:503; Murray to Burton, August 20, 1764, *CA Reports* (1912), 96.

34. Claus to Johnson, May 10, 1764, *Johnson MSS*, 4:418; Gage to Johnson, January 31, 1764, ibid., 315.

35. Claus to Johnson, August 30, 1764, ibid., 516; Claus to Johnson, August 30, 1764, ibid., 11:341–42.

36. Welles & Wade to Johnson, September 17, 1764, ibid., 4:540.

37. J. Welles to Johnson, November 1, 1763, ibid., 4:222–23.

38. Johnson to Commissary General Leake, February 9, 1764, Edmund B. O'Callaghan, ed., *The Documentary History of the State of New York,* 4 vols. (Albany, NY: Weed, Parsons & Co., 1849-51), 2:467.

39. Johnson to John Stuart, March 18, 1764, *Johnson MSS*, 11:103.

40. Gage to Johnson, April 1, 1764, ibid., 4:382.

41. Sosin, *Whitehall and the Wilderness*, 74.

42. Johnson to Gage, March 16, 1764, *Johnson MSS*, 4:371.

43. Gage to Johnson, March 26, 1764, ibid., 4:378.

44. Johnson to Gage, May 3, 1764, ibid., 11:171–72.

45. Johnson to Colden, April 6, 1764, ibid., 4:387; Johnson to Gage, April 27, 1764, ibid., 11:162–64.

46. Gage to Johnson, May 4, 1764, ibid., 175–76.

47. Gage to Johnson, May 16, 1764, ibid., 4:425.

48. Johnson to Gage, April 14, 1764, ibid., 11:128–29.

49. Johnson to Gage, June 9, 1764, ibid., 221–23.

50. Johnson to Colden, June 9, 1764, ibid., 4:443.

51. Gage to Johnson, June 24, 1764, *IHC*, 10:268.

52. Gage to Johnson, June 24, 1764, ibid., 268.

53. Alexander Duncan to Johnson, May 26, 1764, *Johnson MSS*, 4:431.

54. Indian Conference at Niagara, July 9-August 6, 1764, ibid., 11:262–329.

55. Johnson to Colden, August 23, 1764, ibid., 4:511–12.

56. Johnson to Lords of Trade, August 30, 1764, *IHC*, 10:307.

57. Johnson to Gage, August 5, 1764, *Johnson MSS*, 11:324–27.

58. Johnson to Bouquet, September 1, 1764, ibid., 4:517.

59. Bradstreet Articles of Peace, August 12, 1764, ibid., 503–7.

60. Gage to Johnson, August 15, 1764, ibid., 508–9.

61. Bradstreet to Johnson, August 28, 1764, ibid., 11:340–41.

62. Gage to Johnson, September 2, 1764, ibid., 4:521.

63. Congress of Western Nations, September 7-10, 1764, ibid., 526–33.

64. Conference with the Wyandots, September 29, 1764, ibid., 547–48; Bradstreet to Lieutenant Colonel Campbell, October 10, 1764, Hough, *Diary of the Siege*, 288.

65. Indian Conference at Sandusky, October 5, 1764, *Johnson MSS*, 11:373–74.

66. Gage to Johnson, September 16, 1764, ibid., 4:537–39.

67. Gage to Bradstreet, October 15, 1764, *IHC*, 10:345–46.

68. Gage to Johnson, November 29, 1764, *Johnson MSS*, 4:605.

69. Johnson to Gage, December 6, 1764, ibid., 11:491–95.

70. Bouquet to Gage, May 27, 1764, *IHC*, 10:251–52.

71. Gage to Johnson, June 3, 1764, *Johnson MSS*, 4:439; Sosin, *Whitehall and the Wilderness*, 71; *Pennsylvania Archives*, 1st ser., 12 vols. (Philadelphia: Joseph Severns & Co., 1851–56), 4:206; *Michigan Pioneer and Historical Collections*, 40 vols. (Lansing, MI: Wynkoop, Hallenbeck, Crawford Co., 1874–1929), 9:273 (hereafter cited as *MPHC*).

72. Bouquet to John Harris, July 19, 1764, *CA Reports* (1889), 260.

73. Frederick Watson, *The Story of the Highland Regiments* (London: A & C Block Ltd., 1925), 38.

74. Edmund Moran to Evan Shelby, October 21, 1764, Moran Papers, State Historical Society of Wisconsin; Conference with the Senecas, October 17, 1764, *Pennsylvania Colonial Records, 1683-1790*, 16 vols. (Philadelphia: J. Severns & Co., 1851–52), 9:214.

75. Bouquet to Johnson, November 15, 1764, *Johnson MSS*, 4:585.

76. Gage to Bouquet, October 15, 1764, *IHC*, 10:347–48.

77. Bouquet to Gage, November 30, 1764, ibid., 365.

78. Bouquet to Gage, November 15, 1764, *MPHC*, 19: 279–81.

79. Johnson to Croghan, November 6, 1764, *Johnson MSS*, 11:397–98; Croghan to McKee, December 4, 1764, *CA Report* (1889), 312.

80. Bouquet to Captain W. Murray, December 14, 1764, ibid., 313.

81. Bouquet to Gage, December 22, 1764, ibid., 313.

82. Hugh Wallace to Johnson, December 24, 1764, *Johnson MSS*, 4:629.

83. Gage to Penn, December 7, 1764, *IHC*, 10:370–71.

84. Lieutenant C. Graydon to the Governor of Pennsylvania, December 31, 1764, *Pennsylvania Archives*, 1st ser., 4:214.

85. Johnson to Bouquet, December 17, 1764, *Johnson MSS*, 4:620.

86. Gage to Johnson, December 16, 1764, ibid., 618.

10

Conclusion

The fur trade and supplying the British army in North America were vitally important to the colonial economy from 1760 to 1764 because the proceeds of both were used to balance trade with Britain. Furs worth up to £100,000 sterling (about ten percent of exports to Britain) were sent directly to British merchants to balance accounts for merchandise imported into the colonies. British payments ranging from £1.1 million sterling in 1760 to £376,000 in 1764 to pay and supply the troops were made in the form of bills of exchange that also were used to pay British merchants in England for goods imported to the colonies. The two sources, fur and supplying the army, were essential to maintain some proximity of balance between the colonies and Britain.

Above all, Britain wanted peace on the frontier because fighting the Indians was expensive (£753,000 sterling in 1763). After Pontiac's rebellion, the new British policy in fact gave the fur trade back to the French and to the new British merchants in Montreal and Quebec on the assumption that the two groups would have peaceful relations with the Indians. The rights of the colonists were ignored, and to add to their injury, the British taxed the Americans to pay for the army to help the French and keep the colonists out.

The new imperial policy not only deprived the colonial merchants of the furs used to pay for imports from Britain, but also deprived them of the British credits formerly used to pay for the army. From minor deficits or surpluses from 1760 to 1763, the deficit increased sharply in 1764, a shortfall of nearly one-third.

The relative value of the fur trade in the colonial economy is difficult to determine because the flow of goods to the frontier included imports of manufactured goods from England, merchandise (especially rum that constituted fifty percent of the total value of the trade goods) produced in America, and services to move the goods to the Indian market. Evidence is fragmentary and

Table 10.1

Consumption of Rum in the Colonies

Colonists at 20 gallons per adult male	6.4 million
British Army at 23 gallons per soldier	.23 million
Indians at 12 gallons per warrior	.24 million
Canadians	.30 million
Total estimated consumption in North America	7.17 million

even the official British records reflect only a portion of the traffic. For example, the colonists illegally traded food and lumber for French West Indies molasses which colonial merchants distilled into rum. In 1772, when the prohibitive duty was removed, 4.8 million gallons of molasses were imported into the colonies. Similar quantities of molasses smuggled before 1772 were never recorded.

The colonies produced about 4.8 million gallons of rum and imported about 3.8 million gallons annually, much of which was consumed by the colonists. Consumption by the colonists was probably about 6.4 million gallons. There were 1.6 million persons in thirteen colonies with an average of five persons per family or 320,000 adult males who probably consumed about twenty gallons of rum per year for a total of 6.4 million gallons. In 1955, American consumption of liquor was 3.6 gallons per capita while the average family was only four persons, or 14.4 gallons per adult male.

The British army issued a gill (one half pint) or rum daily to each soldier (23 gallons per year) and ten thousand soldiers would consume 230,000 gallons per year. About 250,000 gallons were exported to Canada for 65,000 Canadians (including about 15,000 adult males) and the fur trade. About 240,000 gallons were consumed by the Indians (twelve gallons each for 10,000 warriors in the northern department and a similar number west of the Great Lakes). The colonists, British army, Canadians, and Indians probably consumed more than seven million gallons.[1] The remainder of the 8.6 million gallons of rum (1.5 million gallons) was probably exported to Africa in exchange for slaves and to Britain.

The recorded value of furs exported in 1765 from the continental colonies was £46,000 including 160,000 beaver pelts. Another source lists exports of fur to England as Quebec £25,000, New York £6,000, Pennsylvania £2,000, and Hudson's Bay £10,000 for a total of £41,000. In 1762, before Pontiac's Rebellion, 173,000 beaver pelts were exported (at 5/ each, £43,000) with 94,000 from Canada, 50,000 from Hudson's Bay, 15,000 from New York.[2] However, all of these totals ignore New Orleans, a major export center during the period, and any smuggling that might have occurred. The average value of fur exported to England probably was in the range of £50,000 to £100,000 sterling annually. Cash and bills of exchange obtained from the army for provisions probably exceeded that total as indicated by the transactions of Baynton & Wharton, for a total value of commerce on the frontier in the range of £200,000 to £300,000 sterling. Remittances were made in bills of exchange, cash, or furs received from the Indians, the French merchants and inhabitants, and the British army from Quebec, Montreal, New York City, Philadelphia, and New Orleans.

The value of the goods used to obtain the remittances can be estimated from the claims of the suffering traders, £80,000 sterling in goods lost in 1763. Johnson estimated the total value of the goods used at £307,875 ($61.5 million) including £20,000 in shirts and £7,500 in rum (a gross underestimate). The value of rum consumed by the Indians in the Northern Department was about £24,000 sterling annually. A single shipment of rum to Quebec by Baynton & Wharton was valued at nearly £2,500 sterling. The goods used by the traders and the Indian Department were probably in the £200,000 to £300,000 sterling range as well.[3]

In 1765 British exports to all destinations totalled £14,600,000 and imports were £11,000,000 (including £2,290,000 sterling from the West Indies). Exports from America to Britain totaled £1,250,000.[4] Other sources list American exports to Britain as £1,151,698 in 1765, and imports from Britain at £1,944,114. Military expense in America (some of which was used for Indian Department expense) in 1765, has been estimated at £436,000 for a total of £1,587,000 and a trade deficit of £357,000 sterling (see Table 1.1, p. 8). From this limited amount of data, frontier commerce can be estimated as being equal to about twenty percent of the trade with England in 1765, a considerable portion.

The volatility of the frontier commerce made it economically and politically significant. From 1762 to 1763, the trade with England, including military expense, ranged from a deficit of £109,000 to surpluses of £240,000 and £227,000 sterling. In 1764, after Pontiac's Rebellion, the deficit increased sharply to £763,000 sterling (see Table 1.1, p. 8). The transfer of the £300,000 frontier commerce from the colonial merchants to the French and Scottish merchants in Montreal in 1764 was a major loss to the New York and Pennsylvania merchants and led to the bankruptcy of Baynton, Wharton & Morgan, one of the leading partnerships in Philadelphia.

In the early years, prior to 1750, the French and the colonists went their separate ways in exploiting the North American wilderness with only moderate friction. In the 1750s the friction intensified as the colonists sought to gain a greater share of the wealth obtainable from the Indians on the New York and Pennsylvania frontier. This friction led to the French and Indian War which evolved into the Seven Years' War and the British defeat of France. Faced with a flood of colonial traders and encouraged by the slow progress of the peace negotiations offering the hope that Canada would be returned to France, the French Canadians encouraged the Indians to pillage the colonial traders in 1763. The French anticipated that the Indian uprising would make Canada appear less attractive to the British peace negotiators and would drive the colonial traders out of the market.

After the Capitulation of Montreal terminated hostilities in Canada, including all of the land east of the Mississippi River and north of the Ohio River, the British military command declared that the fur trade was open to everyone, and grants of land west of the mountains were made to discharged soldiers. The colonial traders who had previously been held in check at Oswego and Fort Pitt by the French forces were then free to exploit the wilderness and the Indians.

The Indians were at the end of a long chain of people in western commerce, beginning with the manufacturers in Europe. The middlemen were importers and wholesalers in the ports of New York City, Philadelphia, and Quebec, and in frontier commercial centers in Montreal, Albany, Schenectady, Lancaster, and Carlisle. Hundreds of petty traders were scattered in the western posts and in the forests. More than fifteen hundred men were employed annually by the traders as canoe men, wagon drivers, carpenters, shipwrights, coopers, and blacksmiths. These merchants and their employees were French, Scottish, English, New Yorkers, Pennsylvanians, and Jews from all the provinces. Their ultimate goal was the acquisition of furs from the Indians who in the course of affairs lost their culture, their homelands, and their ability to exist independently of the White man.

The debilitating effect of the alcohol led some Indians to neglect the essential needs of their families. After exhausting their supply of furs to purchase rum, the Indians would even sell their clothing and weapons. An unscrupulous trader would give the Indians some rum and use his goods to buy more furs from the next group of Indians, and the process could continue until the stock of rum was exhausted. On the other hand, once outside the military posts, the trader lived at high risk because the Indians might kill him and take the rum, but he survived with the expectation that some of the Indians would protect him to ensure his return the next year with a new load of merchandise and rum. Diseases contracted from the Europeans caused the deaths of thousands of Indians. Beginning in the sixteenth century, smallpox, typhus, and other epidemics killed from twenty percent to sixty percent of the tribes with each onslaught, although some of the losses were recouped within a few generations. A smallpox epidemic in the northwest in the 1730s had reduced the Indian population severely and although numbers were increasing by 1760, there were fewer hunters for several decades. Smallpox killed proportionally more men than women and children, reducing the number of hunters, and therefore the number of beaver increased in the late 1750s compared to the previous several decades. With a healthy new generation of hunters and a plentiful supply of beaver, the fur trade in the late 1750s was at a peak that continued through the early 1760s when the numbers of animals were once again diminished by increased hunting.

The colonial traders from New York and Pennsylvania, financed by merchants in Albany, New York City, and Philadelphia, were determined to exploit the new area that offered immense profits for those willing to take the risks. For three years, the colonial merchants competed with British and French merchants in the commercial exploitation of the frontier. Although the British tended to join with the French and continue the trading methods that accommodated the Indians, the colonists took a more aggressive path that led to the near extermination of the fur bearing animals through the destruction of the Indian culture with alcohol and the beginning of the movement to drive the Indians westward to make way for White settlement.

The British army was concerned primarily with keeping the peace, and the British commander, Lord Amherst, imposed a heavy-handed occupation after 1760 based on threats, whereas the Indian Department under Johnson, a former successful fur trader from the Mohawk valley, preferred to offer bribes rather than threaten the Indians with punishment.

The new participants after 1760 were discharged army officers from the Scottish regiments that had been disbanded in America after the Seven Years' War. Many became merchants in Montreal and Quebec, forming partnerships with the French upper class merchants. The Scots provided the contacts in England to obtain merchandise, whereas the French had control of the means to exchange those goods with the Indians. Competition was intense between the French and Scots one the one hand and the Pennsylvania and New York traders on the other. Lacking skill in dealing with the Indians, the colonials relied on ample quantities of rum to pave the way to trade, whereas the French were more responsible because of their long established ties with the tribes.

The British army restricted trade to the posts to reduce the amount of rum, which was officially prohibited, because the Indians were more easily cheated when drunk and became violent, leading to the killing of both Indians and Europeans. The French ignored the restriction to the posts, and continued to supply the winterers who lived with the Indians and traded a limited supply of rum or brandy along with other goods on a continuous basis. The colonials were somewhat successful in evading restrictions and continued to sell thousands of gallons of rum outside of the posts.

Encouraged by the French in an attempt to halt the colonial advance, the Indians revolted in 1763. The French, seeing the fruits of their labor slipping away in 1761 and 1762, encouraged the Indians to rob the colonial traders in the forests and to attack the posts. In the summer of 1763, the Indians tried to take all of the posts, but failed to take Detroit, Fort Pitt, and Niagara, the major forts. However, the minor posts were taken and the colonial traders were robbed and either captured or murdered. The Indians did not harm their allies, the French, who sometimes confiscated the colonial's goods. The total loss of the colonial merchants was estimated at £100,000 sterling ($20,000,000). Pontiac's Rebellion was a bloody lesson to the colonial traders that they could not trade with the Indians outside of the garrisoned posts. Deprived of the ability to openly sell unlimited quantities of rum in or near the posts under the protection of the army, the colonial traders could not compete with the French who roamed freely, and the colonials were driven out of the fur trade after 1763.

Prior to the revolt, official reports from America to the British Board of Trade reported the abuses of the colonial traders and the debilitating effect of alcohol on the Indians. After spending an enormous sum of money to suppress the rebellion, the British government was also faced with the heavy cost of maintaining an army on the frontier to prevent future trouble by enforcing regulations to protect the Indians from the colonial traders, which inadvertently favored the French traders. White settlement, the other threat to the Indians, was halted by the Proclamation of 1763 that stopped encroachment on Indian lands.

Whether the substantial losses of the frontier merchants, equal to about six percent of American imports from Britain in 1763, was of any political importance was uncertain. Even minor economic changes can be politically important if they effect powerful interests. The difference in perception of the colonial economy by the various groups was one of the factors leading to the Revolutionary War. When the economy was good, the people were working and most of their needs were met, the merchants were prosperous, and the wealthy enjoyed the fruits of their possessions. When the economy was bad, the people's needs were not satisfied, the merchants lost money, and the wealthy were uneasy because of their concern about retaining their position.

Perception was determined by the media. Even in the eighteenth century, personal experience was tempered with information provided by others; newspapers, pamphlets, and books were the media that created public perception of events. An example was the pamphlet war that erupted in England over the choice between Canada and Guadeloupe as one of the fruits of victory in the Seven Years' War. Perception, not reality, determined policy.

When the transition from a good economy to a period of economic distress was gradual, the controlling establishment had ample opportunity to shape public opinion and create safeguards to protect their position, but when the transition was rapid, as occurred in 1763, when a large group of influential merchants suddenly suffered disastrous losses as a result of the alliance of the Indians and the French against the colonial merchants to drive the colonials out of the west, those suffering from the economic conditions were able to upset the status quo.

The mismanaged British punitive expeditions that ended Pontiac's Rebellion gave the French and the Indians a decisive victory. Although Canada was not returned to France in 1763, the French Canadians had achieved their goal, the resumption of control of the fur trade. The British government had spent a great deal of money financing the punitive expeditions from Fort Niagara and Fort Pitt in 1764 that achieved nothing. Only one skirmish was fought. The Indians forestalled further action by sending messengers to the expedition leaders promising to be peaceful. Bouquet and Bradstreet, the expedition commanders, accepted the apologies, presented the Indians with enormous bribes, and the trade was reopened, but under new terms.

Regulations were imposed that favored the French and virtually excluded the colonial traders, as the British believed that the cause of the revolt was the abuse of the Indians by the colonial traders who sold rum rather than useful goods to the tribes. The British government, hoping to avoid the cost of another rebellion, believed that the simplest solution was returning the trade to the French who had managed it for decades without serious trouble. English commercial interests were still satisfied by transferring the sale of British manufactured goods from the colonists to the new Scottish merchants in Quebec and Montreal.

The impact of the British resolution of the North American problem was devastating to the colonials involved in frontier commerce, a group that included many of the foremost merchants in New York and Pennsylvania and, indirectly, merchants in other colonies. First came the immediate loss of more than £100,000 sterling in merchandise to the Indians during the revolt and, second, the closing of any opportunity to recoup that loss when the trade was given to the French. Supplying the army in 1764 provided New York and Pennsylvania merchants a temporary respite, but when the army began to withdraw from the frontier, the merchants were hit again. Even a major house, Baynton, Wharton & Morgan, went bankrupt.

To many influential men and to the people on the frontier, the perception was that the British government had abandoned their interests in favor of the new British merchants in Canada and the French. In the eyes of the colonial merchants, the British government had replaced the French government in supporting the Indians; the French traders had driven them out of the fur trade; and the Proclamation of 1763 had replaced French claims that had halted land development in the past. What made matters worse was the British attempt to make the colonists pay through a variety of taxes inflicted on the colonists by Parliament for the continuation of the denial of exploitation of the west.

The British government was motivated by the desire to protect the Indians to keep them quiet because of the high cost of repression and a humanitarian concern. The British government was determined to protect the Indians and keep the colonists out of the west, both to protect the Canadian fur trade and the Indians. In addition, the British government was inclined to support the Scottish merchants who were then working with the French to continue a compatible relationship with the Indians, rather than driving them out to make way for White settlement.

By the end of 1764, despite the British government, the French Canadians, and the Indians, the colonial merchants and land speculators were determined to gain access to the west. When the British government replaced the French government in the alliance with the French inhabitants and the Indians to hold the colonists east of the mountains, the merchants demanded compensation.

Instead, in 1765 the British government tried to make the colonists pay for the policy of denial of western expansion.

Many if not most of the individuals who arrived in the thirteen colonies had come in search of religious, political, and economic freedom. Although the argument presented here concerns economic freedom, there is no intent to denigrate the importance of religious and political freedom to the colonists. The goal of the study is to describe some of the economic events that led the thirteen colonies to lose confidence in the British government in 1765. The study assumes that American merchants, land speculators, and farmers shared a deep desire to exploit the land beyond the Allegheny Mountains in the eighteenth century. Before 1760, they were prevented from moving westward by the Indians who were supported by the French fur traders and the French military forces, all of whom received some measure of financial support from the French government. When the British replaced the French government in blocking westward expansion, the anger of the merchants turned from France to Britain.

NOTES

1. John J. McCusker, *Rum and the American Revolution, The Rum Trade and the Balance of Payments of the Thirteen Colonies*, 2 vols. (New York: Garland Publishing, 1989), 2:434, 447, 500; U.S. Bureau of the Census, *Historical Statistics of the United States, Colonial Times to 1957* (Washington, DC: U.S. Government Printing Office, 1960), 772; Virginia D. Harrington, *The New York Merchant on the Eve of the Revolution* (New York: Columbia University Press, 1935), 270, 359.

2. George L. Beer, *British Colonial Policy, 1754-1765* (New York: Peter Smith, 1933), 214; Public Record Office, Group 348, T64, Bundle 276A and 691, 2:20; Murray G. Lawson, *Fur, A Study in English Mercantilism, 1700-1775* (Toronto: University of Toronto Press, 1943), 87-88, 108-9, 134-35; Indian Trade, *Canadian Archives*, C.O. 323, 15:182-84; Note C, *Canadian Archives Report* (1882), 60-61; Colonial Office 378, vol. 2 (extract); Exports, North America, Great Britain, 1768-1772, Public Record Office, Customs 16, 1; Merrill Jensen, ed., *English Historical Documents, American Colonial Documents to 1776*, vol. 9 (New York: Oxford University Press, 1955), 392-93; Harrington, *New York Merchants*, 235-36.

3. Johnson to Lords of Trade, October 8, 1764, *Illinois Historical Collections*, 10:338-39.

4. Public Record Office 348, T64, Bundle 276A.

Select Bibliography

Adam, Frank. *The Clans, Septs and Regiments of the Scottish Highlands*. Edinburgh: W. & A. K. Johnston & G. W. Bacon, 1965.

Alvord, Clarence W., and Clarence E. Carter, eds. *The Critical Period, 1763-1765*. *Illinois Historical Collections*. Springfield: Illinois State Historical Library. vol. 10 (1915).

———. *The Illinois Country 1673-1818*. Springfield: Illinois Centennial Commission, 1920.

———. *The Mississippi Valley in British Politics*. 2 vols. Cleveland: Arthur H. Clark, Co., 1917.

Baynton, Wharton & Morgan Papers. Microfilm. 10 Rolls. Original in Pennsylvania Historical Commission.

Beer, George L. *British Colonial Policy, 1754-1765*. New York: Peter Smith, 1933.

Byars, William V., ed. *B[ernard] and M. Gratz*. Jefferson City, MO: The Hugh Stevens Printing Co., 1916.

Dorn, Walter L. *Competition for Empire, 1740-1763*. New York: Harper Torchbooks, 1940.

Dunham, Douglas. "The French Element in the American Fur Trade." Ph. D. Dis., University of Michigan, 1950. Microfilm in State Historical Society of Wisconsin.

Dunn, Walter S., Jr., "Western Commerce, 1760-1774." Ph. D. Dis., University of Wisconsin, 1971.

Egnal, Marc. *A Mighty Empire: The Origins of the American Revolution*. Ithaca, NY: Cornell University Press, 1988.

Eyck, Erick. *Pitt versus Fox: Father and Son*. London: G. Bell and Sons Ltd., 1950.

Fleming, R. H. "Phyn, Ellice and Co. of Schenectady." *Contributions to Canadian Economics*. vol. 4 (1932).

Gipson, Lawrence H. *The Coming of the Revolution, 1759-1766*. New York: Harper, 1954.

Hamilton, Edward P. *The French and Indian War*. Garden City, NY: Doubleday, 1962.

Harrington, Virginia D. *The New York Merchant on the Eve of the Revolution*. New York: Columbia University Press, 1935.

Henderson, W. O. *Britain and Industrial Europe, 1750–1870*. Leicester: Leicester University Press, 1972.

Hough, Franklin B. *Diary of the Siege of Detroit...* Albany, NY: J. Munsell, 1860.

Innis, Harold A. *The Fur Trade in Canada*. New Haven, CT: Yale University Press, 1930.

Jenness, Diamond. *The Indians of Canada*. Toronto: University of Toronto Press, 1977.

Jensen, Arthur L. *The Maritime Commerce of Colonial Philadelphia*. Madison: The State Historical Society of Wisconsin, 1963.

Jensen, Merrill. *The Founding of a Nation*. New York: Oxford University Press, 1968.

Johnson, Sir William. *The Papers of Sir Williams Johnson*, 14 vols. Albany: The State University of New York Press, 1921–1965.

Kellogg, Louise P. *The British Regime in Wisconsin and the Northwest*. Madison: State Historical Society, 1935.

Kenny, James. "Journal of James Kenny, 1761–1763." *The Pennsylvania Magazine of History and Biography*, vol. 37 (1913).

Lanctot, Gustave. *Les Canadiens Francais et Leurs Voisins du Sud*. Montreal: Bernard Valiquettes, 1941.

Lawson, Murray G. *Fur, A Study in English Mercantilism, 1700–1775*. Toronto: University of Toronto Press, 1943.

Lees, John. *Journal of [John Lees] a Quebec Merchant*. Detroit: Society of the Colonial Wars of the State of Michigan, 1911.

McMillan, Alan D. *Native Peoples and Culture in Canada*. Vancouver: Douglas & McIntyre, 1988.

Martin, Calvin. *Keepers of the Game*. Berkley: University of California Press, 1978.

Parkman, Francis. *A History of the Conspiracy of Pontiac and the Indian War after the Conquest of Canada*. New York: MacMillan Co., 1929.

Pease, Theodore C., and Marguerite J. Pease. *George Rogers Clark and Revolution in Illinois, 1763–1787*. Springfield: Illinois State Historical Society, 1929.

Peckham, Howard H. *Pontiac and the Indian Uprising*. Princeton, NJ: Princeton University Press, 1947.

Phillips, Paul C. *The Fur Trade*, 2 vols. Norman: University of Oklahoma Press, 1961.

Ray, Arthur J. *Indians in the Fur Trade: Their Role as Trappers, Hunters, and Middlemen in the Lands Southwest of Hudson Bay, 1660–1870*. Toronto: University of Toronto Press, 1974.

Robinson, Percy J. *Toronto during the French Regime, 1615–1793*. Toronto: University of Toronto Press, 1965.

Russell, Nelson V. *The British Regime in Michigan and the Northwest, 1760–1796*. Northfield, MN: Carleton College, 1939.

Sellers, Linda. *Charleston Business on the Eve of the Revolution*. Chapel Hill, NC: University of North Carolina Press, 1934.

Shy, John. *Toward Lexington: The Role of the British Army in the Coming of the American Revolution*. Princeton, NJ: Princeton University Press, 1965.

Slick, Sewell E. *William Trent and the West*. Harrisburg: Archives Publishing Company of Pennsylvania, 1947.

Sosin, Jack M. *Whitehall and the Wilderness: The Middle West in British Colonial Policy, 1760–1775*. Lincoln: University of Nebraska Press, 1961.

Stevens, Wayne E. *The Northwest Fur Trade, 1763-1800*. Urbana: University of Illinois, 1928.

Wade, Mason. *The French Canadians, 1760–1945*. Toronto: Macmillan Co. of Canada, 1955.

Wainwright, Nicholas B. *George Croghan, Wilderness Diplomat*. Chapel Hill: University of North Carolina Press, 1959.

Wilson, Charles H. *Anglo-Dutch Commerce and Finance in the Eighteenth Century*. Cambridge: The Cambridge University Press, 1966.

Index

About the Author

WALTER S. DUNN, JR. served as a museum director for forty years. His posts included the Buffalo and Erie County Historical Society and the Iowa Science Center. His books include *Kursk: Hitler's Gamble, 1943* (Praeger, 1997), *The Soviet Economy and the Red Army* (Praeger, 1997), *Hitler's Nemesis* (Praeger, 1994) and *Second Front Now* (Praeger, 1981).

ISBN 0-313-30605-2

HARDCOVER BAR CODE